THE GOLF
INSTRUCTION
MANUAL

THE GOLF INSTRUCTION MANUAL

STEVE NEWELL

A Dorling Kindersley Book

Dorling DK Kindersley

LONDON, NEW YORK, SYDNEY, DELHI, PARIS,
MUNICH, and JOHANNESBURG

Produced for Dorling Kindersley by
Cooling Brown, 9–11 High Street,
Hampton, Middlesex TW12 2SA

Editors Sean O'Connor, Michael Ellis
Designers Elaine Hewson, Alistair Plumb
Photographers Dave Cannon, Steve Gorton
Illustrator Peter Cooling
Proof-reader Stewart Wild; **Indexer** Hilary Bird
Creative Director Arthur Brown

Project Editor Tracie Lee
Senior Art Editor Kevin Ryan
Managing Editor Sharon Lucas
Senior Managing Art Editor Derek Coombes
DTP Designer Sonia Charbonnier
Production Sarah Coltman, Joanna Bull
Picture Researchers Mariana Sonnenberg,
Franziska Marking

First American Edition, 2001
01 02 03 04 05 10 9 8 7 6 5 4 3 2

Published in the United States by
Dorling Kindersley Publishing, Inc.
95 Madison Avenue, New York, New York 10016

DK Publishing offers special discounts for bulk purchases for sales
promotions or premiums. Specific, large-quantity needs can be met
with special editiions, including personalized covers, excerpts of
existing guides, and corporate imprints. For more information,
contact Special Markets Department, DK Publishing, Inc. 95
Madison Avenue, New York, NY 10016 Fax: 800-600-9098.

Library of Congress Cataloging-in-Publication Data
Newell, Steve
    The golf instruction manual / Steve Newell
    p. cm
Includes index.
ISBN 0-7894-7164-7 (alk. paper)
    1. Golf–Handbooks, manuals, etc. I. Title

GV965 .N45 2001
796.352'3--dc21   00-047421

Colour reproduced by Colourscan, Singapore
Printed and bound by
L. Rex Printing Company Limited, China

See our complete catalog at
www.dk.com

CONTENTS

FOREWORD 7
INTRODUCTION 8
HOW TO USE THIS BOOK 12

Chapter One:
ASSESSING AND IMPROVING YOUR GAME 16

CHECKING THE FUNDAMENTALS 18

OFF THE TEE 28
LEVEL ONE 30
LEVEL TWO 38
LEVEL THREE 46
THE PERFECT TEE SHOT 52

IRON PLAY 54
LEVEL ONE 56
LEVEL TWO 64
LEVEL THREE 72
THE PERFECT IRON SHOT 78

PITCHING 80
LEVEL ONE 82
LEVEL TWO 90
LEVEL THREE 98
THE PERFECT PITCH SHOT 104

CHIPPING 106
LEVEL ONE 108
LEVEL TWO 116
LEVEL THREE 124
THE PERFECT CHIP SHOT 130

BUNKER PLAY 132
LEVEL ONE 134
LEVEL TWO 142
LEVEL THREE 150
THE PERFECT BUNKER SHOT 156

PUTTING 158
LEVEL ONE 160
LEVEL TWO 168
LEVEL THREE 176
THE PERFECT PUTT 182

Chapter Two:
FAULTS AND FIXES 184

THE SLICE 186
THE HOOK 187
THE "HEAVY-CONTACT"
  CHIP 188
THE SHANKED IRON SHOT 189
THE SKIED DRIVE 190
THE TOP 191
LOSS OF POWER 192
WEAK SHOT FROM ROUGH 193
THE PUSH SHOT 194
THE PULL SHOT 195

Chapter Three:
THE ART OF SHOTMAKING 196

SLOPING LIES 198
TACKLING PROBLEM SHOTS 202
CONJURING EFFECTIVE ESCAPE SHOTS 204
BETTER WIND PLAY 206
HOW TO HIT HIGH AND LOW SHOTS 208
TWO SIMPLE WAYS TO SHAPE YOUR SHOTS 210

Chapter Four:
PLAYING THE GAME 212

WARMING UP BEFORE A ROUND 214
THE VALUE OF A PRESHOT ROUTINE 216
STRATEGY OFF THE TEE 218
ON THE FAIRWAY AND
  IN THE ROUGH 220
IMPROVING YOUR
  MENTAL APPROACH 222
SIMPLIFYING WINTER GOLF 224
MONITOR YOUR PERFORMANCE 226

Chapter Five:
REFERENCE SECTION 228

BUYING THE RIGHT EQUIPMENT 230
TYPES OF PLAY AND HANDICAPS 236
THE IMPORTANCE OF GOOD
  ETIQUETTE 238
THE GOLDEN RULES OF GOLF 242

GLOSSARY 250
INDEX 252
  ACKNOWLEDGMENTS 256

FOREWORD

GOLF HAS BEEN A PART of my life from an early age. I caddied for my dad when I was about eight years old, started playing soon after that, and managed to get down to scratch by the time I was 14. A year later I was world junior champion, by which time I was pretty certain I wanted golf to be my profession. I was lucky when I was growing up to have the right influences and some wonderful role models, which together instilled in me the importance of practicing good fundamentals and developing a sound swing with good rhythm. *The Golf Instruction Manual* constantly reinforces these same virtues while giving you a clear and easy-to-follow route to a lower handicap.

ADDING UP
The author (left) and Ernie Els examine a score card after another successful round.

I know from playing pro-ams that a lot of amateurs receive little constructive tuition and therefore have no real idea how to develop their game. This is a shame, because there is so much enjoyment to be gained from improving and shooting lower scores. To me, striving to improve is part and parcel of the game's challenge, even at a professional level. And anyone who works through this book is bound to end up playing better golf.

I think the golf swing is like a chain reaction. If you adopt a good address position it is easier to make a better takeaway. If you make a good takeaway you are more likely to get to the top of the backswing in good shape, and so on. The format of *The Golf Instruction Manual* reflects this philosophy. The book contains all the important building blocks of a successful game – it revisits the fundamentals (which are essential to long-term success) and takes you step-by-step through to the advanced stages of each department of the game.

Steve Newell is an experienced instruction writer, and we have worked together on many projects over the last seven or eight years. Steve has put together excellent books for me, and he has produced another superb guide in *The Golf Instruction Manual*. I hope you enjoy the book as much as I did – it is your passport to better golf.

ERNIE ELS

CROWD PLEASER
Golf's popularity has grown spectacularly. Here, spectators flock to watch the action during 1993's Ryder Cup.

INTRODUCTION

THE FACT THAT THIS BOOK is now in your hands suggests that you are well aware of golf's addictive nature. Virtually everyone who seriously embarks upon the game is destined for a life-long affair. Once ensnared in golf's irresistible grip, it is hard to imagine ever not playing, even if everyday commitments make the gaps between rounds painfully long at times.

While it may be rather clichéd to boast of golf's varied playing arena (it's true, every course is different in its own special way) or to highlight the manner in which golfers of unequal ability can compete on even terms due to the handicapping system, these are undeniably two of the attributes that make golf special. They are part of the game's challenge and charm.

Only part, however, because ultimately it is the physical act of playing the game that is so compelling. Stripped bare, golf may appear to be little more than a stick-and-ball game, but surely no other sport asks more telling questions of your mind and body. The scenario involving you, a club, a little white ball, and a 4-in (10-cm) target far in the distance – often out of sight – presents a demanding physical challenge. And there is no under-estimating the skills required to swing a club with accuracy at speeds sometimes in excess of 100 mph (160 kph). This is why a great shot, in which the ball sails toward your chosen target, produces such excitement.

The mental side of the game is equally important, of course. Compared with most other sports, you have an age between shots to contemplate opposite ends of the emotional spectrum. Even during the few seconds in which you stand over the ball, golf's psychological "swingometer" remains hard at work. When you win these mind games – when your swing is on the mark and you produce a good score at the end of a round – it is a wonderful feeling. When you fail, it can be soul destroying because you have no one to blame but yourself. Nevertheless, even on the bad days there is nearly always at least one glimpse of magic – the experience of hitting a great shot or holing a long putt – that lifts your spirits and keeps you coming back for more. This "high" is essentially the catalyst that fuels the desire to become a better player, to experience that feeling not just for one shot, or one hole, but for as much of your playing time as possible.

THE EARLY DAYS

Ever since the first ball was struck (which may have been as early as the 16th century), people have striven to find a way of getting from a teeing ground to a hole with as few strokes as possible. In golf's early days, swing technique was shaped mainly out of circumstance rather than choice. The earliest proper courses (which probably date from the 17th century) were almost certainly the coastal links in Scotland. There, it was soon discovered that a rounded swing,

STUNNING SURROUNDINGS
Golf is a game played amid breathtaking scenery. The Cypress Point course on the Monterey Peninsula, California, is a classic example. Here the ocean very much comes into consideration.

GRAND OLD MAN
*Old Tom Morris was the finest golfer in the
world during the late 19th century, winning
the Open Championship four times. He is
buried at the "Home of Golf": St Andrews.*

whereby the hands and arms swing
the club on a flat plane around the
body, produced a low ball flight and
plenty of run. This suited the windswept
landscape of the Scottish coast.

As photographs of the great
players of the late 19th century
confirm, playing in a tweed jacket
and tie (as was the tradition in the
early years) would have restricted
arm movement, hampering a
free, up-and-down swing of
the hands and arms. Also,
even up until the late 19th
century, the likes of
Mungo Park, Old Tom
Morris, and Allen
Robertson – all great players – would stand with their
feet nearly twice as far apart as today's top golfers, with
their knees bent more than is usual nowadays, and with
the ball way back in the stance (even for the driving clubs).

HOME-CRAFTED EQUIPMENT

Equipment making has always been a highly skilled art,
and many of the top players of the 19th and early 20th
century crafted with their own hands the tools that they
wielded to such great effect. But, by today's standards,
the clubs and balls that were used appear rather primitive.
Clubs were wooden shafted, and the fat, leather-wrapped
handles called for a grip totally unlike the overlapping
and interlocking methods mostly employed today.
Indeed, the club was held in the palm of each hand,
very much like the grip for holding a baseball bat.

Up until the mid-19th century, golf balls were made
of stitched leather stuffed tightly with feathers, hence the
name "feathery ball." These balls were not only
expensive, but their playability was horrendous. Once
wet, they would deform and not fly in a straight line. By
the latter part of the 19th century, balls were being made
of gutta-percha, a rubberlike substance secreted from
percha trees. These "gutties" were cheaper and more
uniform in shape. They also flew better and lasted longer.
Nevertheless, it was impossible to spin them in the way
of today's high-tech balls, and gutties tended to fly on a
low trajectory with plenty of run on landing.

THE MODERN GAME

By the early part of the 20th century, the golf swing
was rapidly becoming more athletic, efficient, and
powerful – not to mention elegant. Harry Vardon
popularized the grip that to this day bears his name
(also known as the overlapping grip), where the
little finger of the right hand overlaps the index
finger of the left. Vardon was also one of the first
golfers to recommend fanning the left foot out at
address to encourage a clearing of the left hip through
impact. Bobby Jones was among the first to advocate
a more narrow stance, as he felt that if the feet were
too wide apart, the lower body became locked in
place, reducing mobility in the swing. Golfers soon
started to stand a little more upright, slightly nearer
to the ball, and with their feet closer together.

All of these subtle changes added up to a
much more upright golf swing. Byron Nelson,
perhaps the first great player with a distinctly
upright swing (which suited his tall stature), won
11 tournaments in a row during the 1945 season, a

TALENTED AMATEUR
*Even though Bobby Jones never turned professional, he was the
dominant golfer of the 1920s, winning four US Opens, three Open
Championships, five US Amateurs, and one British Amateur.*

record that will probably never be matched. Byron's style of play was perfectly suited to the new steel-shafted clubs, which had only just replaced the inferior hickory-shafted clubs (which were much whippier and therefore necessitated an "around-the-body" swing).

The legendary Ben Hogan, who is still regarded by some as the greatest golfer ever, shaped the game not so much in the way it was played but in the manner in which it was practiced. He would hit balls until his hands bled, striving for, and achieving, a level of near-perfection that is still unsurpassed. Many now emulate his selfless work ethic on the practice ranges at professional tour events all over the world. Although he was nearly killed in a terrible car accident in 1949, he fought back to become an even more accomplished golfer than before, winning the three major championships he played in 1953.

Jack Nicklaus, winner of more major championships than any other golfer, has been one of the greatest influences on the game for much of the latter part of the 20th century. When he burst onto the scene in the early 1960s, the great Bobby Jones remarked that "he plays a game with which I am not familiar." But soon everyone wanted to play like Nicklaus – his style spawned a generation of upright swingers with elegant, high-hands finishes (and an arched back in the followthrough). In such a technique, the club travels up and down in more of a straight line, which means that the hands are higher, both in the backswing and followthrough.

One of the most influential modern-day figures in the game is not a player, but a coach: David Leadbetter. His associations in the mid-to-late 1980s with multiple major

WATCHING A MASTER AT WORK
This photograph – taken during the 1956 Canada Cup, which was held in Wentworth, England – shows the great Ben Hogan in action, his high followthrough very much in evidence. Many golf historians believe that Ben Hogan was the ultimate golfer.

winners Nick Faldo and Nick Price popularized a swing less upright than the one employed by Nicklaus. This newer swing is a more rotary action that synchronizes the body-turn and arm-swing more effectively. Today, therefore, most golfers finish their swing in a much more rounded position, with the spine less arched, and the club more across the back of the neck (in an upright swing, the shaft points more toward the ground). This latest swing is more consistent, more sustainable, and places less strain on the lower back than an upright swing.

THE ROLE OF THE COACH
Teaching philosophies have also evolved over the years and become less polarized. Today's great teachers – such as David Leadbetter, Butch Harmon, and John Jacobs – work on essentially the same principles, but each applies individuality and different communication methods to the coaching role. While the standard of golf teaching has improved and become more uniform, golfers of all standards have grown increasingly receptive to tuition.

This is partly because golfers have become familiar with the player/coach culture that exists in sports today and have been inspired by the success of partnerships such as David Leadbetter and Nick Faldo or Tiger Woods and Butch Harmon. Consequently, golfers are eager to harness the expertise of great players and coaches. Thousands of teaching books are bought every year, and

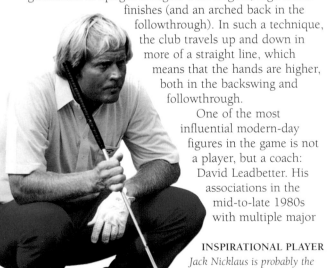

INSPIRATIONAL PLAYER
Jack Nicklaus is probably the greatest golfer who ever lived. He is certainly the smartest thinker and course strategist, which is why his major record is unlikely to be surpassed.

WORLD NUMBER ONE

Women's golf has grown out of all recognition in the last 25 years or so, especially in the US, where professionals play for as much money as the men do in Europe. Karrie Webb is the undisputed world number one and is leader of the US money lists.

research shows that at least 70 percent of all golf magazines are purchased primarily for the game-improvement articles featuring top players and teachers. Golfers wishing to improve can now benefit from high-speed photography that freeze-frames the golf swing in motion, capturing every detail of an incredibly dynamic movement. This technique emphasizes the athletic nature of the game and adds to the aspirational element of striving for a better swing.

YOUR PERSONAL COACH

Today, there is surely not a golfer in the world who does not want to shoot lower scores. Alas, most do not have a personal swing guru to turn to in times of need. But, in a variety of significant ways, this book intends to fulfill that role.

Modern golf instruction is based on wisdom passed down from inspirational teachers over the years – from Harry Vardon to Butch Harmon. The exercises in this book – the largest number of practice drills ever compiled in one book – take and expand upon this wealth of golfing knowledge. The drills are designed to cure faults and promote all the right moves, helping to insure that your practice sessions have a constructive focus and clearly defined goals. Each department of the game is covered – from tee shots to putting, from shotmaking to etiquette – and hundreds of specially commissioned photographs bring into focus every detail of the movements required for a perfect technique. We can sometimes forget that much of what we learn is influenced by imitation, and that is why the images of golfers with superb swings play such a prominent role in this book.

The structure of the book encourages you to assess your ability in each department of the game before you embark on a program of self-improvement. Through a series of tests you will gain an accurate and honest assessment of your game from the tee to the green. Whatever standard you play to, this book offers a way to improve while also explaining how to remedy faults that may creep into your game.

In my view, golf tuition should be inspirational and aspirational. Playing better golf is not just about the practicalities of producing good shots, it is also about the sensations and emotions that the game evokes. I believe this book will inspire you to enjoy the game, as well as teach you how to achieve your goals. The book is designed to educate you about the way you play, to help you understand how the golf swing works, and to make perfectly clear what you have to do to improve. A tremendous amount of work has gone into ensuring that the overall flow and content of the book is logical, and that every page works as hard as possible so that you will gain maximum benefit from all the advice given. I hope you enjoy the book and what it does for your game, and that you will continue to refer to it in years to come. The greatest satisfaction in golf comes from self-improvement, and I am confident that this book will show you the way to fully realize your golfing potential.

SUCCESSFUL DUO

Tiger Woods and Butch Harmon have worked together since Woods was an amateur: no one knows Woods' swing better than Harmon. Vital to their success is that Woods trusts Harmon's judgment.

HOW TO USE THIS BOOK

THIS BOOK has been structured in such a way that using it is like having a personal tutor guide you systematically through every area of the game. Once you have completed all the exercises and learned about almost every other aspect of golf – from shaping shots to etiquette – you will properly understand your swing and what action is required to sustain long-term progress down the handicap ladder.

Chapter One: ASSESSING AND IMPROVING YOUR GAME

Chapter One shows you how to assess and improve your game, beginning with an examination of the fundamentals. Six sections, from "Off the Tee" to "Putting," follow. For each, you take a test, work through a set of drills appropriate to your ability, retake the test, and move up to the next level if you have improved sufficiently.

LEFT-HANDED PLAYERS

ALTHOUGH the instructions in this book are for right-handed players, left-handed players need only reverse the directions. For example: "the little finger of your right hand overlaps the left forefinger" becomes, "the little finger of your left hand overlaps the right forefinger."

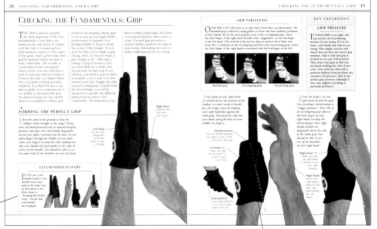

THE FUNDAMENTALS
Before beginning the drills, it is important to assess your fundamentals – grip, aim, stance, and posture.

Logical advice
Step-by-step instructions aid understanding

TESTS
The simple test at the beginning of each section provides an assessment of your ability and determines which of the three levels is most appropriate to you. All six tests (Off the Tee, Iron Play, Pitching, Chipping, Bunker Play, and Putting) are based around hitting 15 balls to a predetermined target.

Level One
The drills in this level are for beginners and less-proficient golfers.

Level Two
Intermediate golfers will benefit most from the drills in this level.

Level Three
The Level Three drills are geared toward more accomplished players.

Summary box
This succinct text gives you a key thought to take with you as you work through the drills

Test in progress
One large image clearly shows you how to perform the test

Performance chart
Once you have your test results, use this chart to work out which level to start at

LEVEL ONE

Although the drills and key checkpoints in this level are tailored to less-accomplished players, every golfer would benefit from working through this section.

Retest yourself

At the end of each section is a "Retest Yourself" box, which acts as a reminder to perform the test again, to see if you are ready to move to the next level

LEVEL TWO

It is likely that many club players will start at this level. However, even highly skilled golfers will find plenty of interest in Level Two.

Graphics

Throughout the book, special lines and arrows illustrate ball flight, alignment, swing path, and so on

Key checkpoints

These short pieces of expert advice offer hints and swing thoughts that will be of enormous benefit to your game

LEVEL THREE

Proficient players will find these drills, which are mostly concerned with fine-tuning, challenging, and rewarding.

Drills

Each drill begins with an introduction that explains the purpose of the exercise. Numbered instructions clearly describe how to perform the drill. An "end paragraph" summarizes what has been learned and sometimes offers extra information

Sequences

Many drills feature sequential images that show how to perform the exercise

THE PERFECT SHOT

These spreads, which appear at the end of each section, show you exactly how the shot in question should be done, as demonstrated by a leading tour professional. The key elements of the swing are broken down and explained, providing an inspirational guide to the perfect shot.

Face-on sequence

Combined images of the swing in action show you how your swing links together

Final reminders

Before you move to the next section, there is a list of the most vital points to remember

"Down the line"

The most important points in the swing, seen from behind the golfer ("down the line"), are carefully examined

Chapter Two:
FAULTS AND FIXES

No matter how good you are, there are times when faults will creep into your game. Do not despair though: this chapter presents the 10 most common faults and shows you how to fix them quickly and efficiently.

Faults
Before you can correct a problem in your game, it is essential to understand what is creating the fault. The text and image here do just that

✗ FAULT: REVERSE PIVOT WRECKS YOUR SWING

Causes
A detailed, annotated diagram provides a close-up examination of the factors at impact that are causing the fault

Weight moving away from target

Correct weight transfer

WHAT CAUSES LOSS OF POWER?

Final thought
This block of text offers extra advice, cross-referenced to a relevant section in Chapter One, for those who wish to try an alternative "fix"

Fixes
An instructive image, graphics, text, and annotation combine to present a clear and straightforward way to fix the fault for good

Chapter Three: THE ART OF SHOTMAKING

There are many situations when it is necessary to adapt your swing. Whether you want to play from a sloping lie, escape from a divot mark, combat a fierce wind, or shape a draw, this chapter gives you all the shotmaking skills you will ever need.

Helpful introduction
Each section begins with introductory text that provides general information about the shotmaking situation, such as "sloping lies," being discussed

Detailed analysis
The technical adjustments required to play from different types of sloping lies (for example) are closely examined using text, freeze-frame images, graphics, and annotation

Swing shape
Layered images not only provide a dynamic element to the page but also show you how your club and body should move as you swing

Extra information
Feature boxes are used if a particular point requires further expansion or explanation

Chapter Four:
PLAYING THE GAME

Golf is so much more than just hitting a ball and hoping for the best. For example, what you do before you strike the ball can be just as important as the swing you make. This chapter covers the areas of the game that go beyond striking the ball, such as preshot routines, psychological factors, and winter golf.

Instructive images
At every possible opportunity, a photograph is used to illustrate the subject in question

Vital photographs
To aid understanding, each portion of text is accompanied by an image that helps illustrate the salient point or points that are being discussed

Special skills
Whenever a particular technical adjustment is required, this is fully illustrated and explained, leaving no room for confusion

Logical groupings
Each aspect of playing the game is broken down into a series of smaller categories

Key checkpoint
Although most key checkpoints are situated in Chapter One, these pertinent slices of advice also appear in later chapters

Chapter Five:
REFERENCE SECTION

What happens if a crow flies off with your ball? What is the difference between a bladed iron and an iron that is peripherally weighted? How is the order of play determined on the tee and on the green? These and many other questions are answered in this concluding section of the book, which covers everything from buying the right equipment to golf's most important rules.

Feature pull-outs
Close-up photographs zoom in on key areas of interest

Descriptive text
Every aspect of the subject in question is described clearly and fully

Chapter One

ASSESSING AND IMPROVING YOUR GAME

CHAPTER ONE has more than twice the number of pages of all the other chapters combined. This reflects the intentions of the book: to give you the foundations of an effective golf game and to build on these to transform you into a more complete golfer. The key concepts throughout are self-assessment and self-improvement. After a discussion of golf's fundamentals, the chapter moves systematically through every department of the game – from tee shots to putting – each starting with a test to establish your level of ability. Then comes a series of progressively more advanced drills, designed to develop your game slowly but surely. Armed with the knowledge and techniques gained from this chapter, you will soon be playing better golf.

PRACTICE, PRACTICE
Tiered practice ranges – such as this one in Tokyo – allow the maximum number of golfers to work on improving and refining their game in a limited space.

CHECKING THE FUNDAMENTALS: GRIP

THE GRIP is almost certainly the most important of the four fundamentals. Given that your hands are the only point of contact with the club, it is amazing how little attention is given to this aspect of the game. Many golfers take their grip for granted simply because it feels comfortable. The trouble is, comfortable doesn't necessarily mean correct: you may well have a fault in your grip and not realize it. If this is the case, it is highly likely that your game is being seriously hindered. It is therefore fair to say that no golfer is too experienced or too skilled to reevaluate the grip. An improved grip can very swiftly hand you a passport to better golf.

However, developing a better grip is not as easy as you might think – perseverance is required. It is perhaps helpful to bear in mind the words of Ben Hogan: "If you don't feel like you've made a grip change, then you haven't made a grip change at all." Although a change of grip is bound to feel uncomfortable for a while, this period need not last long if you rehearse your perfect grip as often as possible, even if only for a few minutes each day. Waggle the club around to familiarize yourself with the new feelings: you will be amazed how quickly the different hand positions start to feel comfortable. The dedication you

show in these initial stages will stand you in good stead for many years to come. A sound grip promotes a neutral clubface position throughout your swing, eliminating the need to make compensations as you swing.

FORMING THE PERFECT GRIP

1 *Rest the club on the ground so that the clubface looks straight at the target. Bring your left hand forward from its natural hanging position, and place the club handle diagonally across your palm, running from the base of your index finger through the middle of your palm. Close your fingers around the club, making sure that your thumb sits fractionally to the right of center on the handle. You should be able to see two and a half of the knuckles of your left hand.*

Right hand
Hold the butt-end of the club steady

Left hand
Lay the club diagonally across the palm of your left hand

LEFT-HANDED PLAYERS

IF YOU are a left-handed player, you should form your grip in the same way as described in the three steps to "Forming the Perfect Grip," except that your hands are swapped.

GRIP VARIATIONS

OVER THE LAST 100 years or so there have been three accepted grips. The baseball grip is ideal for young golfers or those who have arthritic problems in their hands. By far the most popular style is the overlapping grip, where the little finger of the right hand literally rides "piggyback" on the forefinger of the left hand. This method is favored by players such as Nick Faldo and Ernie Els. A variation on the overlapping method is the interlocking grip, where the little finger of the right hand is entwined with the forefinger of the left.

Baseball grip   Overlapping grip   Interlocking grip

GRIP PRESSURE

IF YOUR GRIP is too tight, this can restrict the free-flowing motion of your swing. If it is too loose, your hands may slip as you swing. This simple exercise will insure that you have the correct grip pressure. Take a club and grip it as hard as you can (100 percent). Then relax your grip so that you are barely holding the club (0 percent). Now hold the club with a pressure halfway between these two extremes (50 percent). This is the perfect grip pressure, although it may vary slightly according to personal preference.

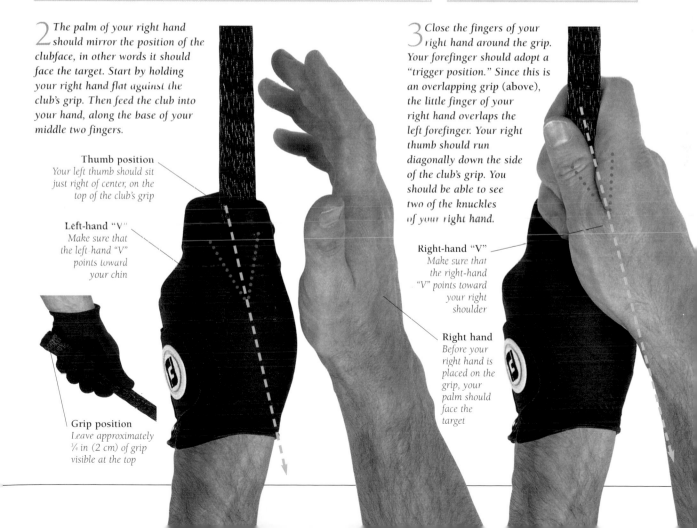

2 *The palm of your right hand should mirror the position of the clubface, in other words it should face the target. Start by holding your right hand flat against the club's grip. Then feed the club into your hand, along the base of your middle two fingers.*

Thumb position
Your left thumb should sit just right of center, on the top of the club's grip

Left-hand "V"
Make sure that the left-hand "V" points toward your chin

Grip position
Leave approximately ¼ in (2 cm) of grip visible at the top

3 *Close the fingers of your right hand around the grip. Your forefinger should adopt a "trigger position." Since this is an overlapping grip (above), the little finger of your right hand overlaps the left forefinger. Your right thumb should run diagonally down the side of the club's grip. You should be able to see two of the knuckles of your right hand.*

Right-hand "V"
Make sure that the right-hand "V" points toward your right shoulder

Right hand
Before your right hand is placed on the grip, your palm should face the target

CHECKING THE FUNDAMENTALS: AIM

IF YOU WERE firing a gun you would naturally take great care to aim correctly. Otherwise you would, it is safe to assume, miss your target. Yet when it comes to hitting a ball, many golfers pay little attention to their aim, while others simply do not know how to aim correctly. If your aim is poor, this will affect not only each shot you play but also your long-term golfing prospects. This is because if you aim incorrectly, it takes a bad swing to hit the ball

toward your target, which means that you will be constantly (unwittingly) making poor swings in an attempt to strike the ball in the right direction. Before you know it, you will have rehearsed a poor swing so often that you will not know any other way. And the longer you swing badly, the harder it is to correct your faults.

More alarming is the fact that if you do take a good swing, you will miss your

target. If you habitually practice perfect aim, however, no compensations or corrections in your swing are necessary to hit the target consistently. This means that your swing will prosper and the game will seem much easier. And the good news is that aiming is extremely simple, but it does require constant checking. Therefore, the principles demonstrated below should be applied to every shot you hit, whether you are practicing or playing an actual round.

TAKING AIM

1 One of the most effective ways to aim correctly is to identify an intermediate target just in front of you, on a line directly between the ball and the target. Then aim the clubface at that mark. This process is called "spot marking," and the likes of Jack Nicklaus and Greg Norman swear by its effectiveness. Once you have identified your mark that is on the ball-to-target line – an old divot mark or a slight discoloration on the ground is perfectly acceptable – make this the focus of your attention.

Aim the clubface directly at the spot. As you can imagine, using this technique produces far more accurate shots than if you were aiming at a target that might well be more than 220 yd (200 m) away.

Mark the spot
A raised piece of turf makes an ideal intermediate target

Target line

2 Once you are satisfied that the clubface is "spot marked," build the remaining elements of your stance around that clubface position. If you want to hit a straight shot, your feet, hips, and shoulders should run parallel to the line along which the clubface is aiming. This position, known as perfect parallel alignment, has a positive influence on the shape and quality of your swing. When you are comfortable over the ball, switch your attentions to your intended target, look back at the ball, and then "pull the trigger" safe in the knowledge that you have aimed the "gun" correctly.

PRACTICE WITH CLUBS ON THE GROUND

THE PRACTICE GROUND is where you develop the "muscle memory" to make a good address position seem like second nature. Equally, if you are careless, you can easily practice the wrong things and damage your swing. This is why you should precisely monitor what you are practicing. With aim, this is extremely simple. Lay two clubs on the ground: one just outside the ball, and the other along the line of your toes. The outer club should point directly at the target – it serves as a useful reference that will help you aim the clubface. The inner club should run parallel to the other club – it helps you align your feet correctly. Together the two clubs form a "railroad track." Check that your hips and shoulders are also parallel to the clubs on the ground (parallel alignment). If you use two clubs on the ground when you practice, you will become accustomed to aiming correctly for every shot.

AIM AND ALIGNMENT *Two clubs on the ground helps you set up correctly for every shot you hit on the practice ground. This helps instill good habits.*

Alignment
Your shoulders and hips should be parallel to the target line

Parallel lines
The alignment of your feet should be parallel to the target line

Target line

KEY CHECKPOINT

GRIP FIRST, THEN TAKE AIM

GOOD CLUBFACE aim can easily be ruined in the process of forming your grip on the club. This means that placing the club behind the ball one-handed and then forming your grip is not a good idea – it is too easy to twist the clubface. It is therefore best to establish your grip and make sure that it is comfortable before you place the clubhead behind the ball. Only then should you aim at your intermediate target. Always bear in mind this simple rule: first grip the club, then take aim, and then fire.

CHECKING THE FUNDAMENTALS: STANCE

THE STANCE IS the aspect of your setup that relates specifically to the width your feet are apart at address and to the position of the ball relative to your feet.

A good stance is crucial because it enables you to strike the perfect balance between stability and mobility. If your feet are too far apart, this will restrict your mobility, which means that you cannot make

the required body-turn (which is essential to a good swing). If this happens, you will lose power and you may find your direction suffers, too. If your feet are too close together, which means that your swing-base is too narrow, you will struggle to retain your balance as you swing and will find it difficult to strike the ball with authority. However, if you spread your feet

the correct distance at address, you will benefit from a stable base, which enhances your balance and offers the mobility to make a powerful body-turn in your backswing. Ball position is equally important. If the ball is placed correctly in your stance, this helps insure that the clubhead meets the ball on the ideal path and angle of attack. You cannot afford to ignore these potential benefits: make sure that you follow the simple but effective guidelines to establishing the ideal stance outlined here.

FORMING THE PERFECT STANCE

1 *Although your stance will change as you move through all the clubs in your bag (see the Key Checkpoint, right), it is a good idea to first establish the correct stance when using a driver. Stand with your feet close together and the ball opposite your left heel. If you stand with your feet side by side as you place the clubhead behind the ball, it is much easier to see where the ball is in relation to your left foot.*

Alignment
Remember, always practice with clubs on the ground so that you can keep an eye on your alignment

Stance
Start with your feet together and with the ball opposite your left heel

KEY CHECKPOINT

HANG TWO CLUBS TO MONITOR THE WIDTH OF YOUR STANCE

YOUR STANCE-WIDTH is a vital part of your setup but it is extremely simple to check. Hold the butt-end of two clubs in each hand, and position one against your left shoulder and the other against your right. Let gravity take its course and note where each clubhead points. If your stance is the ideal width for the driver and long irons, the clubs will point at the inside of each of your heels.

Shoulders
Your right shoulder should be lower than your left

Width check
Your shoulder width and the distance between your heels should be the same

Ball position
For a driver, the ball should be opposite your left heel

2 Draw your right foot back, but do not move your left foot (the insides of your heels should be equal to the width of your shoulders — see the Key Checkpoint, left). Flare out each foot very slightly, rather than keeping them square. This will allow your hips and body to wind and unwind as you swing the club back and forth. It is important to insure that the ball has remained opposite your left instep — the perfect position from which to deliver the clubhead to the ball with a shallow, sweeping blow. This is the ideal width of stance for the driver and all the fairway woods.

KEY CHECKPOINT

THE 1-IN (2.5-CM) RULE DICTATES THE WIDTH OF YOUR STANCE

HITTING A DRIVER requires the fullest, most dynamic swing of all the clubs in your bag – it is not surprising that your stance should be at its widest to offer maximum balance to support such a powerful movement. For the 3-iron through to the wedges, however, your stance should become progressively more narrow, and the ball should gradually edge closer to the center of your stance. Below are three "benchmark" positions from which you can work out the ideal stance for all your irons.

3-IRON: Your feet should be 1 in (2.5 cm) closer together than for the driver, and the ball should be 1 in (2.5 cm) further away from your left instep. This change is necessary to insure that the ball is positioned at the point where the clubhead reaches the bottom of its swing arc.

6-IRON: Your feet should be another 1 in (2.5 cm) closer together, and the ball should be also 1 in (2.5 cm) further away from your left instep.

9-IRON: With a 9-iron, your stance should narrow another 1 in (2.5 cm) , and the ball should again shift 1 in (2.5 cm) back from your left instep. Therefore, there should now be a 3 in (7.5 cm) difference in foot and ball position between this club and the driver.

This "1-in" (2.5-cm) rule should simplify the confusing questions of where to position the ball in your stance and how far apart to space your feet. The correct stance will give your swing a solid foundation, while helping to insure that the clubhead meets the ball cleanly and on the correct angle of attack.

CHECKING THE FUNDAMENTALS: POSTURE

POSTURE DESCRIBES the angles in your legs and upper body at address and how you distribute your weight in your setup. The key elements are: the amount your upper body bends over from the waist; the amount of flex in your knees; and the distribution of your weight on each foot. Together, these factors have a huge influence on the shape of your swing: poor angles and weight distribution invite a bad swing; good angles and weight distribution promote an efficient swing. Since a surprisingly large number of swing faults can be traced back to poor posture, this is undoubtedly one of the most crucial parts of your setup.

ASSUMING THE CORRECT POSTURE

1 Grip a 5-iron as you would normally (see pp.18–19), and spread your feet as if you were about to hit a typical shot (see pp.22–3). Then stand up straight, and, with your hands just above belt-height, extend the club out in front of you. Make sure that you relax: if you are tense now, you will be tense when you prepare to hit the ball, which will be bad for your swing.

2 Bend over from your waist. Maintain the angle between your body and your arms. Keep bending until the clubhead rests gently on the ground.

3 Finally, flex your knees, and push your buttocks out ever-so-slightly (as a result of this your stomach will be pulled in a little). Distribute your weight evenly over both feet. Your legs should feel quite springy. This posture might feel strange at first because you may well have become accustomed to addressing the ball in a completely different way. However, if you rehearse this three-step technique often enough, good posture will soon start to feel more natural. You will also benefit from a better body-turn, the overall quality of the shape of your swing will improve, and you will enjoy better balance.

Spine angle
To form the correct spine angle, bend from your hips until the clubhead rests on the ground

Legs
There should be a comfortable amount of flex in your knees at address

WEIGHT DISTRIBUTION

In an efficient golf swing, your body-weight shifts from your back foot in the backswing and to your front foot in the downswing to add power and to provide balance. But you will not enjoy these benefits if your weight is incorrectly distributed at address. What most golfers fail to realize is that the ideal weight distribution is not the same for every club – it varies depending on the type of strike you are attempting to produce. The driver, for example, works best when you strike the ball with a sweeping blow. Placing your weight so that it slightly favors your right side at address encourages this angle of attack. The principle is the same for lofted woods and long irons.

With the middle and short irons, however, it is a different story. A full swing with these clubs requires evenly spread weight, as this helps promote the necessary (descending) angle of attack.

Unless you are manufacturing a stroke (see pp.208–11), your weight should not favor your front foot at address.

(see pp.208–11)

WOODS AND LONG IRONS
If about 60 percent of your weight favors your back foot at address, this encourages you to shift your weight behind the ball at the top of your backswing. This is essential if you are going to strike the ball with the necessary sweeping blow.

MIDDLE AND SHORT IRONS
For these shorter clubs, you should distribute your weight equally: 50 percent on each foot. This balanced position promotes the correct angle of attack, which – unlike for the woods and long irons – is slightly descending.

KEY CHECKPOINT

ONE HAND-SPAN SEPARATES HANDS FROM THIGHS

IF YOU STAND too far or too near to the ball you will struggle to hit it solidly. Only by finding a happy medium will you be in a position to swing the club freely, without having to make compensations. The three-step guide to assuming the correct posture (see p.24) provides a useful guide to how far you should stand from the ball. However, as an additional measure, check how far your hands and the butt-end of the club are from the tops of your thighs – you should see about one hand-span of daylight. This suggests that you have enough room to swing your hands and arms freely, but not so much that you are reaching for the ball – a happy medium.

Although this hand-span rule provides a useful guideline, there is a bit of room to manoeuver in this area. However, a gap of more than 2 in (5 cm) either side of one hand-span will cause problems in your swing.

SPACE TO SWING *If there is about one hand-span between the top of the grip and your thighs, you are standing the correct distance from the ball.*

GOLF'S SWING ZONES

ALTHOUGH A GOOD golf swing is essentially a continuous, flowing movement, it is possible to break it down into key areas. In fact, when it comes to learning about your swing and improving your technique it is desirable to look at the swing in sections. This will help you understand how the golf swing works and why it is, in some respects, a chain reaction in which one good move often leads to another. Equally, one poor move is usually followed by another. Aside from that, throughout this book you will constantly come across terminology relating to various stages of the swing. It is therefore worthwhile familiarizing yourself with the key "swing zones."

Going back
In the takeaway, progressive rotation of your hands and forearms insures that the clubface remains square to the path of your swing

KEY CHECKPOINT

WEIGHT TRANSFER

IN ALL ATHLETIC SPORTS, good weight transfer is an essential ingredient of an effective technique. Golf is no exception. For full shots, your body weight should move in harmony with the direction of the swinging clubhead – that is, onto your back foot in the backswing and then progressively onto the front foot during the downswing and followthrough. This adds power to your shots.

1 ADDRESS POSITION
The setup, as the address position is also known, is considered mundane for all the wrong reasons and is consequently neglected by most amateur golfers. However, what you do before your swing begins determines both the shape and quality of your swing. The all-important principles of a good address position will crop up again and again throughout this book.

2 TAKEAWAY
The first link in the swing-chain is known as the takeaway. This term encapsulates everything that happens from when the clubhead first moves away from the ball to the time when your hands are just beyond your right thigh.

3 BACKSWING
Technically, the backswing includes the takeaway, but in most golfing circles the backswing relates to the area of the swing where the clubhead is going from halfway back to the point just before the club starts down again (hence the expression "top of the backswing").

7 FOLLOWTHROUGH

Just because the ball has gone, does not mean that this area of the swing is irrelevant. A classic, balanced followthrough is the hallmark of a good player. You can use followthrough imagery to influence the shape of your swing and therefore control the flight and trajectory of your shots.

6 HITTING ZONE

The moment of truth, as it is often described. The hitting zone is the 12 in (30 cm) or so either side of impact, including the point where the clubhead meets the ball. Everything you do in your swing is designed to maximize the quality of the body and club positions you reach in this zone. The optimum swing path through the hitting zone is referred to as: "inside-to-square-to-inside" (see "Swing Paths," right).

SWING PATHS

THERE ARE three basic swing paths through the hitting zone: inside-to-outside, outside-to-inside, and inside-to-square-to-inside. To hit a straight shot, inside-to-square to inside is the correct path. This is the route where the clubhead approaches the ball from inside the target line, then travels square to the target line at the moment of impact, before swinging through inside the line again after impact.

| Inside-to-outside | Outside-to-inside | Inside-to-square-to-inside |

Releasing the club
After this point, your right hand will cross over your left, which means that the clubface rotates counterclockwise and the toe overtakes the heel

5 DOWNSWING

Just as the takeaway is part of the backswing, so the transition is part of the movement known as the downswing. Broadly speaking, the downswing covers the area of the swing from when you start down to just before impact.

Starting down
Your left shoulder moves away from your chin, and your hips start to unwind

4 TRANSITION

This term describes the moment when you change direction from backswing to downswing. This is a critical moment in the swing, and although the club does not travel far relative to the swing as a whole, it is often make-or-break time in terms of the quality of the shot you hit.

OFF THE TEE

THE DRIVER, the most commonly used club off the tee, is also the most powerful club in the bag. Many golfers therefore feel that they should try to hit their drive shots as hard as they can. However, position rather than power is the most important factor off the tee. Professional golfers, who have a far greater awareness of this fact than the average player, hit most of their drives at only 70–80 percent of full power. This is the kind of attitude you should apply to your tee-shot strategy: accuracy, not length, is paramount.

In fact, to help you remember this vital truth, whenever you step on to the tee, you should not simply aim at the fairway in general but should instead identify a more specific target, such as a small mound or discoloured area of grass.

This section of the book will help you hit consistently better tee shots. The merits of teeing off with a lofted wood – which is easier to hit straight yet does not sacrifice much distance – are also discussed. At the end of this section, you should be hitting the ball more solidly, straighter, and – ultimately – further.

THE OFF-THE-TEE TEST

The first step to better tee shots is to assess your current level of ability. This test will do just that. As you perform the test, bear in mind that the key to good tee shots is position, not hitting the ball a huge distance. The test will assess your consistency and accuracy over 15 shots, the average number of drives in a round.

1 *Either: find a fairway that is about 33 yd (30 m) across (the width of an average fairway). Or: go to a driving range and identify two distance boards, or two flags, that are about 33 yd (30 m) apart.*

2 *Hit 15 balls using your driver (right), and see how many come to rest in the fairway. For a true reflection of your ability, run through this step three times, and calculate an average score out of 15.*

○ Remember, accuracy not power should be your priority. As your technique improves, and you strike the ball more solidly, you will find that you hit the ball further with no extra effort.

3 *Use the performance chart (below) to match your average score to one of the three levels. You are now ready to start working through the drills appropriate to your level of ability.*

PERFORMANCE CHART

○ ○ ○ ○ ○
1–5 = Level One
(pp.30–37)

○ ○ ○ ○ ○
6–10 = Level Two
(pp.38–45)

○ ○ ○ ○ ○
11–15 = Level Three
(pp.46–51)

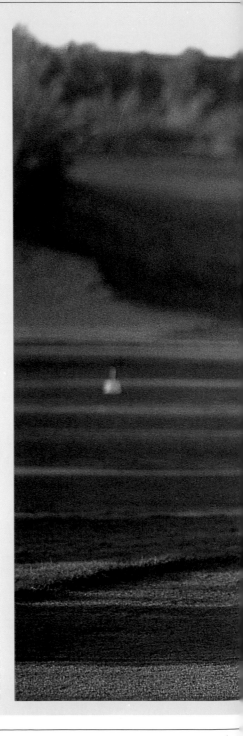

DRILL 1: Use your practice time effectively

I T IS A COMMON SIGHT: every bay at a driving range occupied by keen golfers determined to bash the ball as hard as possible, giving little thought to technique. Although there is nothing wrong with hitting drivers at the range, there has to be a structure and discipline to the procedure, otherwise you might do your swing more harm than good. This drill will give real purpose to your driving practice.

1 *Identify a specific target. If you are focused on where you want the ball to go, you will make a more focused swing.*

2 *Lay one club to the right of a ball, pointing directly at the target. Then lay another club*

parallel to the first, along the line of your toes. This will insure that every time you address a ball you are in perfect parallel alignment (see pp.20–21).

3 *Treat each practice shot as if it is a shot on the course.*

○ Quality not quantity is what good practice is all about. Most golfers would benefit from hitting half as many balls with twice the application to each one. The old saying "practice makes perfect" is only partly true; "perfect practice makes perfect" is more like it.

DRILL 2: Step into a good stance

I N YOUR STANCE, the ideal distance between your feet is usually the same as the width of your shoulders *(see pp.22–3)*. However, if you are especially tall and slim or have short legs, this rule might not apply. If either of these situations are applicable to you, then this fail-safe exercise, which is as easy as walking down the street, will help you establish the perfect base for your swing.

1 *Take the longest club in your bag, your driver, and start walking as you would normally.*

2 *After a few paces, stop walking. It is important that you do not move your feet. This is your normal stride length, which provides optimum balance as you walk. Chances are that this distance between your feet will also provide good balance when you swing a golf club.*

3 *All you need to do now is turn and face the ball, making sure that your feet stay exactly the same distance apart.*

○ Now that you have a sturdy foundation for your swing, do not forget that the ball should be opposite your left heel when using the driver *(see the Key Checkpoint on p.33)*. This helps establish a good upper body posture and enables you to sweep the ball away, which is essential for solid strikes. Good ball contact contributes to extra distance.

DRILL 3: Keep an eye on your stance

HITTING THE BALL consistently well with your driver depends on many factors. One of the most significant of these is making sure that your setup does not change from one game to the next. It is during practice time that you have the ideal opportunity to instill the right habits. Next time you are at a practice range, try this simple exercise.

1 *Before you hit your first practice shot with your driver, it is important to perform a few quick checks to insure that your stance and posture are good (see pp.22–5).*

2 *Once you have found the perfect setup, mark the position of your toes with a couple of small coins, and keep them there for as long as you continue to practice with your driver. This insures that you always stand the correct distance from the ball. Also, if the tee is fixed to the practice mat, you are guaranteed the ideal ball position every time.*

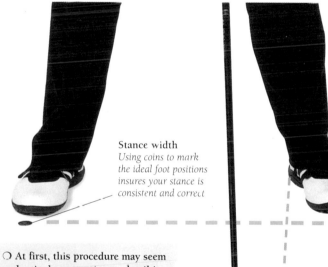

Stance width
Using coins to mark the ideal foot positions insures your stance is consistent and correct

Ball position
Opposite your left instep is the ideal ball position when using a driver

3 At first, this procedure may seem pedantic, but attention to detail is one of the keys to consistent golf – tour professionals are forever monitoring their setup. With most amateurs it is even more vital: when there may be several days between games it is easy to develop bad habits. With a club as unforgiving as the driver, even the smallest errors can be costly.

(Note: this drill can be applied to every club. The longer the club, the further you stand from the ball, so make sure that you repeat this drill with every club change.)

KEY CHECKPOINT

TEE HEIGHT: THE 50 PERCENT RULE

EACH DRIVING CLUB operates best when the ball is teed up at the correct height. However, as the size of driver heads varies greatly (and many people prefer to tee off with a lofted wood – see the Key Checkpoint on p.34), the ideal tee height is not something you can automatically take for granted.

To guarantee that the ball is always teed at the correct height, no matter what club you are using, make sure that 50 percent of the ball is visible above the top edge of the clubface. In other words, the top of the clubface should be level with the ball's equator. This, of course, means that the ball must be teed at different heights, depending on the size of clubhead you are using.

Why is this so important? Well, to strike driving shots solidly you need to swing the clubhead into the ball on a shallow angle of attack, sweeping the ball away with a level blow. You cannot do this if the ball is teed at the incorrect height. Teeing the ball too low means you may hit down steeply into impact; too high and you run the risk of hitting the ball on the upswing.

CENTRAL LINE *Whatever the size of clubhead, establish a tee height where the top edge of the clubface sits level with the middle of the ball.*

DRILL 4: Regain the "swoosh" to help your rhythm

IT IS EXTREMELY FRUSTRATING to suddenly start hitting the ball badly for no apparent reason. This annoying occurrence is usually caused by a slight loss of rhythm or timing and is sometimes triggered by one bad shot. Try this exercise to recapture the best rhythm and timing for your swing.

1 *Hold the clubhead end of the shaft of your driver and make long, rhythmical practice swings back and forth. At the lowest point of your swing, the end of the grip should be about 12 in (30 cm) above the ground. Obviously the club will feel very light, but what you need to focus on is making a loud "swoosh" through the air as the grip end of the club travels into the hitting zone of your swing (where the ball would normally be). You will only produce this sound if your timing is right.*

2 *Now grip the club as normal, but make the same smooth, rhythmical practice swings. Immediately you will feel the weight of the clubhead at the end of the shaft. Try to recreate the loud swooshing sound at the same point in your swing as in step 1.*

❍ The freedom in your swing often deserts you when you are feeling nervous or uptight. Anxiety can very easily prevent you from swinging the club freely and, instead, you start trying to "steer" the ball. This can be disastrous, especially if it happens during an important round. Next time this problem occurs, try this practice exercise, which should help you not only swing your hands and arms more freely but also release the tension in your swing. This will promote a more powerful swing of the clubhead through the ball, and before long you will find that your game is back on the right track.

DRILL 5: Swing through a corridor of tees

THE PURPOSE OF THIS DRILL is to establish whether you swing the clubhead on the right path into and through impact. The correct swing path is vital to your chances of producing an accurate shot, as it helps eliminate sidespin, which causes the ball to curve in the air.

1 *Line up a corridor of tees roughly the width of two driver clubheads apart. Place one tee in the middle of the corridor.*

2 *Swing the club freely through this corridor. The clubhead should clip the lone tee as it swings through. If the clubhead touches either line of tees, you are swinging on the wrong lines. If this happens, taking note of where you ruin the tee formation will help you correct your swing path.*

3 *When you are consistently swinging the clubhead cleanly through the corridor, place a ball on the middle tee. Try to recreate the swing you have been rehearsing. Do not swing harder – you will generate all the necessary power if you swing the club freely on the correct path.*

❍ If you consistently avoid contact with the corridor of tees, you are swinging on the correct path through the hitting area. This will help you hit straighter, and you should notice an immediate improvement in your driving.

DRILL 6: Swing your driver like you would a wedge

ALTHOUGH FEW GOLFERS have trouble hitting a solid wedge shot, using the driver is a different story. Most players want to hit their drives hard, which makes them swing more quickly and lose control. Many golfers also have a fear of the driver, which causes them to change their swing in the false belief that something special is needed to hit this club. All of these thoughts are destructive. An excellent way to overcome these problems and improve the rhythm and tempo of your driver swing is to hit alternate shots with your driver and wedge.

Smooth swing
If you swing your driver just as you did your wedge, your rhythm and accuracy will improve

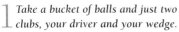

1 *Take a bucket of balls and just two clubs, your driver and your wedge.*

2 *Hit 12 or so smooth wedge shots. Do not worry too much about your aim: focus on striking the ball solidly and with control.*

3 *Now hit two or three shots with your driver. The key to this drill is to try to swing at the same speed and rhythm as you did for the wedge.*

4 *Hit another six wedge shots, followed by two or three shots using your driver. Repeat this step as many times as possible.*

○ The feeling of swinging these two clubs in the same way helps introduce smoothness into your swing, where previously there might have been a flurry of uncoordinated moving parts. The most important point to remember is that you do not have to try to hit the driver harder than you do your wedge: a smooth swing produces all the power you need.

KEY CHECKPOINT

BALL POSITION AFFECTS SWING PATH

BALL POSITION is the forgotten principle of good driving. It is ignored by most golfers, who assume it is too dull to be important. However, where you position the ball in your stance has a huge influence on the direction of your tee shots. There are three basic ball positions: too far forward in your stance, too far back in your stance, and the perfect point.

✔ *Only when the ball is ideally positioned, opposite the inside of your left heel, does the clubhead hit the ball on an online path – the ball will start its flight online, too. It is the simplest of things to keep an eye on, yet ball position has massive benefits to your drives. It would be a shame if you ignored this fundamental part of the game.*

✘ *If the ball is too far forward in your stance (which for a driver is anywhere to the left of your front foot), the clubhead will almost certainly be traveling left of target when it meets the ball, on what is known as an out-to-in path (see pp.26–7). The ball will therefore fly left and then either maintain this flightpath or slice. Neither outcome is desirable.*

✘ *If the ball is too far back (for the driver this is anywhere near the middle of your stance), the clubhead will travel to the right of target when it collides with the ball, in other words on an in-to-out path (see pp.26–7). The ball will fly right and then either maintain this flightpath or hook.*

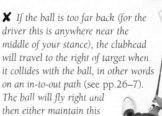

LEVEL ONE

A 3-WOOD MAY OFFER MORE THAN A DRIVER

MANY GOLFERS often assume that the driver will give them the most distance off the tee. However, for a number of players this is not the case.

The driver is a straight-faced club, and because of this it sends the ball on a low trajectory. If you do not generate sufficient clubhead speed through impact, the ball will not spend enough time in the air to achieve a decent length. If this is the case, it is perhaps better to use a more lofted club, such as a 3-wood, which will send the ball on a higher trajectory, therefore creating more airtime and a longer drive.

Another good reason to use a 3-wood is if you have a fault in your swing that means that you do not consistently deliver a square blow to the back of the ball. In this situation, the driver's straight face will create lots of sidespin on the ball, which means losing distance as the shot curves through the air. The extra loft on a 3-wood's clubface helps to nullify this sidespin.

However, if either of these situations apply but you feel that teeing off with a 3-wood is too much of a sacrifice, you might wish to explore the possibility of buying a more lofted driver – something with about 13–15 degrees of loft on the face (*see pp.230–31*).

DRIVER VERSUS 3-WOOD *The clubface of a 3-wood* (left) *has more loft than the clubface of a driver* (right). *This makes a 3-wood more forgiving and easier to hit straight.*

DRILL 7: Get your head and torso behind the ball at address

JUST AS A BOXER plants his or her weight on his back foot before delivering a knockout punch, so a golfer also needs to shift his or her weight in the same way to deliver maximum power to the ball. It is vital to transfer your weight onto your back foot at the top of your backswing. This is much easier if you start your swing with your weight already favoring your right side. Rehearse the following exercise to help familiarize yourself with the mechanics of good weight distribution.

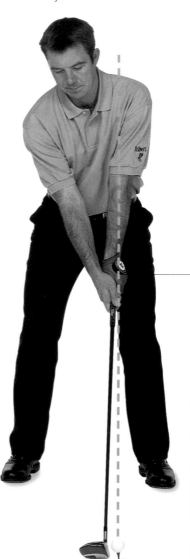

1 Take a driver and stand upright, with your weight spread evenly over both feet. Assume your address position over the ball.

2 Tilt your spine angle away from the target. When you do so, you should feel your balance shift, so that 60 percent of your weight is on your back foot.

3 Check that your head and torso are behind the ball. This should happen naturally as a result of the changes made in step 2.

Stance
This is the correct setup for a driver, with virtually all your upper body behind the ball

○ This exercise makes it easy to load your weight onto your right side and to position your head and torso behind the ball at the top of your backswing. From this position you will find that you can really "punch your weight" and generate much more power. All of golf's big hitters – including the likes of Tiger Woods, Ernie Els, and John Daly – start their swing from behind the ball at address. This helps them produce the huge distances they are capable of generating time and time again.

DRILL 8: Hit the back of the net

WHEN YOU ARE HITTING a few balls into the practice net prior to a game, you do not think about mishitting the shot or guiding the ball. You just swing freely and thump the ball into the back of the net. So why not think exactly the same thoughts when you are actually on the first tee? This visualization drill will undoubtedly help you hit better shots under pressure.

1 *Before you start a round, hit a few shots in a practice net, concentrating only on making a free swing and creating a solid strike. Watch the ball fizz off into the middle of the net.*

2 *Without hesitation, walk straight to the first tee, and, as you play your first shot, think only of the mental image of the ball flying at great speed into the middle of the practice net.*

○ Rather than becoming anxious about the outcome of a shot, or worrying about potential hazards on a hole, simply focusing on "hitting the back of the net" will help you produce much better tee shots. This exercise is a good way to make all your fears disappear and to create a more positive swing.

DRILL 9: Choke down on your driver

TOO MANY GOLFERS are obsessed with hitting the ball as far as possible. Yet most players would drive the ball a lot straighter and, strangely enough, further too if they thought of the driver as a positional club. This quick practice drill will teach you how to hit your drives straighter, with no great sacrifice in terms of distance.

1 *Take your driver from your bag, and adopt your normal grip and address position.*

2 *Alter your grip so that your hands are 1¼–1½ in (3–4 cm) nearer the clubhead and you can see the end of the club's grip clearly protruding above your left hand. This is described as "choking down" on the club.*

3 *Swing as you would normally: you should experience a feeling of greater control. Although you have effectively shortened the length of the club's shaft – which slightly reduces both the arc and the length of your swing – you do not need to feel like you are making changes to your swing. These things happen automatically.*

Grip
Choke down so that 1¼–1½ in (3–4 cm) of the club's grip protrudes above your left hand

Chin
Move your left shoulder under your chin to promote a full turn in the backswing

○ Choking down on your driver is a great trick to have up your sleeve on a really tight fairway. Although you may lose a little distance, the extra control you will enjoy promotes straighter drives, and keeping your tee shots in play on the toughest holes will seem that much easier.

LEVEL ONE

WHY YOU SHOULD WAGGLE

VIRTUALLY ALL professional golfers "waggle" the club before starting their swing. This move varies from one golfer to the next, but all waggles insure that the golfer's hands and arms are soft and relaxed at address, which promotes a free-flowing swing.

The waggle can also give you a sneak preview of the path of your takeaway, which allows you to get used to that all-important first move away from the ball. If, for example, you want to make sure you do not take the club back too much on the inside, you can waggle, watching to insure that the club moves back on the correct path.

Furthermore, the waggle can serve as a preview to the type of rhythm you will achieve in your swing. If, for example, you are feeling nervous (and will therefore tend to swing too quickly), rehearsing a couple of very slow waggles will help settle you down a little and will lead to a smoother start to your backswing. This smoothness should continue through your entire swing.

Develop your own kind of waggle, and use it to get your swing off to a good start. One of the best things you can do for your swing is introduce a waggle.

WAGGLE THE CLUB *Moving the club back and forth – "waggling" – before beginning your swing is an excellent way to ease tension in your hands, arms, and shoulders.*

DRILL 10: If you slice, try strengthening your grip

HOW YOU GRIP the club largely determines how the clubface strikes the ball. If your grip is weak – where the Vs formed by the thumb and forefinger of each hand (*see p.19*) point toward your chin – it is unlikely that the clubface will be square with the ball at the point of impact. In most cases the face will instead be open, which leads to a glancing blow and a weak (often sliced) drive. If these problems sound familiar, this exercise will help you strengthen your grip.

1 *Form your grip on your driver in the normal way.*

2 *Take your right hand off the club so that you have an unobstructed view of your left hand. If your grip is weak, you will only be able to see one knuckle on the back of your left hand.*

3 *To steady the club, hold the bottom of the club's grip with your right hand. Loosen your left hand grip just enough to enable you to rotate your grip to the right until you can see three knuckles on the back of your left hand. Your left thumb should also sit slightly to the right of center on the grip (but should still be pointing straight down). The V formed by your left thumb and forefinger should now be pointing at your right shoulder.*

4 *Apply your right hand to the club's grip so that the V of your thumb and forefinger also point at your right shoulder. You should now be able to see just one knuckle on your right hand and three knuckles on your left hand (never more than that).*

❍ Strengthening your grip is an excellent way to help insure that the clubface is square at impact (to produce more solid strikes). This should eliminate sliced drives. Your new grip will also feel so much more powerful than your old, weak grip. A stronger grip can be of particular benefit to women, as well as seniors and juniors, all of whom might be struggling to generate sufficient distance off the tee.

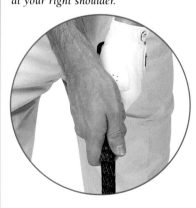

✗ Weak grip

✔ Strengthened grip

Drill 11: **If you hook, try bringing your grip back to neutral**

THE WAY you place your hands on the club's grip controls the behavior of the clubface during your swing. If you are plagued by a persistent hook, chances are that your grip is too strong, which means the clubface will be closed at impact. Basically this is the opposite problem to that of a golfer who slices the ball. One of the best ways to cure a hook is to weaken an overly strong grip so that it becomes neutral. This will help you deliver the clubface square to the back of the ball.

1 *Take your driver from your bag and form your grip as if you were about to hit a tee shot.*

2 *Now remove your right hand from the club. If your grip is too strong, when you look down you will be able to see perhaps four of the knuckles on your left hand.*

3 *Hold the bottom of the club's grip firmly with your right hand. Carefully rotate your left hand grip to the left so that you can only see two or two-and-a-half knuckles on the back of your left hand.*

4 *Now introduce your right hand so that it sits more on top of the grip. While previously you probably could not see any of the knuckles on your right hand, you should now be able to see two knuckles. Also, your right thumb should sit more on top of the grip, rather than to the right (as is the situation if you have a particularly strong grip).*

○ Weakening your grip so that your hands assume a more orthodox position on the club will feel strange at first (like any change to your swing). Initially it is wise to restrict yourself to practice swings, so that you can become accustomed to your new grip. As you become familiar with the hand positions, the clubface will stay more neutral – perhaps even a fraction open – during your swing. This reduces the likelihood of hooking and makes it easier to hit straight tee shots.

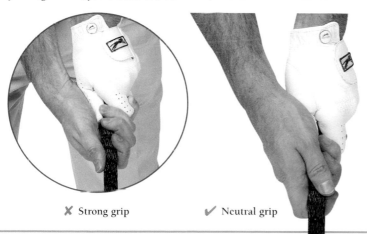

✗ Strong grip   ✔ Neutral grip

KEY CHECKPOINT

POSE FOR A PHOTO TO IMPROVE BALANCE

A GOOD WAY to curb any tendency to hit the driver too hard is to think of one simple word: balance. If, while you swing, you concentrate solely on finishing in a perfectly balanced position (as if you are posing for a photograph for the clubhouse honors board), the chances are that your swing is under control. If you cannot maintain a balanced followthrough, you are almost certainly swinging beyond your limits of control.

PICTURE PERFECT
In a well-balanced followthrough, your weight transfers to your left side, your right heel raises off the ground, and your belt buckle faces the target.

RETEST YOURSELF

Before moving to Level Two, take the test on pp.28–9 again. If you have not improved, it is worth revisiting the Level One drills. However, if the performance chart shows that your tee shots have progressed sufficiently, then you are ready to tackle the more advanced drills in Level Two.

KEY CHECKPOINT

USE EXISTING DIVOT MARKS TO IMPROVE YOUR AIM

WHEN SEARCHING for a spot to place their tee, most golfers try to find an unmarked patch of turf on the tee. However, to do this is to sacrifice a valuable opportunity to aim correctly. Next time you are teeing up, look for an old divot mark that is aiming straight at the target. If you place the ball on a tee just behind the divot mark, you will have a ready-made guide when it comes to lining up the clubface with the target. You can then build your stance around that.

Divot marks can help your swing path, too. Try to find a divot mark that points straight at the target, but this time place the ball on a tee just in front of the divot mark. In your downswing, imagine that you will swing the clubhead into the back of the ball along the line of the divot. This imagery will help promote the correct swing path into impact, which is one of the keys to a good tee shot. This teeing up method has the added advantage of guaranteeing no interference between the clubface and the ball, which means you can achieve the purest of strikes.

HELPFUL DIVOT MARKS *Positioning your ball behind a divot mark pointing at the target (left) will help you aim. A divot mark behind the ball (right) will help you swing on the correct path.*

DRILL 12: Practice a pause at the top of your backswing

WHEN USING THE DRIVER, it is common for golfers to be a little over aggressive when moving from the backswing to the downswing. This very swiftly wrecks any chance of striking the ball solidly. If you find yourself doing this, but cannot shake the habit, this exercise will be of enormous benefit to you.

1 *Start by making a normal backswing, all the way to the top.*

2 *Pause at this point for no more than a fraction of a second.*

3 *As you begin your downswing, try to cultivate a "lazy" feeling, as if this all-important first movement down with your hands and arms is little more than a result of gravity taking its course.*

○ This short pause at the top of your backswing is over in a split second, but it is an extremely valuable time. It allows you to gather together your moving parts – your hands, arms, body, and club – all ready to surge down toward the ball in one combined movement, culminating in a powerful impact. See Drill 16 (*p.41*) for a different way to achieve the same result.

Top of the backswing
Practicing a brief pause at this point means all body parts can work together in the downswing

"Lazy" downswing
The first movement down must not be rushed

DRILL 13: Hit 4 o'clock on the ball

ONE OF THE MOST common faults club golfers experience is the slice, which is brought about by swinging the clubhead across the ball-to-target line and through impact on an out-to-in swing path (*see* pp.26–7). The following drill is a practice exercise that, while requiring you to use a little imagination, is an extremely effective way to insure that you are swinging along the correct path.

1 *Assume your normal address position and look down at the ball.*

2 *Imagine the ball's spherical shape as a clock face, with the target line running from 3 o'clock to 9 o'clock.*

3 *Keep your eyes fixed on a point on the ball correlating to 4 o'clock.*

Target line

Direction of clubhead

4 *As you are swinging, try to move the club down in such a way that the clubhead strikes the ball somewhere around 4 o'clock.*

○ If you swing the club on an out-to-in path through impact, causing a slice, then you are striking the ball somewhere around 2 o'clock. The mental imagery this drill provides will instinctively encourage you to swing the club down on the correct path, attacking the ball from inside the ball-to-target line. After practicing this exercise, you should notice that your shots are flying much straighter – your slice may well become a thing of the past.

DRILL 14: Look for a straight line down to the ball

ANYTHING YOU CAN DO at address to promote a better swing is worth considering. The following practice drill insures that when you set up to hit your driver, the club shaft appears to be an extension of your left arm. Bear in mind that when you come to hitting shots, it is acceptable (when using the driver) for the hands to be over the ball rather than ahead of it. This exercise will help give your swing the best possible start.

1 *Make sure the ball is positioned opposite your left heel.*

2 *Assume your normal posture, but let your left arm hang limp from your shoulder, while holding a driver with your right hand.*

3 *Feed the club into your naturally hanging left hand. You will see that it forms an almost straight line with the shaft all the way down to the ball. This is a good position to start from.*

○ The reason this is such a good starting point is because it makes it easier to keep the club and your left arm working together in the takeaway. Lots of swing problems arise from losing that connection early on, so that the club is not synchronized with your arms and body. This exercise should enable you to regain that link.

DRILL 15: Feel a "turn and a swish" for a natural swing

THERE ARE TWO ELEMENTS that combine to produce the perfect swing: body turn and arm swing. Too much of one and not enough of the other is disastrous – the plane of your swing will be all wrong, and you will struggle to deliver the clubhead to the back of the ball on anything like the correct path

or angle of attack. Too much arm swing, which makes your swing too straight, is a common problem. It is a result of one simple fault: the shoulders not turning enough. If you have had this problem for some time, it can be difficult to put right. This drill, however, should provide a constructive remedy.

1 *Take your driver and stand totally upright, with your arms stretched out in front of you, your hands just below shoulder height.*

2 *Swing the club around yourself, focusing on the rotary motion of your upper body, and letting your hands and arms swish the clubhead back and forth very freely. Make sure that you also feel your weight transferring to the right in your backswing, as your left shoulder turns under your chin. As you make the return swing from right to left, your weight shifts toward the target and on to your left side as you move into the followthrough position. This movement is not unlike a baseball swing and enables you to familiarize yourself*

with a powerful upper-body turn – something that may well have been lacking in your swing previously.

3 *Now stand over a ball and bend from the hips ever so slightly, until the clubhead reaches a point about 2 ft (60 cm) above the ground. Make the same swing, again focusing on the key elements: a proper weight transfer and a free swish of the clubhead through the hitting area. You should feel your arms straightening as the centrifugal force of the swinging club pulls you into the followthrough.*

4 *Bend further still from the waist, until the clubhead rests on the ground, and flex your knees a little. You should now be in the ideal address*

posture for the driver. As you swing, think only of repeating the sensations experienced in steps 2 and 3 – a full turn of the body, good weight transfer, and a wonderfully free swish of the clubhead as you smoothly accelerate down and through the hitting area.

○ If you can recreate the feelings associated with this drill and let the ball get in the way of the swing, rather than becoming too "hit orientated," you will strike the ball sweetly and release the club properly (*see p.27*). You will have achieved a better balance between body turn and arm swing. Drill 16 (*right*) shows how to correct a loss of synchronization between these two elements.

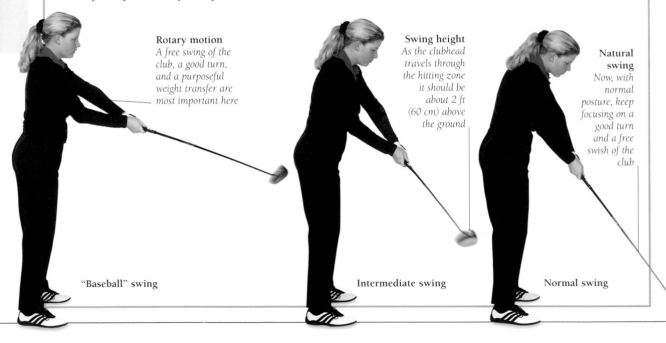

Rotary motion
A free swing of the club, a good turn, and a purposeful weight transfer are most important here

Swing height
As the clubhead travels through the hitting zone it should be about 2 ft (60 cm) above the ground

Natural swing
Now, with normal posture, keep focusing on a good turn and a free swish of the club

"Baseball" swing   Intermediate swing   Normal swing

Drill 16: Synchronize your arm swing with your body turn

LOSING COORDINATION between your arm swing and body turn is a common fault. It can cause a loss of rhythm and make your swing feel clumsy. When this happens, even well-struck shots lack zip. With most golfers, the body moves too early and races ahead of the hand and arm action (the opposite problem is unusual). This is one of the main causes of a sliced drive: the shoulders and upper body unwind too fast in the downswing, throwing the hands and arms outside the ideal swing plane, causing the clubhead to cut across the ball from out to in. If you are slicing your drives, try this drill, which is based on a piece of advice by Harry Vardon, record six-time winner of the Open Championship.

1 *Take your driver and make a normal backswing.*

2 *From the top of your backswing, concentrate on getting your hands and arms swinging the club down to hip height before your shoulders and upper body even start to unwind.*

3 *As you continue swinging downward, your body should start to unwind in harmony with your hands and arms.*

○ This drill eliminates the tendency for your shoulders to spin out too early in the downswing, which throws the club outside the correct path and causes a sliced drive. Improved synchronization will lead to better timing and more powerful ball striking.

Backswing
Swing the club to the top as normal

Body position
Think of your hands and arms swinging down to hip height before your body starts to unwind

KEY CHECKPOINT

THE RIGHT KNEE MAINTAINS ITS FLEX

THE POSITIONING of the right knee is an important ingredient in a successful swing with a driver. Keeping the right knee flexed during the backswing and well into the downswing provides two benefits. First, it creates resistance in the legs and hips as you make your backswing: this gives a major source of power and is an effective way of stopping your backswing becoming too long and uncontrolled. Second, maintaining the right knee flex well into the downswing helps keep your right heel on the ground for longer, which stops your angle of attack becoming too steep. It is a shallow swing that is needed with the driver.

BACKSWING *Keep your right knee flexed to create resistance in your swing. This will stop your backswing becoming too long, which causes a loss of power and control.*

DOWNSWING *Maintaining the flex in your right knee as you swing the club down promotes a wide downswing arc and a sweeping angle of attack, which is ideal for the driver.*

LEVEL TWO

DRILL 17: Keep your left heel grounded to add resistance

WHETHER YOU SHOULD lift your heel off the ground in the backswing – one of the most commonly asked questions about the swing – depends on what type of golfer you are. If you are flexible and do not have a problem making a full backswing turn (or even have a tendency to overswing), then you should probably keep your left heel grounded. This stops your hips turning too far in your backswing and keeps your overall swing compact. You will be able to wind up your body with more resistance from the lower half, resulting in a faster unwinding of the body spring in the downswing. To help you keep your left heel grounded, try this drill.

1 Take up your normal address position, and squeeze a golf ball under the toes of your left shoe. You will feel your weight distribution being tipped toward your left heel, which is good.

2 As you move into your backswing, try to keep your weight on your heel. With the ball under your toes, if you do lift your left heel, your balance will become very rocky indeed.

3 Hit a few shots with the ball under your toes (start with practice swings before moving on to practice drives), then remove the ball, and see if you still keep your left heel grounded.

○ Although the guidelines for lifting or not lifting your left heel are not set in stone, if you are very flexible (often young and/or slim golfers) or tend to overswing, then it is probably worth considering keeping your left heel grounded. However, watch out for the reverse pivot – where your weight moves toward the target in the backswing. Make sure that your weight still transfers onto your right side during the backswing (especially if you have been lifting your heel for some time). If you do decide to keep your left heel grounded, you will be in good company – Tiger Woods, Ernie Else, Fred Couples, and many others do exactly the same.

STANDING ON A BALL
It is almost impossible to retain any sense of balance during your swing if your left heel rises while there is a ball under the toes of your left foot.

DRILL 18: Lift your left heel for a fuller turn

WHILE KEEPING THE LEFT HEEL grounded (*see Drill 17, left*) during the backswing has several benefits for some golfers, others may not find this technique so helpful. Indeed, for anyone who lacks flexibility in the swing and, therefore, struggles to make a full turn – most likely senior golfers or those with a heavy physique – lifting the left heel is probably going to be advantageous. It will enable you to make a more complete turn in your backswing, adding length to your swing and power to your shots. Also, if your swing tends to be too short and quick, letting your left heel come off the ground will give you more time to make a fuller, slower – and therefore more effective – swing. And if you have a tendency to reverse pivot (where your weight moves toward the target in the backswing instead of onto your right side), lifting your left heel will force your weight onto the right side, which is essential in a well-executed backswing. If you think lifting your left heel might help your game, the following practice drill will insure that you develop the correct technique.

1 *Address the ball and start your backswing as normal.*

2 *When you reach the position in your backswing where you feel that your hips and shoulders will not "give" any more, this is the point when the left heel is effectively pulled off the ground to release the right side and to allow for a bigger turn. This is bound to feel unusual if you have never lifted your left heel off the ground in your swing before, but it will work if you let it happen as a consequence of your turning motion, rather than concentrating on lifting it independently.*

3 *To initiate your downswing, plant your heel back on the ground. This starts your weight moving in the right direction – flowing toward the target. The great Henry Cotton, a three-time Open Championship winner, used to stamp his left heel down so firmly to start his downswing that you could actually hear it thump onto the ground as he changed direction.*

○ It is important to remember that lifting the left heel is not an independent movement – the heel should instead lift in response to the twisting motion of your hips and upper body. Lifting your heel should give you a fuller, more powerful swing. And there is the added benefit that planting your heel back down again is a great way to start your weight transferring toward the target, one of the key ingredients of a powerful swing. Jack Nicklaus and Tom Watson are just two of the many famous players who prefer to lift their left heel.

Heel up
Lift your left heel in your backswing

Heel down
Stamp your left heel down to start your downswing

Backswing

Downswing

DRILL 19: Turn your back on the target

GO LOW AND SLOW: that is a great way to start your backswing with a driver. But where do you go from here? This exercise is very useful for anyone who lacks direction in the backswing, or is simply struggling with driving. It involves two key ideas, which together can have a great influence on the quality of your driving.

1 *As you make your backswing, try to turn your back on the target. This will encourage you to make a full turn of your shoulders, will promote a much better weight transfer onto your right side, and will also help you set the club on the correct line at the top of your backswing.*

2 *When you reach the top of your backswing, try to point the club at the target. This idea is particularly beneficial for golfers who slice the majority of their drives. This is*

because these players tend to point the club to the left of the target, which results in an outside the line downswing (see pp.26–7), causing them to cut across the ball through impact and produce a sliced drive.

○ Turning your back on the target insures a good body rotation, which is essential for generating power, while pointing the club at the target means that the club will be online. These two key elements combine to put you in a much better position to swing the club down freely and on the correct path through impact, resulting in more clubhead speed and a more solid contact.

DRILL 20: Miss the heel by addressing off the heel

MANY GOLFERS hit a number of their drives out of the heel of the club, which is a tell tale sign of an out-to-in swing path *(see pp.26–7)*. This causes drives to fly left-to-right through the air. An effective

way to cure this fault is, bizarrely, to address the ball out of the heel of your driver – the very spot on which your problem manifests itself. Try this drill and you will soon see the benefits of this technique.

1 *Place a ball on a tee as if you were about to hit a tee shot. Adopt your usual address position.*

2 *Move the clubhead until the heel of the club is level with the ball, and then make a swing.*

○ This drill is so effective because once you have addressed the ball out of the heel of the club, your hand-eye coordination will "force" you to reroute the club on the way down so that you strike the ball out of the middle of the clubface. American tour professional Fuzzy Zoeller, a former Masters and US Open champion, has addressed the ball out of the heel of the club throughout his career to help him swing down on the correct (inside) line. Even if you do not introduce this technique into your game "full time," it can at least serve as a very fast and effective way to correct a fault that may have crept into your swing.

Address position
For this drill, address the ball out of the heel of the club

DRILL 21· Tilt your spine to pack a power punch

MANY GOLFERS with mid to high handicaps have a fundamental problem with their spine angle at address: not so much in the degree of tilt toward the ball, but in the amount of lean to the golfer's left or right. The most common fault is for the spine to lean toward the target slightly, which places the head and upper body too far ahead of the ball at address (and therefore also at impact). Tee shots hit from this position usually have very little power and do not travel as far as they should. This drill will introduce the ideal spine tilt into your address position, which will undoubtedly help you hit your drives more solidly.

1 *Stand up straight and bend from the waist to address the ball. Although your spine angle is tilted toward the ball, it should be perpendicular to the ground if you were to see yourself from behind.*

2 *Now angle your spine away from the target ever so slightly, so that your right shoulder is lowered a fraction and your left shoulder is raised slightly. This is the spine angle of a good player – the difference is subtle but significant.*

○ If your spine is tilted away from the target at address, chances are that the same will apply at impact. This also means that your head will be behind the ball at impact, which not only provides maximum leverage in your swing but also allows you to deliver a sweeping blow, with the clubhead perhaps traveling slightly upward as it meets the back of the ball. These factors will significantly improve the quality of your drives.

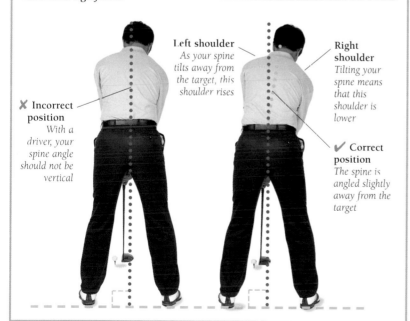

✘ **Incorrect position**
With a driver, your spine angle should not be vertical

Left shoulder
As your spine tilts away from the target, this shoulder rises

Right shoulder
Tilting your spine means that this shoulder is lower

✔ **Correct position**
The spine is angled slightly away from the target

KEY CHECKPOINT

THINK OF YOUR FOREARMS TOUCHING FOR A BETTER RELEASE

NOT RELEASING the clubhead (*see p.27*) through the hitting area is one of the worst faults in a swing. This means there will be very little clubhead speed, just when you need it most. To overcome this problem, simply try to think of your right forearm touching your left forearm as you swing the club through impact. This swing thought will help you release the club on every tee shot you hit, which will mean more clubhead speed delivered to the back of the ball and a marked increase in distance.

FOREARMS MEET *Think of the forearms almost touching in the followthrough, and the clubhead will release correctly.*

RETEST YOURSELF

Before moving to Level Three, take the test on pp.28–9 again. If you have not improved, it is worth revisiting the Level Two drills. However, if the performance chart shows that your tee shots have progressed sufficiently, then you are ready to tackle the more advanced drills in Level Three.

LEVEL TWO

DRILL 22: Shake hands with the target

A GOOD RELEASE of the clubhead through impact (*see p.27*) is part and parcel of a powerful swing. It indicates that the club has been swung freely and with maximum clubhead speed. However, instead of releasing the clubhead, some amateur golfers attempt to guide the club or prod at the ball. Next time you are practicing, try the following exercise to insure that this key move is performed correctly.

1 *Adopt your normal posture but without a club in your hands.*

2 *Let your right arm hang naturally, but fold your left arm behind your back (alternatively, place your left hand in your back pocket).*

3 *Make half-swing movements (to approximately hip height on either side of your swing) with your right arm. The key to this exercise is to feel that you are "shaking hands" with the target as you swing your right arm through the hitting zone.*

4 *When you are comfortable with the hand movement described in step 3, rehearse a few practice swings with your driver.*

5 *Now swing in slow motion, and freeze when your right arm reaches horizontal with the ground in your followthrough. At this point, your right hand should be in line with the target, ready to shake hands. If your hand is pointing to the left or right of the target, or your palm is angled toward the sky or the ground, you need to make some adjustments: try repeating steps 1–3.*

Without a club
The right hand is shaking hands with the target

With a club
The right hand is still shaking hands with the target, indicating a good release of the club

○ If, when you hit your next tee shot, you make sure that you "shake hands with the target," you will release the club better than ever. This is certain to add power to your shots.

DRILL 23: Keep it all together in your takeaway

IF YOU LOSE SYNCHRONIZATION between your arm-swing and your body turn at the start of your swing, it is incredibly difficult to regain in the split second it takes to reach the hitting stage. Here is a fantastic exercise that was popularized by David Leadbetter and Nick Faldo in their time together and has since been adopted by hundreds of golfers hoping that some of the duo's magic might rub off.

1 *Take the driver from your bag, and assume your normal stance.*

2 *Feed the club up through your fingers so that the butt-end of the club rests in your navel and your hands grip the metal of the shaft.*

3 *Rehearse a backswing movement, turning your body and moving the club away from where the ball would normally be, but focus entirely on keeping the butt-end of the club resting against your midriff. Go no further back than the point where your hands reach just beyond your right thigh. Repeat this movement over and over.*

○ When you come to hit shots again, start your swing by recreating the feelings experienced in this drill. This insures that your arms and body move away together, and if they are together at the start they stand a much better chance of being together throughout the swing.

Eyes
Watch the clubhead as it moves back

Grip
Hold the club by the shaft

Club position
Insure that the club continues to rest against your midriff during your backswing

LEVEL THREE

KEY CHECKPOINT

ARE YOU A SWINGER?

THERE ARE two distinct types of player: swingers (*below*) and hitters (*see p.49*). Both styles are effective; the key lies in recognizing which method best suits you.

Great swingers, such as Ernie Els or Davis Love, have stylish swings and a smooth rhythm. They appear to use little effort yet hit the ball a huge distance. The power in a swinger's action comes from the winding and unwinding of the body: this creates tremendous centrifugal force, which is passed out through the arms to the club and onto the ball. To have a good swinger's action you need to be flexible and have a naturally slow rhythm. When making your backswing, think of images associated with slowness and ease. Your downswing should start smoothly, your weight shifting to the left as you start to increase power through acceleration. By the time you get to the bottom of your swing, you should have a sense of the clubhead freewheeling into the back of the ball. This will pull you into an elegant, balanced finish.

SMOOTH SWINGER *Davis Love has one of the most elegant swings in the game and is also among the longest drivers.*

DRILL 24: Create a box at the top of your swing

AT THE TOP OF YOUR BACKSWING, the relationship between your right arm, hands, club shaft and upper body is an important one – never more so than with the driver. This drill will help insure that you are in the ideal position from which to start your downswing.

Perfect position
If your right upper arm, your right forearm, and the shaft of the club form three sides of a box, then your wrists have hinged correctly at the top of your backswing

1 *Swing your driver to the top and freeze right there.*

2 *Now look over your right shoulder. What do you see? The ideal scenario is that the shaft of the club forms a right angle with your right forearm, which in turn forms a right angle with your right upper arm, so that you have three sides of a box. This position encompasses the correct amount of wrist hinge, which is all important with the driver.*

○ Many golfers tend to be too narrow in this part of the swing because their wrists have buckled at the top. This can lead to a loss of control. If you have this problem, at the top of your backswing you will see an angle of less than 90 degrees between the shaft of the club and your right forearm. If this angle is greater than 90 degrees, your wrists are not hinging enough in the backswing. Check the box at the top of your swing to administer the required changes. Your tee shots will almost certainly benefit from keeping this aspect of your backswing in check.

DRILL 25: Turn your left shoulder to where your right shoulder was

ALL KINDS OF MENTAL IMAGERY can help you produce a better swing. Here is an exercise that should insure that you make a 90-degree turn in your backswing, which is a minimum requirement for generating plenty of power with your driver.

1 *Assume your normal address position, but take a brief moment to think about the position of your right shoulder.*

2 *At the top of your backswing, try to turn your left shoulder into the position your right shoulder occupied at address.*

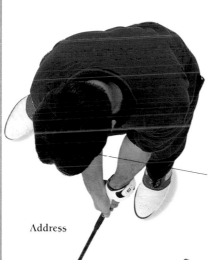

Address

Mental imagery
Concentrate on turning your left shoulder into the position presently occupied by your right shoulder

Backswing

Shoulder position
The left shoulder is now situated roughly where the right shoulder was at address

○ This exercise encourages two very positive things to happen: first, it promotes a better upper body turn; and second, it insures that you transfer your weight onto your right side. Together, these two factors should help you make a more powerful swing with your driver.

KEY CHECKPOINT

ARE YOU A HITTER?

WHILE A SWINGER (*see p.48*) has a flowing action, a hitter has a less aesthetically pleasing swing, but in the end the results of the swing are all that matter.

A good example of a hitter is Tom Lehman, Open champion in 1996, who bludgeons the ball with his strong forearms. Although a hitter's drive does not come from strength alone, muscle rather than mechanics generates most of the power. A good hitter needs to be strong and, usually, to have a brisk swing rhythm. If you are adopting this approach, when you start your backswing, take the club back mostly with your hands and arms, but do not forget to turn your upper body as far as you can. Keep your backswing short, so that the club does not become parallel with the ground at the top. Start down slowly, but pummel the ball with your hands and arms through impact. You should sense that there is a definite hit at the bottom of your swing. Your followthrough need not be perfect, but it must be balanced.

POWER HITTER *Tom Lehman is a powerful man whose swing may not be classic, but it is very effective.*

LEVEL THREE

KEY CHECKPOINT

TEE UP CORRECTLY ON PAR-3 HOLES

MANY GOLFERS tee the ball up too high on par 3s in the mistaken belief that this will enable them to hit nice, high iron shots to the green. However, this assumption is wrong. If you tee the ball up too much and make a good swing, you will hit the ball with the top edge of the clubface. As a result, the ball will then not fly anywhere near as far as it should. Therefore, teeing the ball up too high encourages you to make a bad swing: you have to hit up on the ball in order to strike it with the center of the club.

This does not mean that you should not use a tee on par 3s. Although you must hit irons directly off the grass on the fairway, as a tee gives you a perfect lie, this opportunity should not be wasted.

When using an iron off the tee, the ideal teeing height is such that the ball sits just above the level of the ground. Viewed from grass level, you should only see the cup of the tee. If the grass is lush, you may not even see that, and the ball should look as if it is resting on the tips of the blades of grass. This tee height encourages you to swing the club into the back of the ball, creating ball-then-turf contact – an integral part of a crisp iron shot (*see the "Iron Play" section, pp.54–79*).

PERFECT HEIGHT *For tee shots with an iron, you should tee the ball up so that only the cup of the tee is visible.*

DRILL 26: Close the clubface at address for distance on the run

THERE ARE PLENTY OF SITUATIONS where it is advantageous to get the ball to run more than normal, such as when you are playing into a strong wind and need to generate maximum distance off the tee. Rehearse this super effective drill on the practice ground and you will never be found wanting again on a windswept links.

1 *Place two clubs on the ground: one parallel with the ball-to-target line, and another pointing slightly right to establish a fractionally closed stance.*

2 *Rest the clubhead behind the ball, but do not apply your grip.*

3 *Keeping the clubhead behind the ball, use your right thumb and forefinger to twist the clubface ⅜ in (1 cm) counterclockwise.*

4 *Making sure that you do not upset the new position of the clubface, carefully form your grip as you would normally.*

○ This tiny adjustment means that you can make a normal swing, yet will strike the ball with the clubface in a stronger position. This can add approximately 22 yd (20 m) to a drive into a headwind, due to increased run thanks to a lower ball flight.

The exercise can also be used as a quick fix for a slice at times when you do not want to change your swing – in the middle of a round, for example. This is because this technique helps prevent you hitting the ball with a slightly open clubface, which is the cause of many high, sliced drives.

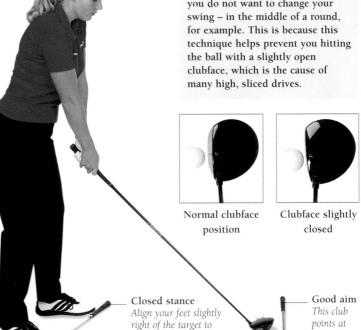

Normal clubface position

Clubface slightly closed

Closed stance
Align your feet slightly right of the target to compensate for the closed clubhead

Good aim
This club points at the target

DRILL 27: Pick and mix your practice drives

A GOOD PLAYER should always be prepared to hit a variety of clubs off the tee in a normal round of golf. You should certainly not automatically reach for your driver on every par 4 or par 5, as it might not be the club that will leave you the easiest second shot. It could, for example, bring into play hazards that would not be a threat with a shorter club. Here is a great exercise you can do at the range that gives you the knowledge necessary to hit different clubs off the tee successfully and provides the confidence to "call the shots" on the course.

1 *Once you have warmed up properly (see pp.214–15), put aside 12 or more balls. Select the three longest clubs from your golf bag.*

2 *Hit the first ball with your longest club – the driver – applying all the principles and skills you have developed throughout this section.*

3 *Hit the second ball with your next longest club, which will probably be a 3-wood. The only change you need make is to tee the ball lower than you did with the driver, so that the top edge of the clubface sits level with the ball's equator (see the Key Checkpoint on p.31). Other than this minor change, your swing should remain the same.*

4 *Hit the third ball with the final club selected – either a more lofted wood or a long iron. You will need to tee the ball lower still, and position it* 1 in (2.5 cm) *further back in your stance. These alterations accommodate a slightly less sweeping angle of attack into impact. One thing that should remain constant with all three clubs is the rhythm of your swing.*

5 *Hit each subsequent shot with alternate clubs until you have worked through all 12 balls.*

○ After you have practiced this drill a few times, you should find that there is no dramatic inconsistency from one ball to the next. You can also use this exercise when practicing other departments of the game, such as iron play. The idea is the same: to prepare yourself for the fact that you never hit the same shot twice in a row on the golf course.

Head position
You should feel that your head stays behind the ball at impact

Coordination
Sense that your body rotates in harmony with the swinging motion of your hands and arms

Impact
Ideal contact means that the ball will be swept away off the tee

LEVEL THREE

THE PERFECT TEE SHOT

ONE OF THE MOST ELEGANT golf swings in the world is that of double US open champion Ernie Els. His super-smooth rhythm is an inspiration to watch. Els is not only a golfer to admire but also an outstanding one to learn from. With a driver in his hands, Els produces extremely powerful shots with apparent ease. This is down to his superb technique, not strength alone. Now that you have completed the drills in the "Off the Tee" section, you are in a good position to pick up pointers from these images of Els in full flow. Watching a master in action is a good way to improve your game.

Downswing
As the arms swing down, the angle between the left forearm and the club shaft momentarily remains the same

Impact
The wrists uncock just before hitting the ball, which unleashes maximum clubhead speed at the moment of impact

Knees
The knees remain braced, providing a stable base to support the unwinding of the upper body and the free swing of the hands, arms, and club

1 ADDRESS
Els has perfect posture, an impressive feat for a man who stands 6 ft 4 in (193 cm) tall. His knees are flexed just the right amount, which gives him a balanced stance. His spine is angled so that his arms hang free from tension, and there is a comfortable space between his hands and the tops of his thighs. This means he has room to swing the club on the correct path. His alignment is also very good. His toes, knees, and hips all run parallel to the target line, and the clubface looks directly at the target.

Backswing
The club travels just beyond horizontal at the top of the swing, which is fine (letting the backswing go beyond this point would make it difficult to control the club, however)

Followthrough
The right hand rolls over the left, indicating a free release of the clubhead after impact with the ball

5 HITTING ZONE

Els makes 300-yd (275 m) drives look easy – evidence that power comes from good mechanics, not brute force. By turning his left side, Els has made room to swing the club into the ball on the correct path. As the clubhead strikes the ball, the club moves back inside the target line.

KEYS TO CONSISTENT TEE SHOTS

OFF THE TEE, the most important consideration is position, not power. Here are a handful of final swing thoughts to help you achieve this aim.

○ *To promote solid contact, tee the ball opposite your left heel.*

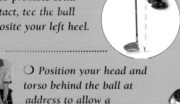

○ *Position your head and torso behind the ball at address to allow a purposeful weight transfer onto your right side during your backswing.*

○ *Turn your shoulders fully in your backswing to help set the club on line at the top.*

○ *Make a smooth transition from your backswing into your downswing. This will allow your hands, arms, and body to work together in harmony to produce a solid impact.*

○ *For a powerful release, feel that your right hand "shakes hands" with the target as you swing the club through impact.*

2 BACKSWING

You can see here how Els has perfectly blended his body-turn and arm-swing, with the appropriate wrist action beginning to set the club on the perfect plane. Note also how his left shoulder is turning under his chin.

3 TOP OF THE BACKSWING

Notice Els' fine upper body rotation, and how his left shoulder is now under his chin. Els' hands are above his right shoulder: a sure sign that his swing is on the correct plane. Also note the braced leg action

4 DOWNSWING

Here Els' hands and arms have swung down almost to hip height, but his upper body has scarcely begun to unwind. This helps slot the club on to an inside track: the perfect prehitting position. From here Els can deliver full power.

IRON PLAY

IRON CLUBS are the precision tools in your bag, each one designed to hit the ball a certain distance. Iron play as a whole encompasses two types of shot: advancement shots, where on a long hole you play for position (in order to make the next stroke easier); and scoring shots, where the flag is the focus of your attention. Whichever shot you look at, trajectory and distance are the primary considerations.

This section of the book will teach you all the skills you need to improve the quality of your ball striking with each iron. It will also raise your levels of accuracy and consistency.

THE IRON-PLAY TEST

Hitting the ball a long way with irons is not an issue, then. Hitting the green, however, is an accurate barometer of your ability, and this idea forms the basis of the iron test. Although there are several irons in your bag, a test encompassing every club would be too time-consuming. Therefore, this test should be carried out with a 6-iron, a club that is neither too demanding nor too easy to use.

1 *Take 15 balls from your bag, preferably of the same make and construction (to minimize inconsistencies). Ideally you should do this test on a golf course, where you can hit balls at a proper green. But it can also be performed at a driving range, where there are flags and greens to aim at. Perform the test on a calm day if possible, since a strong wind may lower your scores to a level that does not reflect your true ability.*

2 *Hit some "range finders" to work out your personal 6-iron distance. Position yourself this distance from a medium-sized green, and hit the 15 balls towards the green (right). See how many come to rest on the green.*

3 *Repeat the above step another two times, and calculate an average figure based on the number of times you hit the green. Compare your results with the performance chart (right).*

○ Always remember that each iron is designed to hit the ball a certain distance – there is hardly ever any call to force an iron shot. All you need to do is take a lower-numbered club and swing with the same rhythm.

LEVEL ONE

LEVEL TWO

LEVEL THREE

PERFORMANCE CHART

○ ○ ○ ○ ○
1–5 = Level One
(pp.56–63)

○ ○ ○ ○ ○
6–10 = Level Two
(pp.64–71)

○ ○ ○ ○ ○
11–15 = Level Three
(pp.72–7)

DRILL 1: Find your range with every iron

EACH IRON in your bag is designed to hit the ball a certain distance. However, every golfer is different, which means that each person will have his or her "personal distance" for each club. The first drill for golfers wanting to improve their iron play therefore involves establishing how far the ball flies with each iron club. This enables you to make more accurate club selection decisions during a round.

1 *Take the same batch of 15 balls that you used to carry out the performance test (see pp.54–5).*

2 *Lay two clubs on the ground to insure that you always have perfect parallel alignment (see Drill 1, p.30, in the "Off the Tee" section).*

3 *Work through your irons, hitting all 15 balls with each club. Once you have hit one "set," pace out the distance to the main cluster of balls, and take a note of the figure. Ignore the longest two or three and the shortest two or three, as these probably do not accurately reflect how far you usually hit the ball.*

○ While a distance chart might give you a rough idea of which club to hit, it is much more valuable to have a precise, personal distance in your mind for each club. (It is a good idea to have a note of these distances in your golf bag.) This will give you increased confidence every time you come to play an iron shot.

One final point. It is not safe to perform this drill at a busy driving range. Instead, find a quiet fairway on a course or go to a practice range when it is deserted. This way you will not be in the firing line when you pace out your distances.

Release
Make your right hand roll over your left through the hitting zone

Perfect strike
The ideal contact is ball-then-turf, which means that there is a divot mark after the point of impact

LEVEL ONE

Drill 2: Establish good ball position for all your irons

IN THE "OFF THE TEE" SECTION, the importance of the correct ball position (opposite your left heel to promote a sweeping blow at impact) was described *(see the Key Checkpoint on p.33)*. Ball position is equally crucial in iron play, as it partly determines whether the clubhead will meet the ball at impact on the correct angle of attack. Obviously there are many different numbered irons, therefore ball position varies as you move through the clubs. This drill will help you appreciate the correct positioning for each iron.

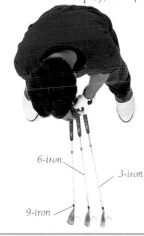

6-iron

3-iron

9-iron

1 Stand as if you were about to hit a long iron shot, with your feet comfortably spaced so as to provide good balance.

2 Take a 3-iron, a 6-iron, a 9-iron, and three balls from your bag.

3 Place one ball opposite you, on an imaginary line 1¼ in (3 cm) inside your left heel. Rest the clubhead of your 3-iron behind the ball. Position the second ball 1¼ in (3 cm) further back, and rest the 6-iron behind that. Then, finally, place the third ball 1¼ in (3 cm) further back still, and rest the 9 iron behind that. These three balls indicate the ideal positions for the clubs that you are holding.

○ Obviously there are more than three clubs in your set. But this all-in-one stance establishes some benchmark positions from which you can gage the ideal ball position for the rest of the irons. Using these positions when you swing helps insure that the clubhead will meet the ball cleanly and on the correct angle of attack *(see the Key Checkpoint on p.61)*.

Drill 3: Frozen at address? Start your swing with a forward movement

THERE ARE MANY REASONS why you might become tense at address and "freeze" over the ball. Whatever the cause – perhaps an excessively tight grip pressure or possibly anxiety about your swing or the upcoming shot – freezing over the ball usually leads to a jerky takeaway, which will ruin your swing when it is barely underway. To become accustomed to the feeling of making a smooth first move away from the ball, try this great drill, which involves starting your swing with a forward movement.

1 Form your normal address position, but with one subtle difference: position the club so that it is hovering just above the ball rather than behind it.

2 Now sweep the clubhead about 30 in (75 cm) forwards (in the direction of the target). Without a pause, swing the club all the way to the top, trying to maintain the smooth rhythm of the initial forward movement. Then swing down into and through impact. Take it easy at first: perhaps try a few practice swings before you hit shots using this technique.

○ If you practice starting your swing with a forward movement, you will become accustomed to not freezing over the ball, and your backswing will be much smoother and less rushed than before. This technique also encourages your arm-swing to work more in harmony with your body turn.

DRILL 4: Let heel-toe weighting teach you good balance

HOW YOU BALANCE your weight at address has a much greater influence on the shape of your swing than you might think. This simple exercise will help you appreciate the relationship between weight distribution and how you swing an iron. It involves addressing a ball with the two extremes of poor weight distribution, so that you can then split the difference and find a happy medium.

1 *Address a ball as you would normally, but place most of your weight on your toes. Now try to make a swing. You will tend to lift your body and head up and backward. You will also try to shift your weight back on to your heels, all to stop you falling forward – just as if you were teetering on the edge of a cliff. You then have to compensate for this sudden extra height by dipping down into impact in an effort to reach the ball. Obviously, this makes your swing very unbalanced, and you cannot achieve any power or consistency.*

2 *Now for the opposite. Put most of your weight on your heels at address. Although this feels strange, many golfers play this way. With your weight too much over your heels, the tendency is to stand too tall at address. Subconsciously your brain knows this, so the natural compensation is to dip your head and body in the backswing, in an effort to restore the correct height into your swing. With your weight tumbling forwards in the backswing, you lose your balance in the downswing and usually fall back on to your heels – just where you started.*

3 *Now try to spread your weight evenly between your heels and toes. This is the perfect balance.*

○ Correct weight distribution encourages good all-round posture, which is reflected in a better-balanced swing. You do not have to dip or lift your body to maintain balance. Without having to make any height adjustments along the way, you can turn your body, swing your arms, and the clubhead will move freely into the back of the ball.

✗ Weight too far forward

Weight on toes
From here you will have to fight the tendency to topple forward in your swing

✗ Weight too far back

Weight on heels
From this position you will have to guard against falling away from the ball in your swing

✔ Correct balance

Weight perfect
From an evenly balanced set-up you can make a good swing

DRILL 5: Find better direction with an intermediate target

IN ORDER TO FIND the target, the ball must start on the correct line. Although this sounds obvious, many golfers tend to be obsessed with thinking about the last part of a ball's journey to the flag, when instead they might be better off considering the initial portion of the ball's flight. This drill requires only a small bucket (or similar object) to improve the initial direction of your shots.

1 *Place a ball-bucket about 5½ yd (5 m) in front of you, along the ball-to-target line.*

2 *Before you hit a shot, aim the clubface directly at the bucket.*

3 *As you swing, think of the ball flying directly over the bucket after it leaves the clubface.*

○ Although it is against the rules to place an object in front of you to improve your aim during an actual round, you can continue to imagine the ball flying over a bucket directly in line with the target. This mental imagery will improve the direction of all your iron shots and will help you find the green more often.

MAKE SURE JUNIORS USE SUITABLE CLUBS

IF YOU HAVE a son or daughter younger than thirteen who is taking up golf, make sure that he or she does not use clubs that are castoffs from an adult. These clubs will be too heavy. It is impossible for a young boy or girl to set a heavy club high enough in the backswing to produce the ideal swing plane; instead, gravity and the weight of the club produce a swing that is way too flat. Sadly, habits formed in early life, good or bad, are hard to change later.

The best solution is to give your aspiring golfer a half set of junior clubs. If this is not possible, women's clubs or cut-down men's clubs (ideally fitted with slim grips to accommodate small hands) will suffice. These clubs should be light enough to allow the youngster to swing the club into a better backswing. Choosing appropriate clubs is discussed in more detail in the "equipment" part of the reference section (see pp.230–35).

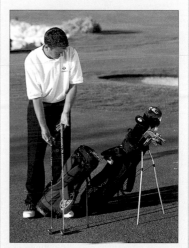

JUNIOR SET *Clubs specifically made for young players are shorter and lighter than adult clubs. Juniors are more likely to swing correctly with such clubs.*

DRILL 6: Video yourself to learn about your setup and swing

IF YOU OWN OR CAN BORROW or rent a video camera, you have an excellent opportunity to examine and improve your swing. This drill focuses on a mid-iron swing, but you can use a video camera to check aspects of your game covered in other parts of this book.

Alignment
Place clubs on the ground and check that your stance and aim are correct

1 *Before you begin filming, you must position the camera correctly. When you are checking your alignment, posture, and swing plane the camera must be looking "down the line." If you imagine a railroad line extending back from the target, with the inner rail on the line of your toes and the outer rail on the ball-* to-target line, then the camera should be midway between these two rails. (It is a good idea to place two clubs on the ground to mark the positions of these "railroad lines.") When checking your ball position, stance, followthrough, and weight transfer the camera must be "face on" (in front of you). It should be exactly opposite the middle of your stance, facing your navel. If the camera position is even a fraction out, it will give you the wrong information about your swing.

Posture
Keep your chin up to allow for a full shoulder turn

Stance
Make sure that your ball position is correct

Camera position
This position is described as "face on," and is very useful for checking your grip, ball position, and stance

2 *Begin by examining your address position. This is the easiest part of your technique to monitor and is conveniently also probably the most important. Many players do not believe that the only static element of the swing is the most vital, but this rule applies to every golfer, from the complete beginner to the tour professional. With the camera positioned directly opposite you ("face on"), and with a mid-iron in your hand, begin filming. When you watch the video, start by checking that the width of your stance is correct: the inside of your heels should be about the same width apart as your shoulders. Now examine the ball position: about two ball-widths inside your left heel is good for a mid-iron. Also insure that your grip is neutral: ideally you should be able to see two knuckles on your right hand and two, perhaps three, on your left hand. If your stance, ball position, and grip are in good shape, you are off to a good start.*

3 *While still in the address position, you must also check that your alignment is correct. Move the camera to your right and place it so that it is looking "down the line." When you watch the video, check that your shoulders, hips, and toes run on a line parallel to the left of the flag, and that the clubface is aiming directly at the flag. Check that there is a comfortable gap between your hands and the tops of your thighs, and that your posture is neither too hunched nor too upright. Look out for the telltale signs of good posture, which include that your right shoulder is over your right toe and that your knees are a little bent.*

4 Now position the camera opposite you and make a few backswings. When you watch the video, check that your weight shifts on to your right foot in your backswing and that your head moves laterally to the right (your left as you watch yourself) – anywhere between 2 in (5 cm) and 4 in (10 cm) is adequate.

Backswing
Check that you complete a full shoulder turn

5 Switch the camera angle again so that it is looking "down the line." Rehearse your backswing, and freeze when your left arm is horizontal to the ground. If your wrists hinge correctly, the club should set on to the ideal backswing plane, whereby the butt-end of the shaft will point at a spot on the ground midway between the ball and your toes.

6 Now hit some shots. Later, you can use the freeze-frame facility on your video player to confirm that your backswing is on the correct plane (as described above). You can also check your downswing: freeze the video when your left arm is horizontal to the ground. The butt-end of the shaft should point at the ball or perhaps a little outside it.

Followthrough
Your right shoulder should be over your left foot

7 Finally, analyze your followthrough. Position the camera across from you, and hit some shots. When watching the tape, check that your right shoulder is roughly over your left foot. This shows that your weight has moved fully on to your left side, as it should.

○ Watching your swing on video can be an alarming experience: what you see is often different from what you feel. But do not be disheartened. If you know what to look for, this process is incredibly informative and beneficial to your long-term progress. Even if you do not have a video camera, it is worth borrowing one every couple of months to see how your swing is developing.

KEY CHECKPOINT

WHEN AND WHY YOU TAKE A DIVOT

ALTHOUGH EVERY iron shot should be struck crisply, with no interference between the clubface and the ball, some iron shots produce a divot and others do not. The reason for this is that to hit a good long iron shot, a sweeping angle of attack – where the clubhead strikes the ball with a shallow blow – is necessary.

Because the ball is swept away, there should never be a divot mark – perhaps just the slightest bruising of the turf. However, with more lofted clubs, good contact demands a progressively more descending angle of attack. Therefore, with a club such as a 6-iron, where the ball is positioned slightly further back in your stance (*see Drill 2, p.57*), the clubhead will meet the ball on a more downward path. This means that the clubhead should first strike the ball and then the turf, taking a divot after the ball has been struck. The more lofted the club, the further back in your stance the ball is placed, and the more pronounced the descending angle of attack becomes. A divot taken with a club such as a 9-iron will therefore be larger than a divot taken when using a 6-iron.

Ball-then-turf contact is what solid ball striking is all about: the divot should start *after* the point where the ball was struck. If you take a divot before impact, lots of turf will be trapped between the clubface and the ball. This is known as "heavy" contact. Taking no divot at all is fine with longer irons, but if there is no divot mark after impact with any club from a 5-iron upward, then you are not striking the ball as you should be Drill 9 (*see pp.88–9*) in the "Pitching" section describes how you can learn about your swing by examining your divot mark.

DRILL 7: Freeze-frame all the right moves

Watch your swing
Carefully observe each of the key positions

Wrist hinge
As your left arm reaches horizontal, your wrists should set the club shaft at a 90-degree angle

A FEW MINUTES swinging a club and rehearsing key positions in the swing can make all the difference when it comes to keeping your swing on track. Therefore, even if you do not have time to hit balls during the week, this "maintenance" exercise will at least stop you becoming too rusty between games. It will help you develop the muscle memory and sensations of a good technique.

1 *Make a "stop-go" swing in slow motion, and freeze-frame the key positions.*

2 *Use the sequence of photographs of Per-Ulrik Johansson (see pp.78–9) to check that your positions are correct.*

3 *Try to become accustomed to the feeling of what you see, thereby introducing "muscle recognition" of the most important positions in a swing.*

○ Although your proper swing is obviously much faster, the more you repeat this drill, the more likely it is that your body will instinctively find the practiced positions. This exercise is doubly effective when performed in front of a full-length mirror, or even some windowed patio doors in which you can see your reflection.

DRILL 8: Split the difference to find the ideal swing speed

G OING TO EXTREMES in your game can often help you find the happy medium. The following practice drill, which is a good example of this theory, might just help you find the perfect balance between control and speed when you swing an iron.

1 *Take a 6-iron and three golf balls. Hit the first ball with every ounce of strength you can muster.*

2 *Hit the second ball as if you want it to fly half the distance of the first. Swing as slowly and lazily as you can.*

3 *With the final ball, split the difference. Make a swing that is halfway between overly hard and ridiculously easy.*

○ Once you have worked through this drill and found the happy medium – a perfect balance between control and power – it is a good idea to spend the next 10–15 minutes becoming as familiar as possible with the tempo of this swing. You will quickly discover that this is the kind of swing that will work most effectively for all of your iron shots.

DRILL 9: Make sure that all your practice swings are for real

THERE IS NO BETTER swinger of a golf club in the world today than Davis Love. He has a wonderfully smooth rhythm and the sort of effortless power that is magnificent to watch. Much of this must stem from one of his favorite swing thoughts, which he has stuck with throughout his long career: "I feel like when I make a practice swing it should be a rehearsal for what I'm getting ready to do. Then when I get the clubhead behind the ball I'm trying to copy the practice swing I just made." This drill shows you how to incorporate this idea into your game.

1 Next time you are practicing your iron shots, before you hit a ball, make a smooth practice swing. Concentrate on your rhythm and on building acceleration through the hitting area.

2 Then address a ball and try to repeat your practice swing. Just let the ball get in the way of the clubhead as you smoothly accelerate down and into impact. There is no hit, as such: it is more of a swinging motion.

○ Since most amateur golfers seem to make better practice swings than they do real swings, this drill can be marvelously effective. You might well be surprised how solidly, and how far, you can hit the ball.

KEY CHECKPOINT

KNOW WHEN TO QUIT

IF LONG IRONS are causing you trouble, you might be better off swapping your two longest irons, say your 3- and 4-irons, for two lofted woods, maybe a 5- and a 7-wood. There is no shame in it: eight-time Ryder Cup player (and captain for 2001) Sam Torrance often carries a 7-wood in his bag.

These clubs are easier to hit and more forgiving than long irons. Your good strikes will be rewarded with a high-flying, relatively long ball flight, and your mishits will not be so bad. And a small-headed, lofted wood is versatile: you can hit it off the tee, from the fairway, and from light rough, where an iron might become snagged. Drill 27 in the "Off the Tee" section (see p.51) will help you hit shots with a fairway wood.

FAIRWAY WOODS *As you move from a 7-wood (left), to a 5-wood (middle), to a 3-wood (right), the loft on the clubface gradually decreases.*

RETEST YOURSELF

Before moving to Level Two, take the test on pp.54–5 again. If you have not improved, it is worth revisiting the Level One drills. However, if the performance chart shows that your iron play has progressed sufficiently, then you are ready to tackle the more advanced drills in Level Two.

DRILL 10: Let a rope teach you new tricks

ONE OF BRITAIN'S most respected teachers, Jim Christine, is a great advocate of the benefits of swinging a rope in practice. Although you might wonder how this could possibly help your game, after trying this drill you will realize that a humble length of rope can improve the rhythm and efficiency of your swing, enabling you to create more clubhead speed with less effort. A worthwhile exercise, then.

1 *Find a length of thick rope about 3 ft (90 cm) long.*

2 *Assume your normal grip and address position. The rope should be just touching the ground.*

3 *Swing your hands and arms upward in tandem with your upper-body rotation. If your backswing is on the ideal plane, the rope will curl gently around your left shoulder. If your backswing is too flat – if your body is doing too much turning, and your arms not enough swinging – you will find that the rope will not make it that high. Conversely, if your backswing is too upright – if your arms are swinging too high, and your body is tilting rather than turning – then the rope will hit you on the head or neck.*

4 *The change in direction from backswing to downswing is one of the most important split seconds in the swing (see Drill 15, p.68), and the rope will teach you a valuable lesson in not rushing this first move down. So, take your time at the top of your backswing: you should feel a slight lag as your weight starts to shift to the left. When your hands and arms start to swing down, the rope will respond to this movement. As you continue to move down, smoothly building up speed, the rope will rapidly catch up with your hands and arms and "snap" straight at the bottom of your swing, like the cracking of a whip. This is centrifugal force taking effect, which means the rope reaches maximum speed at the perfect time: when it is in the hitting zone.*

○ With this exercise you know when you are making a bad swing because the rope reacts differently than described in steps 3 and 4. If you use your upper body too forcibly, the rope will not swing freely through the hitting area. Too much upper body movement will also cause the rope to swing from out to in as your right shoulder throws the rope away from your body and outside the ideal plane. Also, if your weight transfer is poor, the rope will not swing as it should. Note that the positions achieved in the rope exercise and those in a proper swing are remarkably similar. If you can recreate what you did with the rope when using a club, you will swing more easily and hit the ball better. For these reasons it is a good idea to occasionally incorporate this drill into your practice routine.

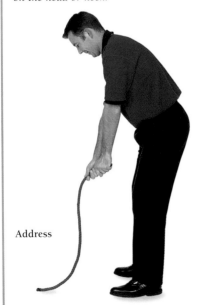

Address

Top of the backswing

The hitting zone

DRILL 11: Monitor your strike when you practice

IF YOU ARE PRACTICING your iron play from grass, rather than on the mats at a driving range, this routine will help you monitor the quality of your strikes. The exercise produces the clearest results when the grass is closely mown.

1 *After placing the ball you are going to hit on the grass, put a second ball about two ball widths outside the ball-to-target line, but in line with the original ball.*

2 *With an 8-iron, hit the first ball. Swing as you do normally.*

3 *Check where the divot mark starts by comparing it to the position of the second ball. With a crisply struck mid-iron shot, the divot mark should start fractionally after the point of impact.*

⊃ The moment of impact happens so quickly that even with the best eyesight in the world you cannot possibly keep track of everything that is going on. However, the kind of feedback provided by this practice exercise gives you valuable information that you can use to improve your technique.

IDENTIFY YOUR GO-FOR-THE-FLAG RANGE

MANY PIN POSITIONS are designed to throw you off. If the flag is close to either side of the green, or is situated just over a front bunker, you have to be very careful about aiming for the flag because if you miss you will probably be left with a delicate shot and very little green to work with. You should therefore determine which clubs are "go for it" clubs and which are "middle of the green" clubs. If, for example, you feel very confident about your accuracy with every club from a wedge to an 8-iron, then when using a 7-iron or lower, you should switch to a "middle of the green" approach. Do not ever be tempted to step out of this comfort zone.

In fact, if club golfers ignored the flag during a round and aimed for the center of each green, there is a good chance that their scores would fall over a period of time.

IRON ATTACK *Be clear in your own mind which clubs you can go for the flag with. Any clubs longer than these are "middle of the green" clubs.*

LEVEL TWO

KEY CHECKPOINT

DOWNSWING SPEED SHOULD MATCH BACKSWING SPEED

BOBBY JONES was a magnificent golfer who, despite retaining amateur status, dominated the game in the 1920s and 30s, winning seven major championships before he turned 30. He was also a guru of golf instruction, shaping the way the game was played at that time. One of his favorite pieces of advice is still relevant and indeed is adopted by many of today's great players. His tip was that you should start your downswing at the same speed as you began your backswing. This avoids the tendency to rush the first move down, which will ruin any golf shot, and gives the hands, arms, club, and body plenty of time to work together. It is such a simple thought, yet is so very effective. That was part of Jones's genius as an instructor.

SAME SPEED *If your downswing starts at the same speed as the beginning of your backswing, the chances of making an unhurried swing, where all body parts move in unison, are greatly improved.*

DRILL 12: Use your shadow to learn about your swing

THIS EXERCISE can tell you a lot about your swing. But it does require one vital ingredient: sunshine. You will be amazed what you can learn from your shadow. However, this is a drill for practice swings rather than hitting shots, as it requires you to take your eye off the ball.

1 *With the sun directly at your back, take up an address position so that the ball is right in the middle of your shadow. Using a long iron, swing to the top of your backswing. Ideally, your shadow should move to your right, so that the ball is in direct sunlight. If this happens, it indicates that your weight has moved on to your right side, an essential ingredient in any successful backswing. If this is not happening, your shadow will tell you as much.*

2 *With the sun still at your back, address the ball again. Have a helper place a club on the ground so that it sits on the top of your shadow's head. As you swing back, watch your shadow and see how your head behaves. It should not move up or down: in any good swing the head always stays almost level from address until impact.*

○ This practice drill is invaluable because weight shift and head position are very difficult to keep tabs on as you swing. Seeing your swing via your shadow can shed a whole new light on your game. The next drill (*right*) reveals another way to monitor head movement.

Checking weight transfer

Checking head movement

DRILL 13: Move your head to the right as your weight shifts backward

THIS DRILL, which requires a helper, enables you to determine exactly how much your head moves during your backswing. It is an especially revealing exercise for any golfers who believe the false assumption that the head should remain completely still throughout the swing.

1 *Address the ball as normal, and position a helper opposite you.*

2 *Instruct the helper to dangle a club vertically in front of him- or herself so that as the helper looks at you, your head is bisected by the shaft. The helper can now monitor the movement of your head as you swing.*

3 *If you are swinging correctly, all of your head should move to the helper's left of the dangling club during your backswing, as you load your* weight on to your right side. *If your head stays where it was in step 2, or worse still, drifts to the helper's right, then your weight is not moving correctly in your backswing.*

4 *If necessary, repeat steps 2–3 until your helper confirms that your head has moved sufficiently to the left of the shaft during your backswing.*

○ Head position is something you should definitely be conscious of, not so much when you are playing, but certainly when you are working on your game.

DRILL 14: Train your head not to move up or down

UNLIKE THE PREVIOUS two drills, which examined the importance of lateral head movement, this exercise concentrates solely on becoming accustomed to not moving your head too far up or down as you swing into impact. This is important because if you lose or gain height during your downswing you will struggle to hit the ball cleanly.

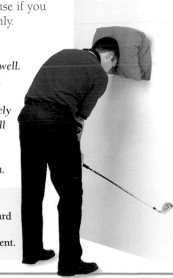

1 *Position yourself so that you are right next to a wall, and assume your normal posture.*

2 *Rest your head on a pillow up against the wall. Your head will hold the pillow in place.*

3 *Rehearse your backswing. Your head should not move up or down.*

4 *Now swing down. Your head should maintain its original height until the point where impact would be. This means that your* spine angle will have remained the same as well. *If these things occur in your proper swing you will swing the club freely into the back of the ball and not have to make adjustments for head movements up or down.*

○ In your backswing, your head must move 2–4 in (5–10 cm) to the right to facilitate a good weight transfer. As you swing into impact, your head may even move a fraction toward the target. So while this drill, which insures that you keep your head still, may seem to advocate something incorrect, it is designed to eliminate excessive up or down head movement.

DRILL 15: Wait, then apply the hit

THE TRANSITION from backswing to downswing is a critical phase in your swing. In the split second when you change direction, you have two choices: you can make a great first move down and successfully store the power in your swing, or you can rush it and forget about producing a good shot. This simple drill will insure that your swing falls into the former category every time.

1 *Make a normal backswing, but have a helper hold the clubhead in position at the top.*

2 *Initiate your downswing by moving your weight on to your left side, unwinding your hips a little. With the helper holding the clubhead firmly in position, you should feel some pressure in your wrists, as the angle between your forearms and the club shaft becomes more acute.*

3 *Now make some practice swings and try to recreate the feelings experienced in step 2. Remember, as you change direction you should feel that the clubhead lags behind for a fraction of a second.*

Wrist pressure
With the club held in position, there will be some resistance in your wrists

Firm hold
The club is held toward the top of the shaft

Top of the
backswing

Beginning of the
downswing

○ This vital move from backswing to downswing is the one that stores the energy in your swing, enabling you to unleash power into the back of the ball as your wrists uncock. It is like the motion of cracking a whip (*see Drill 20, p.72*): if you time it correctly, the clubhead speed at the bottom of your swing will be phenomenal.

Drill 16: Focus with your left eye for solid strikes

IF YOUR UPPER BODY slides toward the target prematurely in your downswing, this is called "getting ahead of the ball." If this happens, you will lose leverage and therefore power because there is no point of resistance at impact. You will probably hit weak shots to the right of the target, and will struggle to hit the ball from the middle of the clubface. This drill might help cure the tendency to get ahead of the ball

1 Place a ball on the ground in such a way that the manufacturer's logo is horizontal to the ground. Turn the ball until the logo sits along the ball's equator. From your address position you should just be able to see the edge of the writing on the ball.

2 Swing to the top of your backswing and focus on the writing on the back of the ball with your left eye only (closing your right eye might help).

3 Maintain this focus until the clubhead makes contact with the ball.

○ This drill will help you instinctively keep your head behind the ball at impact. If your head is behind the ball, your body cannot get ahead of the ball. If you lose sight of the writing on the ball, your head is sliding toward the target in your downswing. Keep trying until you are confident that you can keep your left eye on the back of the ball, then try to apply this principle on the course.

Drill 17: Throw a ball to improve your release

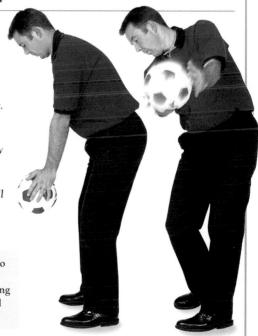

THIS DRILL provides an interesting way to recreate the hand movements required to release the clubhead (see p.27) powerfully through the hitting area. The exercise, which is best performed outside, requires only a ball and a little imagination.

1 Hold a ball with both hands, and try to assume something resembling your normal posture for a mid-iron shot.

2 Move your hands and arms back to hip height. Then swing the ball down and through the hitting zone. Try to spin the ball 30 degrees to the left of the ball-to-target line. To achieve this your right hand must cross over your left in the area where impact would normally be made. If the ball goes straight ahead of you, your hands are moving in such a way that you will not release the clubhead properly when you make a real swing.

○ You do not necessarily need to take a ball with you every time you go to the range, but if you keep the image of throwing a ball in mind as you practice, you might find it easier to release the clubhead freely. It is amazing how a strong mental picture can sometimes trigger the appropriate physical reaction and therefore improve your ball striking.

DRILL 18: Stay square in the takeaway

AS YOU MAKE YOUR BACKSWING, the clubface should stay square to the path of your swing. If this is not the case, you will be forced to make compensations mid-swing in order to present the clubface square to the ball at the point of impact (which is vital for a straight shot). It is therefore prudent to check the position of the clubface in your swing, using this simple drill.

1 *Make your normal takeaway, but stop when your hands are just above your right thigh.*

2 *Compare the position of your clubface with the three images below.*

✔ **CORRECT POSITION**
The clubface is looking just a little to the right of the ball as a result of the correct rotation of the hands and forearms in the takeaway. This is the position you should try to emulate in your swing.

Square face
In a good takeaway, the clubface is square to the path of your swing

✗ **CLOSED CLUBFACE**
As a result of a lack of hand and forearm rotation, the clubface is still looking at the ball, which means it is closed to the path of the swing. Because it is difficult to achieve a more neutral clubface position later in the swing, this kind of takeaway will probably lead to a pull or hook.

✗ **OPEN CLUBFACE**
The hands have fanned the clubface too much in the takeaway. The clubface is looking too far right, which means it is open in relation to the swing path. It will be difficult to bring this back to a square position later in the swing: the result will probably be a push or slice.

O Try to perform this exercise on a regular basis so that you can keep track of the clubface position as you start your swing. Remember, square to your swing path is correct; open and closed are incorrect. The great thing about this move is that you can use it any time you like as a "dry run" to help capture the correct sensations prior to starting your actual swing. This way your first move away from the ball is more likely to be a good one.

DRILL 19: Squeeze your elbows to stay connected

THIS DRILL IS BASED on the concept of developing better synchronization in your swing to insure that your moving parts operate as a team, rather than independent of one another. The exercise specifically examines the relationship between your arm swing and body-turn in your backswing, which often becomes a little disjointed.

1 *Trap a soccer ball, or similar sized and shaped object, between your elbows. Then address a golf ball as you would normally.*

2 *Now make a backswing, squeezing your elbows together to prevent the ball from falling. Stop when the club is horizontal with the ground.*

○ This simple one-two procedure keeps the start of your backswing more "connected," which means that your arm swing and body turn are taking place simultaneously. This retains the width in your swing (which means the clubhead travels in a wide arc that extends away from you), and forces your left side to wind up behind the ball, all the way to the top of your backswing. Rehearse this drill occasionally between shots when you are hitting balls at the range. If you can recreate the feelings experienced in this exercise in your normal swing, you will be a better ball striker.

KEY CHECKPOINT

LEARN TO MOVE ON

EVERYONE HITS bad iron shots. However, a good player can forget a poor stroke and get on with making up for the mistake, while a bad player might dwell on the error and compound it with another bad shot. In this situation, every mishit becomes a potential disaster. It is therefore important to remember that the only shot that matters is the next one. By all means curse yourself when you hit a bad shot, but let that be the end of it. Walk on and make sure that one error does not become the first of many.

SHORT MEMORY *A good player should be able to forget about a poor performance on one hole and instead concentrate on playing the next hole well.*

RETEST YOURSELF

Before moving to Level Three, take the test on pp.54–5 again. If you have not improved, it is worth revisiting the Level Two drills. However, if the performance chart shows that your iron play has progressed sufficiently, then you are ready to tackle the more advanced drills in Level Three.

DRILL 20: Hit at the right time

THE SO-CALLED "late hit" – a feature of every good player's swing – is not a conscious move or technique. It is merely the product of a well-timed downswing whereby the angle between the wrists and the club shaft is maintained from the top of the backswing to late in the downswing, until the wrists gradually unhinge to release the clubhead into the back of the ball at maximum speed. However, as this is something that you swing through very quickly (you cannot "freeze" this position), it is very dangerous to try to copy. This drill will teach you how you can correctly integrate the late hit into your swing to help you release the club with more speed through impact.

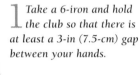

Backswing
Make a three-quarter backswing, and let your right arm fold as usual

Downswing
As you swing down, feel your right arm straighten through the hitting zone

1 *Take a 6-iron and hold the club so that there is at least a 3-in (7.5-cm) gap between your hands.*

2 *Now make some smooth practice swings, and feel that your right arm straightens through the hitting area. Your wrists should unhinge progressively as you accelerate down and through the hitting zone, so that there is a definite "swish" at the bottom of your swing.*

○ Do not be in a hurry to hit shots: it takes a while to become familiar with this technique. Instead, rehearse this drill frequently, then make practice swings with a conventional grip, and finally move on to hitting balls. If you can carry the same feelings evoked during this drill into your actual swing, your ball will think a different golfer is hitting it.

KEY CHECKPOINT

A STRAIGHT LEFT ARM?

OVER THE LAST FEW decades of golf instruction, a few nuggets of advice have echoed around the clubhouses of the world. However, not all of them are correct. One saying that often does more harm than good is to "keep your left arm straight in the backswing." This is often neither practical nor conducive to making a good swing. Probably only a handful of the world's top 50 golfers keep their left arm perfectly straight. This is because to make a full backswing – with a proper pivot and weight transfer – while keeping the left arm ramrod straight, you have to be incredibly flexible. Most tour players allow a little softness in the left arm – with a degree of bend at the elbow – so as to make a full and tension-free backswing. You should, too – unless you are flexible enough to comfortably keep your left arm straight all the way to the top of your backswing. A slightly bent left arm will do your swing no harm, as long as you make sure that the club does not travel way beyond horizontal at the top of your swing.

THE LEFT ARM *For most club golfers, contrary to popular belief, it is perfectly acceptable to bend the left arm slightly at the top of the backswing.*

DRILL 21: Play shots with your feet together

THE GOLF SWING is a complex action consisting of many separate moving parts working together. Nevertheless, it is possible to identify two core elements: arm swing and body turn. Arm swing is often neglected, mainly because many golfers tend to rely too much on the bigger muscles found in the shoulders and torso. Rehearse this drill to insure that your arms play an appropriately active role in your swing.

1 *Take a 6-iron and address a ball with your feet no more than 6 in (15 cm) apart. Grip the club lightly.*

2 *Swish the ball away with a free-flowing swing of the club. Try to swing so that you feel that your arms are doing much more work than your body.*

3 *If you lose your balance, your body is doing too much and your arms too little. Keep trying until you do not lose balance.*

○ It is a good idea to punctuate your practice sessions with spells of hitting 12 or so shots with your feet together. This will remind you of the role of your arms in your swing. It will also promote a free swing of the club through the hitting area, which adds speed to your swing just where it is needed most. If too much upper body motion is a persistent problem, you might want to emulate former US Open champion Hale Irwin, who would occasionally spend days hitting nothing but feet-together iron shots.

DRILL 22: Hit shots with the ball above your feet

SWINGING THE CLUB into the ball on an inside path (*see pp.26–7*) is one of sport's greatest challenges: perhaps on a par with serving an ace in tennis. If you find most of your shots curve from left-to-right through the air, you are not swinging the clubhead into impact on the correct (inside) path. Rehearse this practice drill to help correct this problem and to give your swing a better shape.

1 *Find an incline on your home course that allows you to set up with the ball noticeably above the level of your feet, as much as 12 in (30 cm) if possible.*

2 *Use a 6-iron to hit shots from this position. Instinctively, this immediately establishes a more rounded backswing and encourages a better body turn.*

3 *When you have hit about 12 shots from this incline, find a flat area of ground, and see if you can replicate the swing sensations experienced in step 2.*

○ With a more rounded backswing you can deliver the club to the ball from the inside, promoting a free release of the club (*see p.27*) through impact. You may be pleasantly surprised to discover that a straight ball flight, or even a draw, is not an impossible dream, after all.

LEVEL THREE

DRILL 23: Hitch a ride on both sides of the ball

THE CORRECT ROTATION of the hands and arms is an essential ingredient in a golf swing: without it you can never deliver the clubface square to the back of the ball with enough speed. Anyone struggling to achieve this rotation need think only of "thumbs up" in the backswing and through swing. Rehearse this drill to understand exactly what this means and how to integrate it into your iron play.

1 *Adopt your address position, but without a club in your hand. Now place your left hand in your pocket or behind your back.*

2 *Raise your right arm as if making a backswing, and let your body start to turn. Pause when your forearm is horizontal to the ground. In this position your thumb should be pointing at the sky, and the back of your hand facing behind you. This indicates that the correct forearm rotation and wrist hinge have taken place.*

3 *Swing down and through the hitting zone. Freeze when your forearm is horizontal to the ground. Again, your right thumb should point at the sky, but the back of your hand should face directly in front of you.*

○ The two "thumbs-up" positions – as if you are hitching a ride on both sides of the ball – is what happens when good players release the club properly (see p.27). For these golfers, this is almost an instinctive move, but you might have to work at it before it becomes second nature. After practicing this drill a few times, try to introduce this feeling into your swing. You should notice an immediate improvement in the crispness of your ball striking.

Backswing
Your thumb points upwards when your arm is horizontal

After impact
When your arm is horizontal, your thumb once again points to the sky

DRILL 24: Keep your palm facing down to squeeze your shots

WHEN HITTING IRON SHOTS, all good players decrease loft at impact, which means that the club's shaft is angled towards the target. This produces a powerful ball flight. Poor players, on the other hand, increase loft at impact, which means that the club's shaft is leaning away from the target. This can produce a weak, high ball flight. If the clubhead reaches its lowest point before impact, heavy contact is possible, as is a "thin" (where the ball shoots along the ground). One fundamental difference between these two situations is in the position of the right palm as the club enters the hitting zone. This is because what the right palm does influences what the clubface does. This exercise simulates what the right palm should and should not do in your swing. You can compare the two and become accustomed to positioning your right palm correctly.

1 *The incorrect position. Stand as you would normally to hit a ball. Swing your right arm back, then down toward the hitting zone. At the moment where you would be striking the ball, position your right palm so that it is starting to flip upward. This is how many amateur golfers deliver the clubface to the ball.*

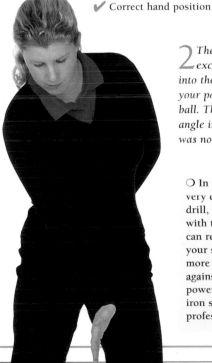

✔ Correct hand position

✘ Incorrect hand position

2 *The correct position. Repeat step 1, except as you swing your right arm into the hitting area, make sure that your palm is angled down toward the ball. This means there will be a slight angle in the back of your wrist, which was not there in step 1.*

○ In an actual swing, this all happens very quickly. But by rehearsing this drill, your brain can become familiar with the correct movements. If you can recreate this right palm position in your swing, you will compress the ball more strongly – literally squeezing it against the clubface – producing a powerful ball flight for all of your iron shots. This is how the tour professionals do it.

MAINTAIN A STRAIGHT LINE AT THE START OF YOUR TAKEAWAY

LOSING COORDINATION in your swing often stems from a bad first move away from the ball. The ideal address position is such that your left arm and the shaft of the club form a straight line down to the ball (*see Drill 14 in the "Off the Tee" section, p.39*). As you start your backswing, that line should remain intact for the first 24 in (60 cm) of the clubhead's journey away from the ball. This promotes a one-piece takeaway, which helps synchronize your arm swing with your body turn.

Wrist hinge
After the clubhead has travelled 24 in (60 cm), your wrists start to hinge

Straight line
Your left arm and the club form a straight line during the takeaway

24 in (60 cm)

ONE-PIECE TAKEAWAY *If your left arm and the shaft of the club form a straight line for the first 24 in (60 cm) or so of the takeaway, there is a better chance of making a synchronized swing.*

LEVEL THREE

KEY CHECKPOINT

FIND A RHYTHM THAT SUITS YOUR PERSONALITY

GOLFERS WITH good rhythm swing at a pace that allows them to generate power while maintaining control of the club. This rhythm also helps them achieve perfect balance from start to finish. But rhythm varies. Some golfers swing fast; others swing slow. Which is best for you?

While there are no strict rules, a useful guideline is to think about what type of person you are. If you are a naturally lively person who tends to do everything quickly, then the chances are that your ideal swing rhythm is relatively brisk. Golfers such as Nick Price and Jose Maria Olazabal fit into this category. If, on the other hand, you tend to go through life at a fairly sedate pace, then a slower swing speed will probably suit your game. Think of golfers like Ernie Els and Fred Couples.

SLOW SWING *Fred Couples is a naturally laid-back person. This is reflected in his swing, which is blessed with a wonderfully slow tempo.*

DRILL 25: Flex your knee to add resistance to your swing

FOR MOST GOLFERS, keeping the right knee flexed throughout the backswing stops the hips turning more than 45 degrees. This provides a point of resistance against which the upper body can "wind up." The following simple practice exercise will help you focus on maintaining your right knee flex.

1 *Take any iron, and assume your normal address position. Make sure that you introduce the appropriate amount of flex in your knees (see p.24). Take your left hand off the club.*

2 *Rehearse a backswing. As you do so, shift your weight on to your right leg, keeping the knee braced. At the top, your head should be over your flexed right knee.*

3 *Repeat step 2 several times, always focusing on turning your upper body and shifting your weight on to your right knee.*

4 *Now put both hands on the club and try to replicate the same feelings in your proper backswing. If your knee straightens in your backswing, you are probably reverse pivoting, where your weight moves on to the left side instead of the right. If your knee slides to the right you are probably swaying off the ball too much. These situations are to be avoided.*

Top of the backswing
Your head should be positioned directly above your right knee

○ By keeping your right knee flexed throughout your backswing, your hips can only turn so far, which enables you to wind your upper body tight, like a spring. The tighter you wind up in the backswing, the faster your upper body will unwind in the downswing, and the more power you will generate. (Note: older or less supple golfers will probably not be flexible enough to coil their upper body sufficiently and therefore need to allow their hips to turn more than 45 degrees. This will help provide the necessary twisting motion.)

Drill 26: Learn about trajectory by examining the launch angle

B Y NOW YOU PROBABLY have a good idea how high or low the ball flies with each iron you hit, but are you aware of the ball's launch angle? This is the trajectory of the shot in the first 20 yd (18 m) or so of its flight – a distance that is traversed so quickly that your head usually does not come up in time for you to see where the ball is going. However, establishing the launch angle for each iron is far more important than you might think, as it enables you to make informed club selections when, for example, overhanging branches are partly blocking your way to the target. It is also useful when you need to control the trajectory of your iron shots on a breezy day. The following exercise will prepare you for such eventualities.

1 *Find a spot on a golf course where you can hit shots so that there are overhanging branches between you and the target.*

2 *Drop 12 balls about 20 yd (18 m) behind the branches.*

3 *Select a long iron, a mid-iron, and a short iron and hit the balls toward the target, alternating between the three clubs. Note which clubs send the ball under the branches and which do not.*

○ The information gained from this drill will allow you to establish a mental picture of the ball's launch angle with each iron. This knowledge will be very useful when you are playing a round. The "Shotmaking" section (*see pp.196–211*) will examine in greater detail the skills required to manipulate the flight of a golf ball. This will further enhance your versatility in situations that demand creativity.

see pp.196–211

KEY CHECKPOINT

KEEP CHECKING YOUR PERSONAL DISTANCES

I F YOU HAVE worked through all the drills in this section, you will undoubtedly be a much better iron player than you were when you performed Drill 1 (*see p.56*). This means that, because of the improved quality of your ball striking, your personal distances for each club will have increased. It is therefore a good idea to repeat Drill 1 periodically, especially if your handicap and scores are lowering. This helps insure that you are not inadvertently selecting the wrong clubs, which could easily result in costly errors. Always remember to ignore the longest and shortest few balls hit with each club, as these do not accurately represent your normal average length. Instead, pace out your distances to the center of the main cluster of balls.

see p.56

DISTANCE CHECK *Take time to regularly reassess your personal distances. This only takes an hour or so and will greatly improve your club selections.*

THE PERFECT IRON SHOT

PER-ULRIK JOHANSSON has one of the most correct swings on the European tour, and as a result he is a highly consistent performer. Johansson has the ability to swing every iron with exactly the same tempo, letting the club do the work for him. Swinging with a consistent rhythm is a vitally important lesson to learn – it is one of the most significant aspects of iron play. As you follow the sequences of Johansson swinging an iron featured below, you will see that there are many points to be learned from his iron play, and these will remind you of some of the key points covered earlier in this section.

Backswing
Johansson has coiled his body perfectly – he is in a great position at the top of his backswing

Hips
Note how Johansson's hips unwind – they do not slide – in the downswing

Legs
A stable leg action provides a good base for the powerful unwinding of the body and a free swing of the arms

1 **GREAT POSTURE**
Johansson's posture is perfect at address, which goes a long way to promoting his very correct action. This is because the angles established at address to a large degree determine the shape of the swing. His alignment is also perfect; the feet, hips, and shoulders being parallel to one another. This in turn promotes an on-line swing path. So, together, posture and alignment have significant benefits.

2 PERFECT PLANE

Here, a perfect body-pivot combined with the appropriate hand-and-arm swing produces a backswing that is on the ideal plane. The club does not reach horizontal at the top of the backswing, but it does not need to: Johansson has completed all the body-turn he needs and his wrists have hinged fully.

3 CONSTANT SPINE ANGLE

As Johansson approaches impact, his spine angle is the same as it was at address. Maintaining this angle means that he does not need to make height adjustments mid-swing to return the clubface to its address position. This helps him strike the ball out of the middle of the clubface.

4 LEFT SIDE CLEARS

Johansson gives himself plenty of room to swing the club freely into impact on the correct path. This is the result of clearing his left side out of the way quite early in his downswing. If the left side fails to clear, the arms and club become trapped too far on the inside. Johansson has no such problems.

Impact
The centrifugal force generated from the swinging motion causes the arms to straighten

5 TOTAL CONTROL

Johansson swings at about 80 percent of his power potential – whether he is using a 2-iron or an 8-iron – and relies on smooth acceleration through the impact area to generate all the distance he needs. His perfectly balanced followthrough is a testament to the great control he possesses in his swing. This sense of balance should be a key feature of your followthrough, too.

KEYS TO ACCURATE IRON PLAY

PINPOINT ACCURACY should be your objective with every iron in the bag. These four keys will remind you of some of the primary moves essential to achieving this goal.

❍ *To give you extra confidence on the golf course, use your practice sessions to establish exactly how far you hit each of your irons.*

❍ *Make sure that the clubface remains square to the path of your swing in your takeaway. This way you will not have to make adjustments later in your swing in order to hit a straight shot.*

❍ *If you retain the flex in your right knee as you make your backswing, your hips will turn no more than 45 degrees, allowing you to effectively coil your upper body.*

❍ *Swing each iron with the same rhythm and trust the loft on the clubface to produce the exact shape of shot and yardage you require. Swinging longer irons harder does not help you hit further; in fact it results in poor striking and loss of accuracy.*

PITCHING

THE PITCHING WEDGE comes into operation anywhere from approximately 38 yd (35 m) to 120 yd (110 m) away from the green. From this position, a tour professional will more often than not land the ball close enough to the flag so that only one putt is required. Most amateurs, however, are just happy to hit the green. Even allowing for the remarkable skills of top tour players, this difference is too big.

For one thing, distance is not an issue: you do not need to worry about generating lots of power. Also, because a shorter swing is required, accuracy and control should be much more attainable.

THE ART OF PITCHING

Theory is all well and good, but you need

to turn your pitching aspirations into reality. Although there are similarities between pitch shots and other iron shots, there are nuances in technique and touch that are unique to pitching. This section of the book will provide you with all the necessary knowledge to master these skills. But first you must perform the all-important test, which will accurately establish your current level of ability with a pitching wedge.

THE PITCHING TEST

You are likely to be using your pitching wedge when you are 38 yd (35 m) to 120 yd (110 m) from the green (although this upper limit is higher for the likes of Tiger Woods). However, forgetting the two extremes of pitching, somewhere midway between these two parameters is a good distance from which to gauge your ability. Therefore, shots of about 82 yd (75 m) form the basis of the pitching test.

1 *Locate an average-sized green, ideally with the flag positioned centrally. Pace out approximately 82 yd (75 m) from the flag into the fairway.*

2 *Hit 15 balls from a good lie with your pitching wedge (left). Walk up to the green and note how many balls* finish within seven paces of the hole. (Note: if you are performing this test at a driving range, you will not be able to actually walk on to the green and check your results. However, it is better to make your best guess from a distance [as to how many balls are within seven paces of the hole] than not do the test at all.)

3 *Hit two more batches of 15 balls, and calculate your average score. Then use the performance chart (below) to establish your current level of ability.*

○ Accurate pitch shots can save you several strokes during a round. They will not only set you up for a greater number of birdie opportunities on par 4s and par 5s but also help you salvage valuable pars when your long game goes awry.

PERFORMANCE CHART

○ ○ ○ ○ ○
1–5 = Level One
(pp.82–9)

○ ○ ○ ○ ○
6–10 = Level Two
(pp.90–97)

○ ○ ○ ○ ○
11–15 = Level Three
(pp.98–103)

LEVEL ONE

LEVEL TWO

LEVEL THREE

DRILL 1: Think of distance not direction

ONE OF THE BIGGEST problems golfers have with their approach play is not knowing precisely how hard to hit shots of different distances. Drill 1 (*see p.56*) in the "Iron Play" section discusses the importance of knowing your personal distances for each club. It is critical that you practice with this information in mind.

1 Next time you are at the range and you want to work on your pitching, identify a specific target, whereby you know exactly how far it is from you. Do not aim at something beyond the distance you can comfortably hit with a wedge.

2 Hit pitch shots to this target, and judge every one in terms of distance. Whether the ball comes up short, long, or perfect will provide you with feedback you can use to make adjustments to the feel of your swing.

○ The essence of a good pitch shot is being able to see a target and make an appropriate length swing to produce the required amount of carry through the air. If your wedge shots are flying in all directions, then your technique needs work. But, assuming direction is not a problem, which it should not be with such a short shot, getting the right distance is your priority. Distance technique is further refined in Drill 13 (*see p.92*).

DRILL 2: Open your stance

WHEN PLAYING most shots, perfect parallel alignment – where your toes, hips, and shoulders all run along the same line – is required. However, as explained in the introduction to this section (*see pp.80–81*), pitch shots are not like any other iron shot. To be a good pitcher your stance needs to be slightly open, and this drill will help you make the appropriate change.

1 Address the ball as you would to hit a normal iron shot, with your stance parallel to the target line. Place two irons on the ground to help you find perfect parallel alignment.

2 Now draw your left foot back about 2 in (5 cm), to open your stance. Make sure you keep your shoulders square, though. This element of your setup must remain the same.

Open stance
Draw your left foot back approximately 2 in (5cm)

○ This small adjustment has two key benefits to your pitching. Firstly, it creates more resistance in your legs and hips, shortening your backswing so that the club does not reach a point where it is horizontal with the ground. This is preferable when pitching, as a shorter swing equals more control. Secondly, because you are making a shorter swing, you need assistance to clear your left side out of the way in your downswing. An open stance provides this help and produces a better impact position.

DRILL 3: Find the bottom of your swing for crisp strikes

CONTROLLING THE DISTANCE you hit your pitch shots is impossible unless you learn to strike the ball consistently out of the clubhead's sweet spot. To do this, the ball must be positioned at the bottom of your swing arc – the point where the clubhead first comes into contact with the turf. Anywhere else in your stance and you have to make unnatural compensations to avoid hitting the shot heavy or thin. This straightforward drill will help you locate the bottom of your swing arc and will confirm the ideal place to put the ball in your stance.

1 *Stand in a closely mown area of grass and make a well-disciplined practice swing – not a half hearted swish, but a dynamic movement that closely resembles your actual swing.*

2 *Take note of where the clubhead first comes into contact with the ground. This is the perfect place to position the ball in your stance.*

3 *It is a very good idea to make regular checks on this aspect of your swing. You can also use this drill to find the bottom of your swing for every iron club in the bag. This will help you identify the correct ball position for all your irons.*

CHECK BALL POSITION
Hit balls placed along a line that indicates the bottom of your swing. The divot mark should start slightly in front of the line.

Divot-mark
The beginning of the divot mark is the best place to position the ball

KEY CHECKPOINT

GRIP AS YOU HOLD A CHILD'S HAND

SHORT SHOTS tend to create greater anxiety than almost any other shot. This usually leads to tension, especially in the grip. But what is the ideal grip pressure? Well, Sam Snead – who holds the record for the most tournaments won by any professional golfer in history – said you should grip a golf club using the same pressure you would to hold a live bird.

Another analogy is that you should hold the club as if you were holding a child's hand while crossing a road: you hold the hand tight enough not to let the toddler break free, but soft enough so as not to cause discomfort. This is the ideal grip pressure for holding a golf club: firm enough to provide a secure hold on the club, but soft enough to promote flexibility in the wrists, which allows you to make a free-flowing swing. Holding your wedge at the correct pressure will undoubtedly improve your pitching. The Key Checkpoint on p.19 describes another way to attain the correct grip pressure.

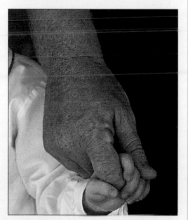

SOFT HOLD *Imagine the grip pressure you would use to hold a toddler's hand. This is very close to the grip pressure you should use when pitching.*

DRILL 4: Keep your hands soft for a free flowing swing

IF ONE THING IS GUARANTEED to hamper your chances of making a good swing, it is tension. It only takes a little extra tightness in your grip for tension to spread into your arms and shoulders. This tends to lead to a poor first move away from the ball (see Drill 3, p.57), and your whole swing will lack fluidity and rhythm. This is disastrous for a pitch shot. Lee Trevino, who won six majors in his career, used to say that just before he took the club away he consciously eased his left-hand grip to free up the muscles in his hands, arms, and upper body. If he did not do this he felt his swing was in danger of becoming a little tight and too short. Many golfers are guilty of doing the opposite to Trevino, actually tightening their grip just before they start to swing.

1 Address a pitch shot as you would normally.

2 Just before you take the club away from the ball, ease the grip pressure in your left hand by about 10 percent. Use this pressure release as the trigger to start your backswing.

Grip pressure
Hold the club lightly and keep your hands relaxed

○ The difference between relaxed and tense hands and arms is enormous. Soft muscles work much better in a swing than tight muscles, so a relaxed setup leads to a much improved takeaway: the left arm extends away from the ball more correctly, and the right arm folds as it should. Also, the wrists hinge more readily, which sets the club on the correct plane in the backswing.

DRILL 5: Find your personal speed limit

HOW HARD SHOULD YOU HIT a full wedge shot? As with most things in golf, this varies, depending on the individual. This drill shows you how to find the correct amount of force you should use – a speed limit, so to speak. You can then apply this to every pitch you hit, using the length of swing and changes of club as necessary to regulate the distance you will hit your shots.

1 Hit pitch shots in three-ball batches. Start with a very easy swing, using barely 50 percent of full power.

2 Swing the club using progressively more force with each batch of balls. Build up gradually.

3 Eventually you will start to lose control, not just in terms of balance but also in the consistency of your ball striking and the accuracy of your shots. If all three balls are coming off the clubface differently or are flying erratically, you have exceeded your speed limit. When this happens, drop down a level. The amount of force used on the batch of balls hit just before you lost control is how hard you should hit a full wedge shot.

○ No one can tell you your personal swing speed limit: you have to find out yourself. This practice exercise allows you to do just that. Once you have this information, it is a simple matter to determine how far you hit a full wedge shot. Knowledge of your personal speed limit and distance with a wedge will help you manage your game more efficiently and should lead to lower scores. The more you know about your swing, the better your pitching will be.

DRILL 6: Swing down on the path of your backswing

SOMETIMES THE SIMPLEST of thoughts can clear your mind and clarify your swing objectives. With pitching, for example, it is easy to become so obsessed with hitting the target that you actually forget what you have to do in your swing. This simple drill will provide a clear swing thought that will improve your pitching.

1 *As you start your swing, be conscious of your takeaway path. Ideally, the clubhead should move straight back for* *the first 12–18 in (30–45 cm) and then gradually arc inside in response to your body-turn (see p.26–7).*

2 *Perform a couple of "practice run" backswings to help establish a strong visual reference.*

3 *Make it the sole objective in your downswing to swing the club into impact on exactly the same path that it went back on. Do not think about anything else.*

Downswing
Try to swing the club down on the same path it went back on

○ Swing path is one of the most important ingredients of a well-struck pitch shot. If you can combine the proper swing path with the correct angle of attack (*see the Key Checkpoint on p.101*), you will soon find that your pitch shots become much more precise.

LEVEL ONE

KEY CHECKPOINT

HAVE A TRIGGER TO START YOUR SWING

MOST GOLFERS find that the closer they are to the flag, the more anxious they become. And anxiety usually leads to tension and a poor swing. That is when you need a trigger to start your swing smoothly. A lot of the greatest players in history have relied on a "swing trigger." Gary Player, for example, kicks in his right knee just before he takes the club away; Jack Nicklaus turns his head to the right – different move, same principle. Next time you are practicing your pitching, take time to try out a few swing triggers of your own – trial and error is the key. Maybe either of the two moves mentioned above will suit you. Perhaps a final waggle of the club or a little nudge forward of your hands at address will do the trick. And do not forget the possibility of easing the pressure in your left hand, as discussed in Drill 4 (*see p.84*). Keep experimenting until you find a trigger that feels comfortable. Having a swing trigger means that you will never freeze over the ball.

HEAD TURN *Simply moving your head slightly to your right just before beginning your backswing is an effective way to trigger the start of your swing. It will also facilitate a fuller body turn.*

DRILL 7: Make a right angle in your backswing

POOR PITCHING IS OFTEN the result of either too much wrist hinge in the backswing, where the hands pick the club up too abruptly; or too little wrist hinge, where the wrists remain stiff as the club swings back. Either situation damages your ball striking because if you cannot set the club correctly in the backswing, you will never produce the ideal angle of attack into impact. This drill will insure that the appropriate wrist hinge takes place in your backswing – and at exactly the right time.

1 *Take your pitching wedge and address the ball as normal.*

2 *Begin your backswing, but freeze at the point where your left arm is horizontal. Compare your position with the three images shown below.*

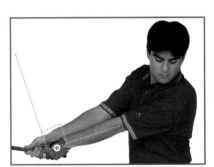

✗ OBTUSE ANGLE
The angle between the left forearm and the club is too wide: the wrists have not hinged sufficiently (a common problem). Set your wrists a little earlier in your takeaway.

✔ RIGHT ANGLE
The wrists have hinged correctly and at the right time. The shaft of the club and the left forearm form a right angle.

○ Working on this aspect of your swing is time well spent. Correctly hinging your wrists in your backswing helps promote the ideal angle of attack in your downswing, enabling you to strike your pitch shots with authority.

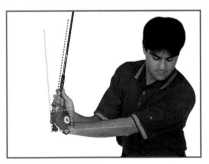

✗ ACUTE ANGLE
The wrists have done too much too soon, and there is a poor body turn. Try to keep your wrists passive for longer and to get the club a little wider as you turn your upper body.

DRILL 8: Check your swing plane halfway back

THIS DRILL uses the same "frozen" position employed in Drill 7 (*left*). It will show you a very simple way to check if your swing is on the correct plane in the backswing, which is vital to your chances of making a good swing.

1 *Position either a mirror or a helper to your right. Assume an address position whereby you would be hitting away from the mirror/helper.*

2 *Begin your takeaway, but freeze when your left arm is horizontal.*

3 *Use either the mirror or your helper to check your position. If your wrists have hinged correctly (see Drill 7, left), the butt end of the club's grip will point at a spot on the ground between the ball and your toes (slightly closer to the ball than your toes). This is the perfect swing plane. If the grip is pointing too far – say more than 4 in (10 cm) – either side of this spot, your swing requires corrective action.*

⟳ This drill, together with Drill 7 (*left*), is extremely important to the future success of your pitching. If you can be correct in this early stage of your swing, it is so much easier to develop a repeatable action. Certainly, if you take the time to perfect this part of your swing, the targets set by the drills in Levels Two and Three will be much more achievable.

Wrists
The correct wrist hinge is vital to a good swing

Swing plane
If you are swinging on the correct path, the butt end of the club will point between your toes and the ball

KEY CHECKPOINT

CHOKE DOWN TO INCREASE CONTROL

ANY OPPORTUNITY to enhance the control in your pitch shots has to be seized. One good way to do this is to hold the club about 2 in (5 cm) further down than you would normally. This might not seem much, but choking down on the grip (*see Drill 9 in the "Off the Tee" section, p.35*) brings your hands slightly closer to the clubhead, which gives you greater control over it. If you control what is happening to the clubhead, you can control the ball better, too. Try choking down on your wedge, and you should notice an improvement in your pitching.

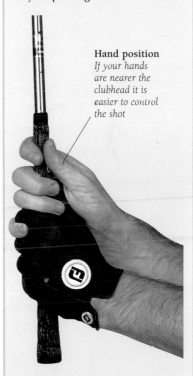

Hand position
If your hands are nearer the clubhead it is easier to control the shot

CHOKE DOWN *When choking down on a pitching wedge, the right hand is almost in contact with the metal of the shaft. This aids control.*

DRILL 9: Check your divot marks for swing information

THE DIVOT MARK (or lack of one) you leave in the ground after playing a pitch shot can tell you a great deal about the shape and quality of your swing. Each divot mark is like a fingerprint that reveals one or more of the individual traits of your game. Knowing how to interpret what your divot mark is telling you can lead to some dramatic discoveries and, more importantly, clues as to how you can hit better pitch shots. Use the information in this drill to decode the information your divot marks are giving you.

DEEP DIVOT MARK AND HEAVY CONTACT

Taking a divot is part and parcel of good short-iron play. However, if your divot marks become too deep (right) and your ball striking is very erratic, it is obvious that you are doing something wrong. These symptoms suggest that your swing is too narrow, causing you to swing the clubhead into impact on an excessively steep angle of attack. This means you will be chopping down into the ground behind the ball. If these problems sound familiar, this short exercise will improve the quality of your ball-striking immensely.

1 Make sure the ball is not too far forward in your stance – in other words, close to or directly opposite your left heel – as this might cause you to hit behind the ball.

2 To shallow your angle of attack and start striking the ball more cleanly, try to delay hinging your wrists in your backswing.

❍ Shallowing your angle of attack immediately establishes a wider arc to your swing and encourages the club to come into the ball on a less severely downward angle. You will still take a divot, but the divot mark should not be so deep and, more importantly, should occur after you have struck the ball.

NO DIVOT MARK AT ALL

Chances are that you are trying to help the ball into the air with a scooping motion if many of your shots leave no divot mark at all in the ground (left), and you are also occasionally hitting very heavy shots, where the ball flies barely half its proper distance. These problems indicate that the clubhead has traveled beyond the lowest point in its swing arc (see Drill 3, p.83) and is on the way up at the moment of impact. This is the worst possible angle of attack for pitching. Try this quick and easy drill to correct this destructive fault.

1 Check that the ball is positioned correctly – in the middle of your stance. This alone will help promote the required descending blow.

2 Examine the weight transfer in your swing. If you are hitting up on the ball, you are probably hanging back on your right side in your downswing. Eliminate this problem by insuring that your weight flows on to your left side as the club swings down toward impact. With your weight traveling in the same direction as the club, you can hit down on the ball.

❍ You should notice right away that you start taking a divot after you have struck the ball. This is an immediate signal that you are back on the right track.

DIVOT MARK POINTS LEFT OF THE TARGET

Target line

When a pitch shot finishes left of the target, there is every chance that the divot mark will be pointing that way, too (right). This problem is caused by the clubhead approaching the ball from outside the correct line (see pp.26–7) and travelling to the left of the target through impact.

1 Narrow your stance by about 2 in (5 cm). This encourages your arms to play a more active role than your body (see Drill 21 in the "Iron Play" section, p.73), which in turn encourages a more correct swing path.

2 When you are at the top of your backswing, start down with your hands and arms. Try to feel that your downswing consists of more hand and arm swing and less body movement. This will enable you to swing the club into impact from slightly inside (see pp.26–7), which is ideal.

○ Once you have effected the suggested changes in this drill, you should find that instead of the ball (and your divots) flying left, everything is now back on line.

DIVOT MARK POINTS RIGHT OF THE TARGET

A divot mark pointing right of the target (below) is much less common than the mark pointing to the left, especially at amateur level. This

Target line

○ These adjustments create more room in front of you, which promotes a more correct line of attack in your downswing.

problem is caused by your hips not clearing out of the way as they should in your downswing. This means that the clubhead becomes trapped on the inside, which leads to a severe in-to-out swing path (see pp.26–7). Therefore, when the clubhead approaches impact it will travel to the right as it makes contact with the ball. This means that the ball will fly to the right of the target. The following drill will eliminate such tendencies.

1 Firstly, check that the ball is not too far back in your stance (nearer your right foot than your left foot) because this ball position can create an excessive inside-the-line attack, and cause your shots to fly to the right of the target. Remember, the center of your stance is the perfect ball position for pitch shots.

2 Open your stance so that your toe-to-toe line runs slightly left of the target (see Drill 2, p.82).

3 At the top of your backswing, initiate your downswing by turning your hips so that there is plenty of space for your hands and arms to swing on the correct path.

RETEST YOURSELF

Before moving to Level Two, take the test on pp.80–81 again. If you have not improved, it is worth revisiting the Level One drills. However, if the performance chart shows that your pitching has progressed sufficiently, then you are ready to tackle the more advanced drills in Level Two.

DRILL 10: Pitch to a catcher

JUST ABOUT THE SCARIEST SHOT in golf, certainly for most amateurs, is the pitch shot over a bunker. Strictly speaking, it is no different from a pitch with nothing in the way, but of course it never feels like that: psychologically, this is an intimidating shot. Often, the fear of landing the ball in the bunker becomes a self-fulfilling prophecy, and you end up hitting the exact shot you most wanted to avoid. However, the positive mental imagery this drill provides will help eliminate the fear of such shots and will allow you to function normally. This means that pitching over a bunker will soon become much less problematic.

1 *Find a position on the course where you have a pitch shot of approximately 44 yd (40 m) to the flag, with a bunker between you and the green.*

3 *As you hit the shot, concentrate 100 percent of your mental capacity on lobbing the ball to the person on the green. Try to give him or her an easy catch.*

2 *Instead of worrying about hitting the ball into the sand, as perhaps you might have previously, imagine someone standing on your landing area on the green, waiting to receive the ball.*

○ Even though it may seem unwise not to think about technique as you play your stroke, with "fear shots," mental imagery is a powerful process. By focusing your mind on something positive rather than negative, your body is free to play the shot as if the bunker were not there.

DRILL 11: Hit the bucket to improve your accuracy

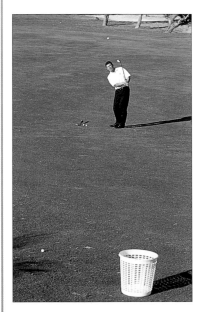

IT IS EASY TO HIT pitch shots on the practice ground and be satisfied with a loose grouping in the distance. In reality, this is not good enough: pitch shots should be incredibly accurate. You should be looking to knock pitch shots close to the flag every time: merely hitting the green is not good enough. Try this exercise to completely transform your attitude about pitching.

1 *Place a large bucket on the range, about 33 yd (30 m) away, and think of this as your target. From such a short distance you will almost certainly find it beneficial to pitch with your most lofted wedge (see the Key Checkpoint on p.91), because greater loft allows you to be more positive while not having to worry about hitting the ball too far.*

2 *Now hit a few pitch shots, and try to get the ball into the bucket (without the ball bouncing on the turf*

first). This forces you to be very specific about your target and subconsciously raises your expectations.

○ By challenging yourself in this way you ultimately demand more of yourself, which is how you become a better pitcher of the ball. Next time you are on the course, think of the flag in the same way as you did the bucket. You will soon find yourself pitching consistently closer.

DRILL 12: Feel controlled aggression through the ball

PITCH SHOTS are predominantly "touch" shots played from a distance, which means many golfers become a little tentative with the strike. You cannot afford to do this. Yes, pitch shots are control shots, but they still need to be struck with authority. Watch the likes of Jose Maria Olazabal or Nick Faldo, both great pitchers of the ball, if you need confirmation of this fact. Here is a simple exercise that will help you make a more authoritative strike.

1 *Take your pitching wedge and find a thick area of rough.*

2 *Make some smooth practice swings. Build up speed gradually in your downswing, and feel as if you are swishing the clubhead through the long grass. Be very positive and get used to the feeling of the clubhead zipping through the hitting area. If you become too tentative, the clubhead will become caught in the grass. However, do it properly and the clubhead will rip through the grass and enable you to swing through to a full finish.*

○ The next time you hit a pitch shot you should try to recreate the feeling of the clubhead swinging positively through the hitting zone, except that this time there will be a ball in the way rather than a thick patch of grass. This controlled form of aggression will help your ball striking enormously.

LEVEL TWO

KEY CHECKPOINT

SMART GOLFERS CARRY THREE WEDGES

IF YOU WERE to take a peek into any tour professional's golf bag you would find at least three different wedges, perhaps even four. If professionals feel it necessary to have this many wedges all to hit from 38 yd (35 m) to 120 yd (110 m) from the green, then so should you. Wedges will be discussed again in the reference section (*see p.234*), but now is a good time to stress the importance of carrying several types. This is because during a round you will have to play many different wedge shots. Lofts on wedges start from around 46 degrees for a standard pitching wedge and move up through the gap wedge and sand wedge to the lob wedge, which has a loft of around 62 degrees. Having this array of wedges is smart thinking, because it means you will have a club for every situation. Drill 24 (*see p.102*) shows you how to determine your personal distances for these clubs.

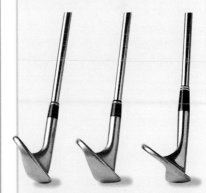

CLUB SELECTION *There is probably not a single tour professional in the world who does not carry at least three different wedges, and you should do the same. A good selection of wedges, to cover a variety of situations, would include a regular pitching wedge (left), a sand wedge (center), and a lob wedge (right).*

DRILL 13: Match your swing length to every pitch

IF GOLF WAS AN EXACT science you would be able to leave yourself with your ideal distance pitch shot every time – and you would never hit a bad shot. But golf is not like that, and inevitably you have to play pitch shots from a variety of distances during a normal round. This is part of the game's charm and challenge.

The following drill will improve your ability to match the correct swing to shots of different lengths. Drill 23, (*see p.101*) shows another way to do this. It will also help you establish your favorite pitching distance, which will make you better at seeing a certain length shot and matching the correct swing to it.

1 *Arm yourself with a bag of balls and however many pitching clubs you have in your bag (you should have at least three: your pitching wedge, another slightly more lofted wedge, and your sand wedge).*

2 *Find a quiet green. Starting from about 38 yd (35 m) from the flag, drop a ball, move 5½ yd (5 m) back, drop another ball and so on. Stop when you are about 120 yd (110 m) from the green.*

3 *Starting with the shortest shot, simply work your way back from the target, pitching each ball towards the flag. As there are 5½-yd (5-m) gaps between each ball, you will have to alter your swing very slightly for every shot. You may also want to swap clubs at the appropriate time, going with progressively less loft as the shots become longer.*

○ Since you only have one chance at each shot on the course, this practice drill accurately recreates the challenge of a proper round (this idea is elaborated on in Drill 25, p.103). It also reveals the exact distance from which you feel most comfortable pitching. Somewhere along the line of balls you should have hit upon a distance where you felt most confident.

This distance represents a strength in your game that you can deliberately play to. For example, if you are on a hole where the green is out of range in two shots – say on a long par five or if you have hit a poor drive into trouble on a par 4 – your first consideration should be to leave your second shot in a position whereby you can pitch from your favorite distance. This is one area of the game that tour professionals are very good at exploiting, which is one reason you see them hit so many of their pitch shots close to pin-high. Once you have practiced this drill, there is no reason why you cannot do the same.

DRILL 14. Hit three shots with one swing

THE KEY CHECKPOINT on p.91 discusses the merits of carrying at least three, or even four, wedges in your bag. The following drill, which teaches you how to hit three different length pitch shots with the same technique, will help you appreciate why this is such a sensible plan. It is an easy exercise to carry out and can only be of benefit to you when you are on the course playing a proper round.

1 *Hit 10 balls with your most lofted wedge.*

2 *Use exactly the same swing to hit another 10 balls, but this time use your gap wedge, which probably has a loft of around 56 degrees.*

3 *Hit 10 more balls, again using the same swing, with your regular pitching wedge.*

4 *Walk up to the three clusters of balls, and make a note of the different distances. Your regular pitching wedge shots might fly about 100 yd (90 m), gap wedge shots around 75 yd (70 m), and the most lofted wedge shots will reach no more than 50 yd (45 m).*

○ Although your personal figures for each wedge might differ from those suggested in step 4, you now have three specific-length wedge shots that require no change in your swing. Drill 23 (see p.101) and Drill 24 (see p.102) show you how to produce three different-length shots using just one club.

LEVEL TWO

KEY CHECKPOINT

WHICH BALL SHOULD YOU USE?

THERE ARE three main ball categories, and it is important that you are aware of the differences to insure that perfectly decent pitch shots do not go unrewarded simply because they are inappropriate for the type of ball you are using. Ball types are also discussed in the reference section (see p.235).

CONTROL BALL: Most golfers would gain more than they would lose by switching to a control ball. Any distance lost off the tee will be more than made up for by the enhanced control you will enjoy around the greens. You will find that a well-struck wedge shot spins back more, which gives you the confidence to attack the flag when you are playing well. The downside is that a badly struck shot, and even normal bunker shots, will scuff and cut the soft cover, which is made of balata (an artificial rubber compound). However, providing expense is not an issue, these balls are well worth the money.

DISTANCE BALL: What you gain in length with a distance ball you lose in control. This means that around the greens you have to work a little harder to compensate. In summer months you should pitch the ball well short of the pin and allow for some run. Whenever possible, load your shots with plenty of height and maximize the backspin you generate to give yourself some degree of control. Only in the winter months, when the greens are soft and receptive, can you start pitching the ball well up to the pin.

COMPROMISE BALL: This type of ball occupies the middle ground between control balls and distance balls. You cannot expect a compromise ball to spin back as much as a control ball, but on all except the hardest putting surfaces you can expect reasonable spin and control. However, even with your most lofted club, you will not be able to stop the ball dead unless the greens are very spongy. On the plus side, you will not be losing much yardage off the tee, as these balls will fly almost as far as a distance ball. This balance between distance and control suits golfers who are unwilling to make too great a sacrifice in either area.

DRILL 15: Follow the professionals' swing path

A GOOD PITCHING ACTION relies on a slightly open stance (*see Drill 2, p.82*), but you have to be careful that this does not allow faults to creep into your swing. Some golfers have a tendency to take the club back too much on the inside, which leaves them trapped at the top in a very flat, behind-the-body

position. From this situation it is inevitable that the club will be thrown outside the correct line (*see pp.26–7*) resulting in a pull or even a shank. This practice drill involves a slight exaggeration of a perfect pitching swing, but as an exercise it helps eliminate that damaging inside-to-outside loop.

1 *Stick the shaft of an old club, or a rolled-up umbrella, in the ground about 2 ft (60 cm) to the right of the toes on your back foot. Position it so that it leans at the same angle as the club at address (have a helper check this for you).*

2 *Practice mini-swings in which the clubhead travels above the umbrella during your backswing and under the*

umbrella on your downswing. Do not be in a hurry to hit shots too soon: become familiar with the feeling of the clubhead traveling on this path. It might feel strange at first, but every swing change will seem unusual at first.

3 *Continue rehearsing this swing, slowly building up to full speed. Then remove the umbrella, and hit some shots, recreating the feelings experienced in step 2.*

○ After practicing this drill, you should notice a difference in the quality of your ball striking and also in the accuracy of your pitch shots. Drill 16 (*right*) addresses the problem of a flat swing in a different way.

DRILL 16: Force the club upward in your backswing

RILL 15 *(left)* discussed how easy it is to let the club swing too flat from an open stance, which destroys your chances of swinging the club on the correct plane. While Drill 15 was for the practice ground only, this exercise can be rehearsed just about anywhere. This drill trains you to swing the club on the correct plane going back, which increases the likelihood of a good swing path coming down.

1 *Stand with your buttocks resting lightly against a wall or similar object (such as a tall fence or hedge). Pretend that you are about to hit a proper pitch shot.*

2 *Now rehearse your backswing, making sure that as you swing back and upward the clubhead does not come into contact with the wall. If you can get to the top of your backswing without the club hitting the wall, while keeping the clubhead no more than 3–4 in (8–10 cm) from the wall, you are swinging on the correct plane. If you have been swinging the club too far on the inside, this will probably feel quite strange. But rest assured that this swing path represents the correct movement, provided you continue to make a good shoulder turn.*

3 *Step away from the wall and hit a few pitch shots. Try to imagine that you are still up against the wall.*

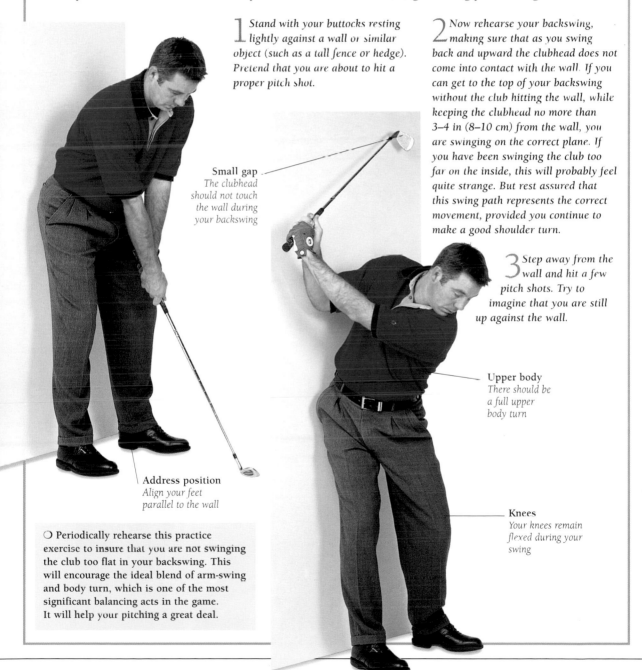

Small gap
The clubhead should not touch the wall during your backswing

Address position
Align your feet parallel to the wall

Upper body
There should be a full upper body turn

Knees
Your knees remain flexed during your swing

○ Periodically rehearse this practice exercise to insure that you are not swinging the club too flat in your backswing. This will encourage the ideal blend of arm-swing and body turn, which is one of the most significant balancing acts in the game. It will help your pitching a great deal.

DRILL 17: Practice your body turn, the hub of your swing

WHEN PLAYING SHORT SHOTS it is easy for your hand and arm action to become independent of your body turn, which can upset the timing of your swing. Whenever you play a pitch shot, whether it is from 120 yd (110 m) or 38 yd (35 m),

you must ensure that your hands and arms swing the club up and down in harmony with the appropriate body action. Here is a good drill that you can rehearse between hitting pitch shots at the range. All you need is one of the clubs from your bag.

1 *Trap a club across your chest and fold your arms to hold it in place.*

2 *Assume good posture for a wedge shot, making sure your knees are flexed and your spine angle is correct (see pp.24–5).*

3 *Turn your body to simulate a backswing movement, your left shoulder moving under your chin. Keep turning until you see the end of the shaft move behind the ball.*

4 *Turn your body back again as you would in a downswing, until your chest faces the target. Because your spine is tilted forward at address, during your backswing your left shoulder will be lower than the right shoulder; during your downswing, your right shoulder will be lower than the left.*

5 *Now hit some shots, and try to feel the same body motion you created in steps 3 and 4 in your proper swing.*

○ It is worth reiterating that even on short shots you have to keep your body moving. You should think of your upper body as the hub of the swing, with your hands and arms swinging in harmony with your body turn.

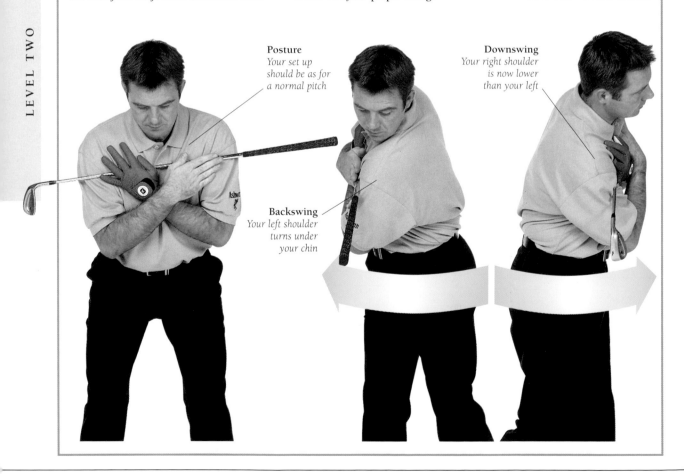

Posture
Your set up should be as for a normal pitch

Backswing
Your left shoulder turns under your chin

Downswing
Your right shoulder is now lower than your left

DRILL 18: Preset impact to train a crisp strike

A SLIGHTLY DESCENDING angle of attack is essential for accurate short-iron play *(see the Key Checkpoint on p 101)*. This produces the right kind of strike – ball then turf – which in turn creates lots of backspin, and with backspin comes that much sought-after ingredient: control. Try this exercise to help promote the correct angle of attack.

Body
Your hips and torso should be slightly open at the point of impact

Hands
Your hands should be ahead of the ball at impact

1 *Address the ball as normal, and then preset your impact position by opening your hips slightly and lifting your right heel off the ground a little. Make sure that your hands are ahead of the ball and that the shaft of the club is leaning forward.*

2 *Make your swing and try to return to the position created in step 1. It should be easier to replicate a good impact position because you started from a good impact position.*

3 *Once you have repeated step 2 a number of times, try hitting a few shots using this presetting technique.*

○ Complete beginners and high handicappers will struggle with a drill like this, but if you have a bit of golfing experience you will certainly benefit from the feeling of presetting your impact position.

Impact position

Address position

RETEST YOURSELF

Before moving to Level Three, take the test on pp.80–81 again. If you have not improved, it is worth revisiting the Level Two drills. However, if the performance chart shows that your pitching has progressed sufficiently, then you are ready to tackle the more advanced drills in Level Three.

LEVEL TWO

KEY CHECKPOINT

SOFTER METALS PROVIDE MORE FEEL

ALL TYPES of equipment will be discussed in depth later in the book (*see pp.230–35*), but now is the right time to consider the possibility of using a wedge with a clubface made of a metal compound other than steel, to give you more feel around the green. (Wedges with different lofts are discussed in the Key Checkpoint on p.91.) The most popular alternative to steel is beryllium copper because it is softer than steel (and pleasing to the eye). This softness allows you to gain more backspin on the ball. This means that, especially if you are using a soft-covered ball (*see the Key Checkpoint on p.93*), you can make your pitch shots "sit down" incredibly quickly on almost any green. For this reason it is well worth having at least one alternative-metal wedge in your bag – probably the most lofted of your wedges, as this is best suited to the most delicate shots.

Soft metal
Wedges with beryllium copper heads are popular because they provide extra feel

FEEL THE CONTROL *Since the essence of a great short game is touch, you can only benefit from having a wedge featuring a soft metal clubhead, as the ball comes off the face with more spin.*

DRILL 19: Free up your swing

IF YOU STRUGGLE to get your swing off to a smooth start, this exercise might just release the tension in your swing and help you wield the club more freely. It also removes the tendency to hit at the ball too aggressively, which can cause problems in your swing.

1 *Tee up five or six balls in a row, approximately 4 in (10 cm) apart.*

2 *Address the first ball in the line. For the purposes of this drill, use either a pitching wedge or a 9-iron.*

3 *Hit each ball without stopping between balls. Start with a half swing and build up gradually. From the time you address the first ball, the clubhead should not stop moving until the last ball is dispatched.*

○ At first you might struggle to hit every ball out of the middle of the clubface. However, provided you maintain a flowing, easy rhythm, after a couple of tries you will notice certain things happening to your swing. Your rhythm will indeed be smoother and more natural. Your swing will not be restricted by tension, and as a result you will start to feel what it is like to release the club more freely through the ball. Once you are confident that these feelings are ingrained in your swing, try to replicate them when you hit pitch shots during a round.

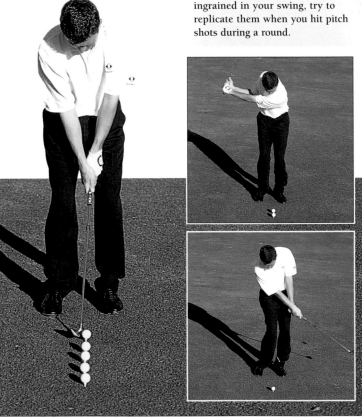

DRILL 20: Think of gradual acceleration in the downswing

MICKEY WRIGHT, probably the greatest female golfer of all time, once said: "You cannot start a car from a dead start and put it immediately up to 70 miles an hour. No matter how powerful your engine, you must have a gradual acceleration of speed. So it is in the golf swing." Mickey was referring to the need to build up clubhead speed gradually in the downswing. Another way to look at this is to think of a rollercoaster as it begins its plunge downwards. At first it descends quite slowly, but gradually it picks up speed until, when the rollercoaster reaches the bottom of the dip, it is traveling at full speed. Although pitch shots are control shots, gradual acceleration is still required in the downswing to produce a proper strike. A rollercoaster analogy forms the basis of a useful way to work on your swing.

1 *Forget targets and distance for the time being. Simply set up a shot at the practice range, and make what feels like a comfortable-length backswing with a pitching wedge.*

2 *Imagine that your hands, arms, and the club are the cars of a rollercoaster, that the top of your backswing is the highest point on the rollercoaster ride, and that the ball is at the bottom of the ride's dip.*

Make sure the "rollercoaster cars" start their descent slowly and then pick up speed gradually but purposefully. At the bottom of the ride the clubhead should reach top speed. After that your hands, arms, and the club (the rollercoaster cars) are simply freewheeling to the finish of your swing.

○ For the purposes of this drill, it is not important to concern yourself with hitting toward a target. The idea is to develop smooth acceleration in your swing (see Drill 12, p.91), rather than to work on your accuracy.

Beginning of the downswing
Your hands and arms should start down smoothly

Followthrough
Your hands, arms, and club freewheel through to the finish of your swing

Halfway down
The club should be gradually accelerating

Hitting zone
The club should be moving at optimum speed

DRILL 21: Hover the club for a free and easy takeaway

IF YOU ARE PITCHING from rough, it is easy for the clubhead to become caught in the grass during your takeaway. You can prevent this happening if you hover the clubhead behind the ball at address. This technique, advocated by two-time US Masters champion Bernhard Langer, guarantees a smooth, uninterrupted start to your swing, which can only enhance the rhythm of your entire swing. However, it takes a bit of practice.

1 *Place a ball in light rough and address it with your pitching wedge just as you would normally, with the clubhead resting on the ground.*

2 *Raise the clubhead so that it is hovering in a position approximately level with the ball's equator. Do this by standing a little taller from your spine, rather than lifting the clubhead up with your hands alone.*

3 *You are now in a good position to sweep the clubhead back freely.*

○ This drill also promotes a cleaner strike because it slightly raises the bottom point of your swing, preventing the heavy impact that is a common fault in the rough. Without interference from grass behind the ball, your backswing will now be a smooth, uninterrupted movement.

DRILL 22: Try right-armed swings to train a better release

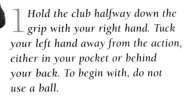

WITH GOLF'S SHORTER SHOTS there can be a tendency to want to guide the ball towards the target. But this usually ends in misery because you cannot possibly strike the ball with any conviction or confidence if you are trying to guide the ball. Ironically, your preoccupation with greater accuracy usually results in a missed green. To produce a good pitch shot, you have to release the club properly (*see p.27*) and trust your swing. This practice drill will help you attain a free release of the clubhead through the hitting area.

1 *Hold the club halfway down the grip with your right hand. Tuck your left hand away from the action, either in your pocket or behind your back. To begin with, do not use a ball.*

2 *Make a three-quarter-length backswing. Allow your right elbow to fold as it does in a proper golf swing.*

3 *Swish the clubhead in your downswing so that the club is freewheeling through the hitting zone.*

4 *When you are confident with this one-handed swing, try hitting a shot. Tee up the ball (to give you the best chance of a clean strike) and reproduce the movements described in steps 2 and 3. You will be surprised at the quality of shot you can hit.*

○ When you attain the correct freedom of movement in your one-armed swing, you will find that your right arm straightens through the impact area, due to the centrifugal forces built up in the swinging motion of the club. It is this feeling that you need to cultivate in your actual pitching swing.

DRILL 23: Swing around the clock to vary your distance

To PRODUCE A PITCH SHOT of a certain distance requires a length of backswing that enables you to swing down and through the hitting zone with smooth acceleration (*see Drill 20, p.99*). A good way to determine which backswing length matches which distance is to work through the following drill. It requires you to make three different length backswings based on the numbers on a clockface.

1 *Address a ball as normal and imagine that the ball is at 6 o'clock on an imaginary clock face and that your head is at the center. With your first shot, swing your arms back until your hands reach 9 o'clock. Then smoothly accelerate into your downswing and through impact. Note how far the ball flies. (Use the same wedge throughout this drill.)*

2 *With your next shot, stop your backswing when your hands reach 10 o'clock. Swing down with the same smooth acceleration and see how far this ball travels.*

3 *Finally, make a swing in which your hands move all the way to 11 o'clock in your backswing and check the distance this ball achieves.*

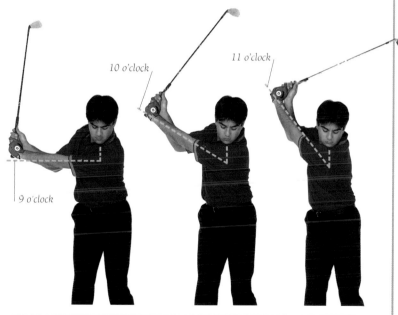

10 o'clock

11 o'clock

9 o'clock

○ You should use the same amount of acceleration in your downswing for all three shots: it is the length of your backswing that determines how far the ball will travel. Armed with the knowledge gained from this exercise, you can think of every pitch shot you play during a round as merely a function of swing length. Rather than guessing about how hard to hit each shot, you simply have to judge whether it is a 9 o'clock, 10 o'clock, or 11 o'clock swing.

THE GEOMETRY OF A GOOD PITCH SHOT

A PROPERLY STRUCK pitch shot requires a fairly steep angle of attack. But it is not necessary to work on this aspect of your swing in isolation, since you need only adhere to the fundamentals dealt with in the Level One drills (*see pp.82–9*) to insure that your angle of attack is correct. In particular, check that your stance is very slightly open, that the ball is in the middle of your stance, and that your wrists are set correctly in your backswing. If all of these factors are in order, you will produce the necessary downward blow, which gives a clean contact and lots of backspin. As explained in the section on iron play, the divot mark should start after the point of impact (*see the Key Checkpoint on p.61*). If the mark occurs before the point of impact, the turf will be interfering with a clean strike. If there is no divot-mark, you are not hitting down on the ball properly. Drill 9 (*see pp.88–9*) shows that divot marks can teach you much about your swing.

DIVOT MARK *A descending angle of attack will automatically create a divot mark. This mark should start just after the point of impact.*

DRILL 24: Hit three shots with one club

DRILL 14 (see p.93) demonstrated how you can hit three different length pitch shots with the same swing. This might be the easiest way to play different length pitch shots, but for more advanced players, there is another way. By manipulating the clubface and adjusting your stance accordingly, it is possible to vary the trajectory and length of your pitch shots using just one club. If you like the sound of that, the following drill outlines the points you should work on next time you are at the practice range.

1 *Hit a few standard pitch shots. Note the trajectory of the balls' flight and the distance achieved.*

2 *Now try to hit a low-flying wedge shot, which can be useful in windy conditions. To do this, place the ball back in your stance with your hands forward so that the club's shaft is angled slightly. This delofts the clubface. To insure that this lack of loft is maintained through the hitting area, keep your hands and wrists firm so that they do not hinge as much as normal. Grip the club a fraction more tightly than usual as well, since this* will restrict your hand and wrist movement. It should feel like more of a shoulders-and-arms swing than a hands-and-arms swing. Finally, think of your hands and the club finishing low.

3 *Now aim for a much higher shot, which could be used to clear an obstruction between you and the target. To achieve this shot, move the ball forward in your stance to a point opposite just inside your left heel. The clubhead will then meet the ball on a relatively shallow angle of attack, delivering lots of loft at impact, so that you end up with a higher ball flight.*

Rather than gripping the club quite tightly, as you would with the low-flying wedge shot, hold the club more softly to promote a longer, more flowing swing. As with the low shot, let your followthrough reflect your intentions and aim to finish with your hands high.

❍ Hitting three shots with one club is a more advanced technique, requiring skill and practice. The major benefit is that, if you have a favorite wedge – a club that feels great in your hands – you can use it in a variety of situations.

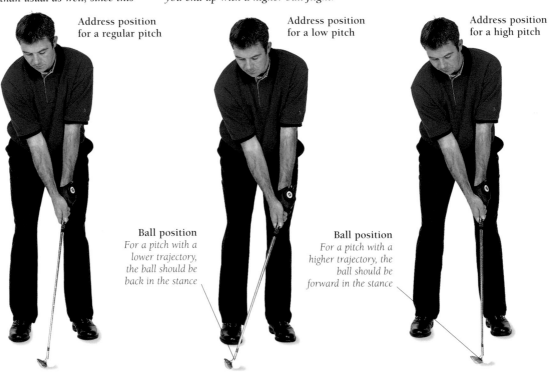

Address position for a regular pitch

Address position for a low pitch

Address position for a high pitch

Ball position *For a pitch with a lower trajectory, the ball should be back in the stance*

Ball position *For a pitch with a higher trajectory, the ball should be forward in the stance*

DRILL 25: Aim at multiple targets when you practice

WHEN YOU PLAY a round of golf, you only ever get one attempt at each shot. Once you have hit that shot, chances are you will not get another like it in the same round. The pressure on your pitching is perhaps the greatest of all the shots, because you are aiming at the most well-protected area of the course where all manner of hazards, such as sand or water, guard the green. Work on this "multiple target" drill in your practice sessions so that on the golf course you will be up to the challenge of hitting the right shot first time.

1 *Identify as many separate targets as possible within your pitching range: five or six is just about the right number, but as few as three will still be sufficient. The targets should be at a variety of distances and in various directions.*

2 *With a bucket of balls by your side, hit the first ball at the first target, the second ball at the second target, and so on. Try not to rush. Make sure you treat each shot just as you would if you were playing a round. The key is not to hit the same shot twice in a row.*

○ By not hitting more than one shot at a time at a particular target, your swing never has the luxury of getting into a groove as it can do if you beat dozens of balls in the same direction. In that sense, this drill is much like playing a proper round. If you can hit good pitch shots in this practice routine, you will know you can do it on the course, too.

KEY CHECKPOINT

BE WARY OF TOO MUCH BACKSPIN

THE KEY CHECKPOINT on p.101 describes how, through a steep angle of attack, clean contact, and a high degree of loft on the clubface, it is possible to generate lots of backspin on pitch shots. On a receptive green this can make the ball "suck back" quickly. However, there are times when lots of backspin will hurt you more than it helps.

Take, for example, a green that slopes upwards from front to back: as soon as the ball lands it will spin back down the slope. If the flag is at the back of the green, lots of backspin will make it difficult for you to hit the ball close to the hole. It is sometimes wiser to play a less lofted club, such as a 9-iron, and hit the shot a little softer and lower to generate less backspin. Of course, backspin will help you place the ball close to the hole if the flag is at the front of the same green. In this scenario you can pitch the ball into the middle of the green and be confident it will spin back down the slope toward the hole.

SOFTER SWING *If you want the ball to run rather than stop quickly on the green, take a less lofted club and make a softer swing. This generates less backspin.*

THE PERFECT PITCH SHOT

SUPREME ACCURACY in his long game is one of the standout features of Nick Faldo's golf, but his pitching is often overlooked. This is a shame because it is every bit as good as his long game. There was certainly no better pressure pitch in the 1990s than Faldo's 82-yd (75-m) shot on the 18th during his 1995 Ryder Cup singles match against Curtis Strange. The ball finished 4 ft (1.2 m) from the hole, and when he sunk the putt the Cup was virtually secured for Europe. This magnificent pitch shot was the product of a wonderful sense of touch combined with a sublime technique, where his body-turn and hand- and arm-swing worked in perfect harmony. Every golfer can learn from Faldo's pitching style, as captured by the following sequences.

Wrists
A 90-degree angle between the shaft of the club and the forearms indicates the perfect amount of wrist hinge in the backswing

Body position
Faldo's body-turn is perfectly synchronized with his arm-swing, enhancing his control of the shot's distance

Legs
Faldo's leg action is very stable, which is one of the big improvements he made during his Leadbetter-inspired swing change in the mid-1980s

1 ADDRESS

You can see that Faldo's alignment for this pitch shot is very slightly open: a line drawn along his toes would run left of parallel to the target line. (His stance would become more open for shorter pitches and less open for longer pitches, where a fuller swing is required.) Note how the clubhead is barely touching the ground, as if he is resting it on an eggshell. This helps remove tension from his address position – you can see that his hands and arms look relaxed and soft. This also facilitates a smooth first move away from the ball.

4 FOLLOWTHROUGH

Faldo's followthrough is the same length as his backswing, showing that he has accelerated the club smoothly but briskly through impact. When professionals play these shots, they put plenty of spin on the ball by really "zipping" the club into the back of the ball. The shot soars along the perfect trajectory and then drops like a falling stone, which ensures little forward momentum on landing.

KEYS TO SHARP PITCH SHOTS

W HILE CONTROL is vital for pitch shots, you must still remember to make a positive swing. The following handful of reminders will help you combine these two key elements while you are pitching.

❍ *Choke down on the grip by about 2 in (5 cm), and make sure that your grip pressure is soft. These factors will enhance your control over the clubhead.*

❍ *Open your stance to stop you swinging back too far and to help you clear your left side out of the way at impact.*

❍ *Feel that you create the same amount of acceleration in your downswing on every pitch shot you hit, using the length of your backswing to vary the distance the ball flies through the air.*

3 IMPACT

Has hitting a golf ball ever looked so easy and controlled as this? Just as Faldo's body wound up as his hands and arms swung upwards in the backswing, his downswing is controlled by harmonizing the unwinding of his body with his arms and hands as they swing down and through impact. This smooth, controlled acceleration brings him into the wonderful impact position shown here.

2 BACKSWING

Note how Faldo's hand- and arm-swing works with this body-pivot: as he turns his body, his hands and arms follow. While this is happening, his wrists are hinging, setting the club into the perfect position. The lower half of his body is relatively passive: his knees have remained flexed, and his hips have resisted the turning motion of his torso.

❍ *Since you must hit down in order to create height and spin on your pitch shots, think of generating ball-then-turf contact to promote the ideal impact factors.*

CHIPPING

IT IS A WIDELY held belief that all tour professionals are masters of the short game (they know that this is where the money is). They must be highly skilled around the greens because even the best golfers in the world cannot find the green every time with their approach shots. Indeed, they often miss the target as many as five or six times in a round.

On average, you might miss many more greens than that, which shows how vital chip shots are. A nicely played chip gives you an outside chance of a "chip-in" birdie, which will send you off to the next tee with a spring in your step. Even if you do not hole the shot, the ball should finish close to the hole. This takes the pressure off your putting –

a significant factor when you are under pressure to produce a good score. Altogether, a sharp chipping technique can save you between five and 10 strokes per round.

DELICATE CHIP SHOTS

A proficient chipper must control the four key ingredients that combine to determine where the

ball comes to rest on the green: height, carry, spin, and roll. Everything you read and do in the forthcoming section is designed to enhance your understanding of these elements, and to give you the necessary skills to master them. By the end of this chapter you will have a versatile short game, spanning a range of clubs.

THE CHIPPING TEST

*T*here are dozens of different kinds of shots you can play around the green. However, the following test uses just one shot-type and asks the one simple but incisive question that matters most: how sharp are you around the greens?

1 Find a green to which you can play chip shots of approximately 11–22 yd (10–20 m). Ensure that there is more green than fairway between you and the flag, and do not position yourself so that it is necessary to chip over a bunker.

2 Make a circle of tees – with a radius of about 1 yd (1 m) – around the hole. Use your wedge as an approximate measuring device. It is best to use only five or six tees because if you place too many around the hole they can deflect balls from their natural course. This makes it difficult to obtain accurate results from the test.

3 Take your 9-iron or pitching wedge and chip 15 balls towards the flag (left). Your objective is to get as many balls as possible inside the tee circle. Repeat this step another two times, average your scores, and use the performance chart (below) to determine your current level of ability.

○ Even at the highest level, the ability to turn three shots into two is one of the keys to consistent scoring. This is why chipping plays such an important part in your game. No matter how confident you are in your ball-striking ability, you cannot hit every green – so you will need to be able to chip and putt.

PERFORMANCE CHART

○ ○ ○ ○ ○
1–5 = Level One
(pp.108–15)

○ ○ ○ ○ ○
6–10 = Level Two
(pp.116–23)

○ ○ ○ ○ ○
11–15 = Level Three
(pp.124–9)

LEVEL ONE

LEVEL TWO

LEVEL THREE

DRILL 1: Organize your setup to make chips seem easy

IF YOU HAVE A FUNDAMENTAL problem striking your chips cleanly, then the prospect of playing any shot from around the green can be intimidating. If this is the case, it is likely that your setup is to blame. Many problems, in every department of the game, can be traced back to what you do before you start your swing, and even those who consider themselves reasonable chippers would be wise to take this opportunity to revisit the basics. This simple exercise – which can be done at home, in the garden, or at the course – will insure that you have the correct address position.

1 *Stand with your feet, hips, and shoulders slightly open to the target (if you imagine the target as 12 o'clock, align yourself to 11 o'clock). Your feet should be only 6–8 in (15–20 cm) apart.*

2 *Place the ball back in your stance: opposite your right instep.*

3 *Settle your weight to favor your leading foot. A ratio of 40 percent of your weight on your right foot and 60 percent on your left is ideal for a standard chip shot.*

4 *Place the clubhead behind the ball and move your hands forward so that your left arm and the shaft of the club form a straight line down to the ball. The clubface should be positioned so that it is aiming straight at the target.*

○ The correct setup position for a chip shot can be summed up like this: ball back, hands and weight forward. It is worth pointing out that the chip shot is one of the few strokes in golf where the impact position is virtually identical to the address position. Improving your setup by working on this drill will, therefore, also improve the quality of your impact position.

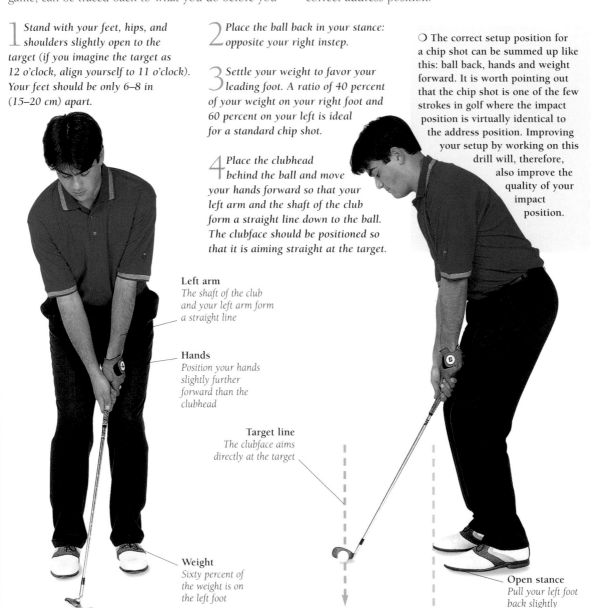

Left arm
The shaft of the club and your left arm form a straight line

Hands
Position your hands slightly further forward than the clubhead

Target line
The clubface aims directly at the target

Weight
Sixty percent of the weight is on the left foot

Open stance
Pull your left foot back slightly

DRILL 2: Go back low, then release and hold

DRILL 1 *(left)* demonstrated the perfect setup; now for the perfect swing. The technique described in this exercise applies to a medium-length chip of about 13 yd (12 m). However, to play shots of different lengths, you can still apply the same techniques described in this drill – the only thing that changes is the length of your backswing (shorter to send the ball a lesser distance; longer to send it a greater distance).

1 *Take a pitching wedge and assume the address position described in Drill 1 (left). Be meticulous about your setup and, to begin with, perform this exercise without a ball.*

2 *Sweep the clubhead away, mostly using your hands and arms, and maintain your body's connection to this motion. The clubhead should stay low to the ground for the first 12 in (30 cm), and your wrists should hinge softly to bring the club up. Your backswing should stop when your hands reach 8 o'clock (see Drill 23 in the "Pitching" section, p.101)*

3 *As you change direction, from backswing to downswing, you should feel a softness in your hands and wrists, which is often referred to as "lag". This puts your hands in a dominant position as you lead the clubhead on a downward path into the ball. Effectively, lag prevents the clubhead from overtaking your hands before impact.*

4 *When you are familiar with these movements, you can then move on to hitting a ball. Simply try to recreate the swinging motion described in steps 2 and 3.*

5 It is important to remember that your body must move, even in a swing that is as short as this. As your arms swing back and forth, your body rotates backward and through – everything works in harmony. If your body is motionless in your downswing, the clubhead will pass your hands before impact, and the club will meet the ball on an upward path, which is far from desirable. How your body should move during a chip shot is examined in a different way in Drill 3 (see p.110), and in Drill 13 (see p.117).

DRILL 6: One ball and one club at a time

VISUALIZATION IS A VITAL COMPONENT of an effective short game. However, although it is important to see shots in your mind's eye (visualizing the path of the ball through the air and along the ground), you still have to select the club to match your mental image. This drill will give you a crystal clear understanding of how the ball reacts relative to the amount of loft on the club.

1 *Select an even patch of ground about 5½ yd (5 m) to the side of a green, with about 5½–7½ yd (5–7 m) between the apron of the green and the flag.*

2 *Count out nine balls of the same make and construction and line up nine clubs, ranging from a 3-iron to a sand wedge.*

3 *Start with the 3-iron, and hit a chip shot. Note the amount of height (not much) and run (lots) on the shot. Work your way through the clubs until you play the final ball with your sand wedge, which will provide plenty of height but little run.*

○ Throughout the exercise, use exactly the same, standard chip shot technique (*see drills 1–5, pp.108–11*). You do not have to change your swing each time you change club; instead, the different lofts on the clubs will produce shots of a different nature. Always pay close attention to the ball's height, carry, spin, and roll. Then, when you are on the course, you will be able to select the most appropriate club for every chip.

KEY CHECKPOINT

THE "TEXAS WEDGE" SHOT IS SOMETIMES BETTER THAN A REGULAR CHIP

PUTTING FROM off the green (known as the Texas Wedge shot) can be an effective alternative to a chip if it is used in the correct circumstances. It is certainly not a cowardly decision, as some golfers seem to view it.

If your ball is lying on the fairway near to the green, and the grass is closely mown between you and the putting surface, you will be amazed how easy it is to knock the ball inside a 2-ft (60-cm) radius of the hole. This takes all the pressure off your next putt. This is partly because most people find it is easier to judge the distance of a long putt than a chip. Also, you are unlikely to completely mishit a putt. With a lofted club, however, it is easier to make a hesitant swing and send the ball only halfway to the hole. The only adjustment you need to make to your putting technique (*see the "Putting" section, pp.158–83*) when putting from off the green is to stand a little taller to facilitate a longer, freer swing of your hands and your arms.

However, there are some occasions when you should not attempt this shot: if the ball is lying in rough (you cannot make a decent strike); if there is rough between you and the green (you cannot expect a ball to run through long grass); if the grass is wet from early morning dew or rain (the ball will be quickly slowed down by the surface moisture); or if you are more than about 20 yd (18 m) from the putting surface (even if the fairway is closely mown, you will have to hit the ball so hard that you are unlikely to strike it properly).

PUTTING OFF THE GREEN *If the conditions are right, the Texas Wedge is a useful alternative to a standard chip shot. You might be surprised how accurate you can be.*

LEVEL ONE

DRILL 7: Clip a tee to promote a free swing

IN A FULL SWING, the clubhead is traveling so fast that there is no danger of the club stopping at impact. But with chipping, where the swing is short and delicacy is often required, it is easy to stub the clubhead into the ground behind the ball. The turf instead of the ball then soaks up the energy. This drill shows you how to be more positive in your approach to chipping, encouraging you to make a freer swing of the clubhead.

1 *Tee up a ball about ⅜ in (1 cm) off the ground. Address the ball as you would for a normal chip, using your pitching wedge.*

2 *Make a smooth, free swing of the club: focus on flattening the tee into the ground at impact (left). This encourages you to accelerate the clubhead through the hitting area. Try to ignore the ball. When you succeed in flattening the tee, you will produce nicely flighted chips.*

3 *Repeat step 2 a few times and then dispense with the tee.*

○ If you can translate the freedom in your swing when the ball was teed up into your actual swing, you will never "quit" on a chip shot (which is so often the cause of heavy contact). Instead, you will find that you can make a positive move through impact, while still retaining control.

DRILL 8: Use upturned umbrellas to increase accuracy

TO BE A GOOD CHIPPER, you have to control the height, carry, spin, and roll of the ball. The following exercise is based on a popular practice drill, but with an added twist to enhance your judgement of two of the four key elements: height and carry. One of the good things about this exercise is that you do not have to be at the golf course to gain full benefit from it: your garden at home will do just as well.

1 *Stick two open umbrellas into the ground, approximately 5½ yd (5 m) apart.*

2 *Place a batch of balls about 5½ yd (5 m) from one of the umbrellas.*

3 *Using your pitching wedge, alternate hitting one ball to the closer umbrella and the next ball to the further umbrella. See if you can land every ball in an umbrella (the balls do not necessarily have to stay in). Try a less-lofted club for an even stiffer challenge.*

○ This drill is a particularly effective way to improve your ability to see a particular length chip and find your range first time. This is what you have to achieve on the course, where you only ever have one chance to get the shot right.

DRILL 9: Rehearse, look, and hit

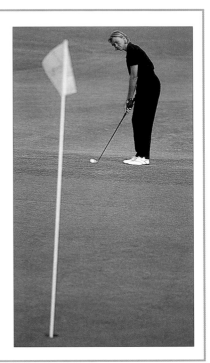

MANY GOLFERS CHIP POORLY because they fail to make use of their natural "touch" and hand-eye coordination. By practicing chipping as outlined in the following drill, you will use these attributes to improve your performance around the greens.

1 *Set yourself up with a chip shot about 11 yd (10 m) from the flag.*

2 *Make a couple of practice swings, but keep your eyes firmly fixed on the target, not on the ground. Try to get a feel for the length and force required to send the ball the correct distance.*

3 *Then address the ball, take one look at the hole, and hit the chip. Do not hesitate any longer than you have to, just recreate the same swing that you practiced, only this time with the ball in the way.*

❍ By taking a practice swing while looking at the target, your eyes pass visual signals to your brain. In turn, your brain sends the appropriate message to your hands and arms. This information needs to be fresh, so one look at the hole before you hit is enough. If you take too long, you will lose the visual and physical feedback gained from the practice swing. This is a great way to chip when you are on the course: rehearse, look, hit – and let your instincts take over.

DRILL 10: Monitor your swing path when you chip

A CHIP SHOT involves a short swing, and the clubhead travels through impact at a much slower speed than with a full iron shot. Even so, it is still very hard to monitor the exact path of the clubhead into and through impact. The following drill can provide you with this crucial information.

1 *Place any club from your bag approximately one clubface length the other side of the ball, lying parallel to the ball-to-target line.*

2 *Take your pitching wedge and address the ball, remembering the importance of a slightly open stance. Keep your hands and weight forward, and the ball back in your stance (see Drill 1, p.108).*

3 *Now play a chip shot. In a correct swing the clubhead will not strike the obstruction in the backswing, downswing, or followthrough. The club should travel on an inside arc during the backswing, then parallel to the obstruction through the hitting zone, before arcing to the inside again in the followthrough. This is an "in-to-in" swing path (see pp.26–7).*

❍ This exercise gives you immediate feedback on your errors. If you strike the obstruction in your backswing, the clubhead is traveling too far outside the correct line. To rectify this, take the club back more on the inside. If you hit the obstruction in your followthrough, your swing is excessively in-to-out through the hitting zone – the result of taking the club back too far on the inside in the takeaway. To cure this, take the club back more on a straight line, and swing the clubhead to the left of the target through impact. This practice drill is an excellent way to straighten out your chipping.

DRILL 11: Throw some balls to read the roll on the green

THIS IS ONE OF MANY drills in this section designed to train you to visualize shots before playing them. It uses the simple action of throwing a ball to improve your understanding of height and roll. A better grasp of these key concepts will be of great benefit to your chipping.

1 *Stand about 30 yd (27 m) from a flag. Have to hand at least 10 balls and a selection of clubs, from a 7-iron to a sand wedge.*

2 *Lob a ball underarm, and try to finish as close as possible to the flag. Use a low trajectory, which will produce plenty of roll. After a couple of tries you should find your range quite accurately.*

3 *Now throw a ball underarm high into the air so that it bounces near the flag and does not roll far. You will find it much more difficult to get the balls to finish close to the flag. Not only that, but the general dispersion of the "high" balls will probably be more erratic.*

4 *Keep throwing balls, always varying the height and roll.*

5 *Now hit some chip shots. Think of the trajectory and roll you achieved with your throws, and try to recreate these by selecting clubs with different lofts. Again you will find that the low shots nearly always finish closer than those hit high.*

○ On the course, whenever possible, use a low trajectory and get the ball to roll as early as possible in its journey (although the first bounce should ideally be on the green). Only when hazards force you to take a more aerial route should you play a high-flying chip.

THE ANATOMY OF A GOOD CHIP SHOT

ONE OF THE FIRST things you should know about chipping is that the way the ball behaves through the air and on the ground varies enormously from club to club. As a general rule, loft creates height and backspin, which combine to reduce roll. This means that the most lofted clubs in your bag, such as the wedges, produce lots of carry and not much roll, whereas clubs such as the mid-irons produce little carry and lots of roll. Long irons produce nearly all roll and almost no carry.

If you want to be more specific, however, the following simple table might help when you are trying to visualize a shot and attempting to match a club to your requirements. These figures are a useful guide, but bear in mind that extreme ground conditions, such as those encountered after a heavy frost, might alter these percentages.

Club	Carry	Roll
7-iron	25%	75%
9-iron	50%	50%
Pitching wedge	65%	35%
Sand wedge	75%	25%

RETEST YOURSELF

Before moving to Level Two, take the test on pp.106–7 again. If you have not improved, it is worth revisiting the Level One drills. However, if the performance chart shows that your chipping has progressed sufficiently, then you are ready to tackle the more advanced drills in Level Two.

DRILL 12: Add and subtract hours to accelerate into impact

IN HIS HEYDAY, Tom Watson was probably the best player of the chip shot in the world. He maintains that one of the worst chipping faults is making too long a backswing and then decelerating into impact. This he compares to a boxer pulling his punches. Try this drill, which – like Drill 23 (*see p.101*) in the "Pitching" section – is based on the principle of determining your swing length using positions on an imaginary clockface. It will also help you learn to accelerate into the ball on every chip shot.

1 *Make a backswing with your pitching wedge where your hands swing to 7 o'clock. Then accelerate down through the hitting zone, and swing your hands through to 4 o'clock. This insures that your followthrough is longer than your backswing. Note how far the ball travels.*

2 *Now add an hour to the backswing so that your hands swing back to 8 o'clock. To compensate for the extended backswing, take an hour off your followthrough so that your hands reach 3 o'clock. Again, your followthrough is proportionately longer than your backswing. This extended swing will make the ball travel further.*

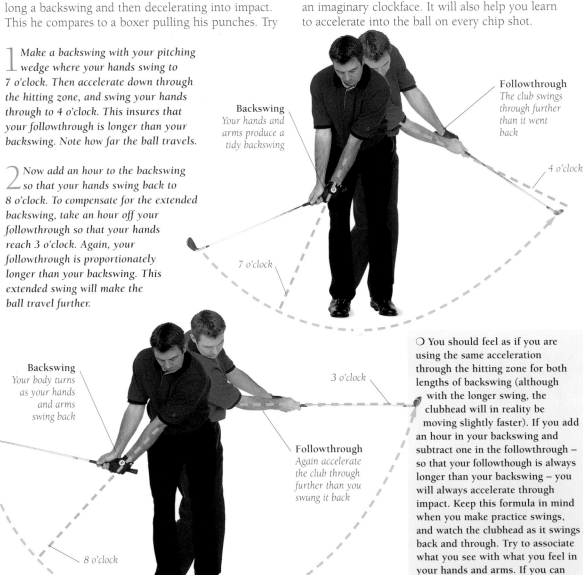

Backswing
Your hands and arms produce a tidy backswing

Followthrough
The club swings through further than it went back

4 o'clock

7 o'clock

Backswing
Your body turns as your hands and arms swing back

3 o'clock

Followthrough
Again accelerate the club through further than you swung it back

8 o'clock

❍ You should feel as if you are using the same acceleration through the hitting zone for both lengths of backswing (although with the longer swing, the clubhead will in reality be moving slightly faster). If you add an hour in your backswing and subtract one in the followthrough – so that your followthough is always longer than your backswing – you will always accelerate through impact. Keep this formula in mind when you make practice swings, and watch the clubhead as it swings back and through. Try to associate what you see with what you feel in your hands and arms. If you can replicate this when playing shots, you will not "pull your punches."

Drill 13: Rock the shaft to keep your body and arms together

THE RELATIONSHIP BETWEEN your upper body and your arms is critical for any golf shot, even chip shots. These two core elements of your swing must work together to insure reliable and consistent shots. If you can maintain the harmony in your body's motion during the swing, you will strike the ball the same way every time, which makes it easier to judge the distance of your chip shots. This drill trains your body and arms to work together.

1 *Trap a club under your armpits so that the shaft is horizontal across your chest. Take a 9-iron or pitching wedge and assume your normal address position, while keeping the horizontal shaft in place.*

2 *Rock the shaft up and down by turning your body smoothly back and through. Let your arms respond* to this turning movement, and you will find that the club tracks a neat path back and forth, with the clubhead just brushing the ground as it travels through the hitting area. The shaft should stay trapped against your chest throughout. If it becomes dislodged, your arms are working independently of your body turn, and your ball striking will suffer.

○ When you are comfortable with this movement, remove the horizontal shaft and hit 20-yd (18-m) chip shots with no target in mind. If in your proper swing you can recreate the same feelings experienced in this drill, you will hardly ever mishit a chip shot.

KEY CHECKPOINT

CHOOSE SHOTS THAT REFLECT THE TYPE OF BALL YOU USE

YOUR CHOICE of ball, which is discussed further in the reference section (*see p.235*), has a direct influence on what shots you can and cannot play around the green.

CONTROL BALL: Just about every chip shot is available to you if you play a balata-covered ball. These balls spin more and consequently run less than a ball designed for distance, which means you can pull off the very difficult shots when there is little green to work with. But there are pitfalls. For example, if you have a chip to a long green with the pin at the back, a crisp strike with a lofted club will give lots of backspin, which makes it very easy to leave the ball short. In this situation, a smart control-ball club selection would be an 8-iron. Less loft equals less backspin, so you can play a chip-and-run and the ball will roll towards the hole.

DISTANCE BALL: There is no problem playing chip-and-runs with this type of ball. Your difficulty is to impart much backspin with a distance ball, because it is designed for length and durability. Do not expect to emulate the professional who gets the ball to bite and slow down, or perhaps even spin back, on the second bounce. A distance ball is most problematic when you have little green to work with. If, for example, you are chipping over a bunker, you may have to accept that you cannot get the ball to stop close to the pin.

COMPROMISE: There are many balls, of differing construction, that bridge the gap between control and distance balls. They offer durability and a degree of control.

LEVEL TWO

DRILL 14: Use less loft on an upslope

WHEN YOU WORK on your short game, it is not enough to play all your shots from a perfect lie. After all, that is not what happens in a real round of golf. You have to put yourself in difficult spots if you are going to learn how to play the tough shots. This drill shows you how to chip from an upslope lie.

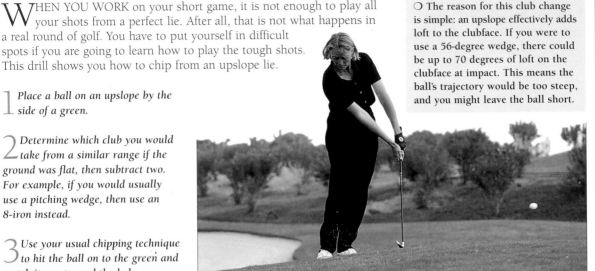

○ The reason for this club change is simple: an upslope effectively adds loft to the clubface. If you were to use a 56-degree wedge, there could be up to 70 degrees of loft on the clubface at impact. This means the ball's trajectory would be too steep, and you might leave the ball short.

1 *Place a ball on an upslope by the side of a green.*

2 *Determine which club you would take from a similar range if the ground was flat, then subtract two. For example, if you would usually use a pitching wedge, then use an 8-iron instead.*

3 *Use your usual chipping technique to hit the ball on to the green and watch it run toward the hole.*

DRILL 15: Practice on a downslope to heighten your skills

PLAYING FROM AN UPSLOPE *(see Drill 14, above)* is an easy proposition compared to chipping on a downslope. Hitting good chips from a downslope demands a very sound chipping technique. Therefore, when you revert to chipping from a flat lie, the shot seems much easier and your confidence soars. If you work on this drill, you will find that all your chip shots – not just those on a downslope – will improve greatly.

1 *Place a ball on a downslope to the side of a green.*

2 *Put the ball 2 in (5 cm) further back in your stance than usual, and move your hands further forward than normal. These two adjustments allow you to strike the shot cleanly but deprive the club of even more loft. The best solution is to use your most lofted club: the sand wedge. This means that you can still deliver about 45 degrees of loft to the ball, even on a severe slope. This should be enough to create a relatively soft landing chip shot – one with sufficient height for the ball not to run out of control.*

3 *Keep most of your weight on your lower foot, and insure that your hands are ahead of the clubhead, as you swing down the slope. Do not try to help the ball into the air – focus on hitting down through impact. Trust your technique to create the necessary height.*

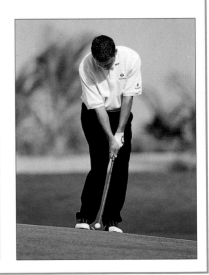

○ A downslope naturally delofts the clubface, resulting in a flatter trajectory than normal. This makes the shot very difficult. When you are striking the ball cleanly from the downslope, try some chips on even ground – these shots will never have seemed so easy.

Drill 16: Play off a hard surface for a clean strike

Drills 14 and 15 (*left*) highlighted the benefits of practicing from a tough spot to improve your overall technique. This exercise is based on the same theory. Although it is challenging at first, the drill ultimately improves your chipping action and makes playing normal chip shots seem simple. This will give you lots of confidence around the greens, which is a valuable asset to have.

1 *Place a ball on a hard, bare surface, such as tarmac, tiling, concrete, or paving stones – anything that has no give in it. Use an old pitching wedge that you do not mind scratching.*

2 *Put the ball back in your stance and push your hands forward and body weight on to your left side – refer to the keys to a good setup outlined in Drill 1 (see p.108).*

3 *Hit some short chip shots of no more than 20 yd (18 m). For now, a target is irrelevant: the aim of this exercise is to strike the ball cleanly from an unforgiving surface. Keep your hands in front of the clubhead all the way into the hitting area. This will help prevent the clubhead hitting the bare surface before it reaches the ball. After a few tries you should achieve some success. Next time you play a chip shot from grass, it will look far more inviting.*

○ Do not rehearse this exercise with a sand wedge. The bounce (the rounded sole of the clubhead) raises the leading edge off the ground, which makes it virtually impossible to get the clubface to the bottom of the ball. Instead, the wide flange tends to bounce over the bare lie so that the leading edge of the clubhead strikes somewhere around the ball's equator, sending it shooting low across the ground. For this reason you should never choose a sand wedge to play a shot from a bare lie on the course. Always go with a club that has a straighter leading edge, such as a 9-iron or pitching wedge. Clubs such as these will help you get the clubface under the ball and will promote a better strike. Smart club selection sometimes makes all the difference.

Impact
The clubface should strike the ball first, not the bare surface

Hands
At impact your hands should be ahead of the ball

KEY CHECKPOINT

ANALYZE YOUR LANDING ERRORS

DRILL 17 (right) is an invaluable aid in helping train you to hit your chosen landing area on the green. However, if you consistently struggle to hit the mark, you need to analyze your mistakes and learn from them. Try not to chip away without pausing for thought, hoping you will improve but not knowing how. Here are some clues that will help you learn more from the shots you miss.

TOO MANY SHOTS LAND SHORT: This is the most common problem among poor chippers. You are probably decelerating into impact and making a tentative swing. Alternatively, you could be reading the shot wrongly – visualizing a landing area too far up the green and taking a club that has not enough loft on it (for short shots, less height means less carry). Try visualizing a landing area nearer to you, or take a more lofted club and pitch the ball further up the green.

TOO MANY SHOTS LAND LONG: Look at the length of your swing. You might be taking too long a backswing and accelerating into the ball. You should be making a shorter backswing, but still accelerating in the hitting zone. Also look at your club selection. It might be wise to use a less-lofted club, aim to land the ball nearer to you, and allow for some run on landing.

TOO MANY SHOTS LAND LEFT OR RIGHT OF THE TARGET: This indicates a fundamental problem with your technique. Check that you are aiming accurately. Also look at the path of your swing through impact (see Drill 10, p.114) and revisit Drill 1 (see p.108) to establish the correct address position.

DRILL 17: Be a record breaker

THE PRINCIPLES of trying to visualize a shot in your mind's eye and then matching that to the appropriate club and length of swing were explored in Drill 6 (see p.112) and Drill 11 (see p.115). The following drill is a great way to further enhance those skills, although you do need to be at a course. You will need three or four old vinyl records. (You can use small towels if you do not have any unwanted albums.)

1 Scatter the records around a green, making sure that they are well spread out.

2 Choose a spot to the side of the green and select your preferred chipping club.

3 Hit some chip shots, trying to land each ball on to one of the records. Do not aim at the same record twice in a row. Instead, alternate between shorter and longer chip shots as much as possible. If you can hit a record regularly – say one in five times – from a distance of about 8 yd (7 m), you can be very pleased with yourself. And, if the balls that do miss the target pitch within a 2 ft- (60 cm-) radius of the record, this is a good indication that your chipping is improving.

○ When you need to pick out your landing area on the green during a round, imagine that there is a record for you to aim at. Then go ahead and try to break it. This visualization technique will help you focus on something positive, rather than, for example, a bunker or a thick patch of rough between you and the green. Positive thoughts nearly always enhance performance.

DRILL 18: Practice the flop shot

FROM MOST POSITIONS on the course there will be a selection of shots to choose from. But this is not always the case. You may have to chip over a bunker, for example, which will mean very little green to play with. In such a situation you need to play the flop shot, which provides lots of height and a soft landing. It is also a fun shot to practice.

1 *Place a ball in light rough where there is a bunker between you and the green. Take your most lofted club: the sand wedge.*

Feet alignment / Clubface alignment
Target line

2 *Open your stance so that your feet and body are aligned well left of the target. You also need to open the clubface so that it is aiming right of the flag. These technical adjustments are the same as those you would make for a greenside bunker shot (see Drill 1, p.134).*

3 *Make a swing twice as long as you would for a shot of the same distance from a good lie on the*

fairway. Try to slide the clubhead through the grass under the ball – treat the grass as you did the tee in Drill 7 (see p.113). Do not try to help the ball into the air: there is plenty of loft on the clubface, so trust it to do the job for you.

○ The main obstacle to playing this shot well is not having the confidence to make a much longer swing than you might think necessary. You have to practice to become accustomed to the feeling of the grass cushioning the blow at impact. This produces a floating trajectory, and the ball tends to land softly and not run far.

KEY CHECKPOINT

SHOTS FROM ROUGH HAVE LESS BACKSPIN

THIS SECTION on chipping has stressed the importance of understanding the relationship between height, carry, spin, and roll. It is therefore worth emphasizing the effect rough has on your chip shots. That it is more difficult to strike the ball cleanly when it is in the rough you will undoubtedly know all too well from experience. But one thing that tends to be forgotten in the heat of a round is that you simply cannot generate much backspin from rough. Therefore, when playing a chip shot from the rough, you should anticipate approximately twice the amount of run on landing compared to an identical length shot from the fairway. It is important to take this into consideration when you are picturing the shot in your mind and trying to identify an appropriate landing area. Long grass equals more run – there is no escaping this fact, so it makes sense to allow for it.

ROUGH CHIPS *Whenever your ball is in the rough around the green, it will be impossible to gain any backspin. Therefore, allow for more run on landing.*

LEVEL TWO

KEY CHECKPOINT

AIM FOR FLAT SPOTS ON THE GREEN

EVEN WITH the best planning in the world, once the ball leaves the clubface, the outcome of any shot is to some degree down to chance. The ball might, for example, bounce badly (through no fault of your own) or be affected by a gust of wind. Therefore, if there is anything you can do to eliminate some of the unpredictability that is part of every shot, you have to take the opportunity to do so. One way to do this when chipping is always to aim for a flat part of the green. This way you can more accurately predict the first bounce and how the ball will behave from then on, reducing the margin for error. Your misjudged chips will be less wayward, and your well-judged chips will finish consistently closer to the hole. If the ball does not land on a slope or on top of a hump, it is easier to judge the first bounce and determine where the ball will finish. Whenever possible, try to take this into consideration as you make your club selections.

AVOID SLOPES *One of the many things you should take into account when chipping is to try to land the ball on a flat portion of the green.*

DRILL 19: Try a less-lofted club when the green slopes up

MOST GOLFERS leave the ball short when they chip to a green that slopes upwards from front to back. This drill will show you how to predict the effect of a sloping green on a chip shot and will demonstrate how to use this slope to your advantage. Once you have worked your way through this exercise, sloping greens will not seem so daunting.

1 *Find a green with a slope upward from front to back.*

2 *Place a ball on a good lie on the apron of the green (the closely mown grass between the rough and the putting surface).*

3 *Take your pitching wedge and hit chip shots towards the back of the green. Forget the actual flag position (unless it happens to be at the back, of course).*

4 *Now swap clubs to something in the region of an 8-iron, and play the shot using exactly the same technique.*

❍ With a pitching wedge, it is difficult to get the ball up to the back of the green because the amount of loft on the clubface creates too much spin, which causes the ball to "die" on the slope. With the less-lofted 8-iron, however, a flatter trajectory and less spin makes it much easier to get the ball running up the slope. But do not forget that you require a shorter swing with the 8-iron to produce a shot of the same length. This in itself makes it easier to produce an appropriate length shot. Next time you are faced with a difficult chip shot to a sloping green, try using a less-lofted iron.

DRILL 20: Have a chipping contest

WHAT MAKES THIS DRILL so beneficial to your chipping is that it introduces the intensity and pressure of a competitive round into your practice sessions. Trying to better an opponent in a point-scoring game such as this is an excellent way to sharpen your skills.

1 *Team up with another golfer, and find a green surrounded by as many interesting features as possible, such as bunkers, slopes, and different levels of rough.*

2 *Take turns to nominate a place around the green from which you will both chip (using a sand wedge).*

3 *Have one attempt at each shot, and the closest to the pin scores a*

point. Make sure that you constantly move to different locations around the green so that you do not become overly familiar with one situation. Keep score as you go.

○ This exercise is great fun, which is what practicing should be. It also gives your short game a sharp edge, improving your imagination and powers of execution.

KEY CHECKPOINT

REMEMBER, LOFT EQUALS HEIGHT AND SPIN

IT IS AMAZING how often golfers leave chip shots short of the hole. The most common explanation for this is playing a club with lots of loft while not allowing for the fact that the ball will run only a short distance when it lands. Remember, loft equals height and backspin (*see the Key Checkpoint on p.115*). If you choose to play your chip shots with a lofted club, you have to carry the ball roughly three-quarters of the way to the pin (even further if the greens are soft). If you want to take this high-trajectory route, be positive and make sure that you pitch the ball well up. On the other hand, if you want the ball to run, take a less-lofted club, such as an 8-iron. Whichever option you choose, make your decision before you take a club out of the bag — do not become caught in two minds.

Also consider the condition of the putting surface. In winter, when greens are often slow and soggy, use less loft than you would in summer. This will encourage the ball to run out toward the flag.

RETEST YOURSELF

Before moving to Level Three, take the test on pp.106–7 again. If you have not improved, it is worth revisiting the Level Two drills. However, if the performance chart shows that your chipping has progressed sufficiently, then you are ready to tackle the more advanced drills in Level Three.

LEVEL TWO

DRILL 21: Use a weak grip to keep the face open

SOME OF THE WORLD'S greatest chippers play short, delicate chip shots with a weak left hand grip. This technique helps keep the clubface open through the hitting zone – which promotes a higher and softer-landing ball flight – enabling the most delicate of chips. Using a weak left hand grip is a technique that is well worth practicing – give this routine a try next time you are working on your chipping.

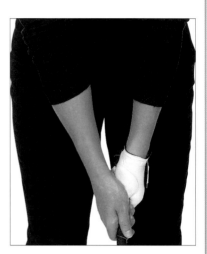

1 *Place about 12 balls on a good lie on the fairway.*

2 *Play a standard chip shot with a pitching wedge using your regular chipping technique. Observe the way the ball travels through the air and the amount of roll there is after landing.*

3 *Now weaken your grip by rotating your left hand, so that you can barely see the second knuckle on the back of your left hand.*

4 *Hit another chip shot. Since your weak grip effectively keeps the* clubface *more open through impact, this should translate into a slightly higher, floated trajectory with much less run on landing.*

5 *Alternate between hitting some chip shots with your regular grip and others with a weak grip.*

○ This drill is a good way to enhance your feel for the way the ball reacts to the position of the clubface at impact, which is one of the key ingredients for controlling the ball around the greens.

DRILL 22: Play from a circle around the green

MANY PLAYERS PRACTICE their short game by hitting a few chips from the same spot, but as you improve you should give yourself greater challenges to become truly "match fit." This is a particularly effective practice drill because it recreates some of the situations you might encounter during a round. Once you have practiced this exercise, you will be better prepared for the real thing.

1 *Drop 10 balls around a green. Make a point of varying the quality of the lie. Place some on the closely mown apron of the green and others in the first cut of rough (with a few sitting up and some nestling down). If there are sloping lies, position one ball on a downslope and another on an upslope.*

2 *Work your way around the green, trying to chip each ball as close as possible to the hole. Have several clubs to hand so that you can visualize each shot and match the correct club to each situation (see Drill 6, p.112).*

○ Analyse your performance as you work through this exercise. How many balls finish within 2 yd (2 m) of the hole (therefore leaving you an achievable putt)? What is the general pattern of your poor chips: do they finish mostly short or long? It is important to learn from your mistakes and make improvements next time.

Drill 23: Try the "Bellied Wedge" shot from the collar of rough

ONE OF THE MOST perplexing dilemmas for golfers is when the ball rests against the collar of rough bordering the apron of the green. Even though you are close to the putting surface, a putter does not seem to be the most appropriate club. But then again, neither does a wedge, since the grass behind the ball gives the impression that a clean strike will be impossible. The solution is a shot called the "Bellied Wedge," which involves striking the equator of the ball with the leading edge of the clubhead.

1 *Take your pitching wedge and adopt your putting grip (see Drill 1, p.160) and posture (see Drill 2, p.161). Choke down on the club, as this brings your hands closer to the clubhead and enhances your control of the stroke.*

2 *Hover the clubhead so that the leading edge is level with the ball's equator (see the Key Checkpoint on p.129). This insures that the clubhead will not become caught in the rough.*

3 *Keep your head and body as still as possible, and make a firm-wristed*

stroke back and forth. Make sure your wrists barely hinge – this is known as a "dead-hands" technique.

4 *Strike the middle of the ball with the leading edge of the clubhead. The ball might hop a little at the start of its journey, but it should roll much like a putt thereafter, making it relatively easy to judge distance. After a couple of tries, you will be amazed how well you can judge line and length.*

❍ Many amateurs feel that this shot is too difficult to attempt. But it is a great way to play a ball resting against the collar of rough. Drill 25 (see p.127) reveals another way to deal with this difficult lie.

see Drill 1, p.160; see Drill 2, p.161; see the Key Checkpoint on p.129; see p.127

KEY CHECKPOINT

PRACTICE HOLING EVERY CHIP YOU HIT

IT IS EASY to be a little defensive on chip shots, which can mean leaving the ball short. Train yourself out of this tendency by practicing an aggressive and positive outlook, aiming to hole every chip shot you hit. This attitude has two clear benefits. Firstly, if you get the ball running toward the hole, there is always a chance that it might drop in (the hole never comes back to meet the ball, remember). Secondly, if the ball misses the hole you can observe its progress past the hole, which will give you a clue as to whether your return putt will break or run straight.

Thinking positively gives you every chance to realize your potential, which will result in a higher standard of chipping. Often it is when you are overly defensive that you hit your worst shots.

THINK POSITIVELY *Aim to hole every chip you hit. Raising your expectations is often a great way to lift the standard of your overall game, too.*

DRILL 24: Try chipping using your putting technique

ANY IDEA THAT MIGHT MAKE the short game easier is well worth considering. The technique described in the following drill is employed by some of the world's best players, which is reason enough to give it a try. It can be applied to a variety of clubs, from a pitching wedge down to an 8-iron, depending on the circumstances. Chipping using your putting technique might improve your chips immeasurably.

Hands
Adopt your normal putting grip in a chipping stance

Grip
Choke down on the club's grip for extra control

Takeaway
Sweep the club away with your hands and arms

Impact
Keep your hands ahead of the club into impact

1 *Adopt your putting grip (see Drill 1, p.160) instead of your regular full-swing grip.*

2 *Nudge your hands ahead of the clubhead and ball at address. The shaft of the club should now be leaning noticeably toward the target.*

3 *Now simply replicate the swing action you would use for a long putt. As you swing your arms back and through impact, it is important that your hands remain ahead of the clubhead.*

○ Adopting your putting grip when chipping minimizes wrist action, which has three benefits: it simplifies the stroke, increases the consistency of the strike, and enhances your feel for distances. Because the ball receives very little backspin from this shot, as soon as it comes into contact with the green, it will roll just like a putt. The shot works best when you are faced with a delicate chip shot from short range: when there is up to about 7½ yd (7 m) between you and the flag. At first this technique will feel strange, but it will allow you to play a superb "feel" shot.

READ THE GREEN WHEN YOU PREPARE FOR A CHIP

GOLFERS HAVE no hesitation in lining up a putt and assessing the amount of break. Curiously, very few do the same with chipping, even though it is no less relevant. So, when you visualize chip shots, take into account the effect that slopes on the green will have on the ball's path to the hole. This sounds quite obvious but is often overlooked, and that can result in a perfectly played chip shot finishing off target. So make sure that you read a chip just as you would a putt.

SEE THE LINE *Let your actions reflect your intentions; you should read the green if you want to chip in or at least leave the ball extremely close to the hole.*

DRILL 25: Try the "toe poke" with a putter

YOU MIGHT HAVE SEEN a few tour professionals striking the ball with the toe end of the putter when playing a shot from the collar of rough around the green. This technique might seem unorthodox, but there is considerable logic to the shot, which is known as a "toe poke". Although it is close to the flag, the collar of rough creates a very awkward lie. The tendency is to play too delicate a shot from this position, leaving the ball well short. The toe poke is a useful remedy for this dangerous inclination.

1 *Place a ball against the collar of rough beside the apron of a green. Now, instead of reaching for your wedge, take your putter out of your golf bag.*

2 *Hold the putter so that the toe end of the club is hovering behind the ball's equator. The end of the club should also be pointing toward the hole.*

3 *Make a short, sharp, stabbing stroke and aim to strike the center of the ball. You will find that there is no interference from the grass behind the ball – the primary reason for playing the shot in this way. The ball will pop into the air before the topspin takes effect, allowing it to roll on to the putting surface.*

○ Drill 23 (*see p.125*) highlighted the other way to deal with this situation. Should you prefer the toe-poke with a putter, the only reservations concern the distance the ball needs to travel – anything over 6½ yd (6 m) is too far – and the type of putter used. This shot only works with a putter that has a relatively flat toe end. If the toe end is rounded, the ball tends to come off in unpredictable directions. However, if you bear these considerations in mind, this shot is worth trying.

LEVEL THREE

KEY CHECKPOINT

LEAVE THE PIN IN IF YOU WANT TO HOLE A CHIP

FROM A CHIP SHOT off the green, a ball is more likely to drop in the hole when the flag is still in place. This was proven beyond doubt by Dave Pelz, a former NASA space scientist who has chosen to apply his considerable intellect to the game of golf. Using scientific instruments, he has measured almost every conceivable aspect of a ball's behavior, from the moment it is struck to the time it stops moving. His studies have entailed rolling thousands of balls at various speeds into different parts of the hole, both with the flag out and with the flag in. The results were conclusive: taking the flag out before you play a chip may do a lot for your ego, but it will do nothing for your chances of holing the shot. Remember, there is no penalty for hitting the flag if you are playing from off the green.

FLAG IN *Scientific research by one of the most intelligent men in golf has shown that the ball stands a better chance of dropping in the hole if the flag is left in.*

DRILL 26: Play a mini-hook shot to give your chips more run

THIS ADVANCED chip shot is best described as a miniature hook. The thing to understand about this shot before you attempt it is that a hook produces right-to-left spin, which makes the ball run further than normal. This makes it a very useful shot to have in your repertoire when you have a lot of green between you and the pin. Work on the following three points to perfect the shot.

1 *Select a short iron, such as an 8-iron. Position the ball well back in your stance, opposite your right toe, and place your hands well in front of the clubhead (even more so than for a normal chip shot). Also, feel that you align your body a little right of the target, with the clubface aiming straight at the flag.*

2 *Take the club back on a path that is distinctly more on the inside than for a regular chip shot.*

3 *Then swing the club into impact on the same path, so that the clubhead travels right of the target through the ball. This in-to-out path – coupled with the fact that the clubface*

will be closed (relative to your swing path) – will impart the necessary right-to-left spin. The ball will fly a little lower than an ordinary chip with the same club, and will roll more.

○ With this chip shot, you only have to make a short swing to send the ball up a long green, and short swings are easier to control. It is basically an alternative to chipping with a 6-iron – the advantage being that the shorter shaft on an 8-iron helps to enhance your control. The additional run created by this technique may take you by surprise at first, but after a few attempts you will quickly learn to judge the extra distance.

DRILL 27: Practice the chip with a lofted wood

A FEW YEARS AGO, chipping with a lofted wood was a rarity. But since the likes of Tiger Woods and Greg Norman have played this shot in major competitions, it has moved rapidly from obscurity to credibility. This practice drill demonstrates how you can use the lofted wood with surprising effectiveness for shots close to the green.

1 *Take a 3- or 4-wood, and choke down on the grip so that your lower hand almost touches the metal of the shaft.*

2 *Adopt your normal chipping set-up, only stand a little taller to accommodate the longer club. You will also need to stand a little further from the ball than when using a wedge (otherwise your hands and arms become tucked into your midriff, giving you no room for movement).*

3 *Now make your regular putting stroke (see the "Putting" section, pp.158–83), swinging the clubhead back and forth low to the ground and with very little wrist hinge. It is principally an arms-and-shoulders*

swing, which means the clubhead will brush the ground through impact. The ball spends virtually no time in the air and rolls quickly over the green.

○ The prime situation for a chip with a lofted wood is similar to when you might opt to putt from off the green (see the Key Checkpoint on p.112). That is, when the grass is closely mown, and there are no obstructions between you and the putting surface. The lofted wood chip is more versatile than a putt, however, mainly because there is extra loft on the clubface. This means that you can get the ball to move more easily over uneven or damp surfaces.

KEY CHECKPOINT

HOVER THE CLUB ON ROUGH CHIPS

IN THE SECTION on pitching, the benefits of hovering the clubhead at address were discussed *(see Drill 21, p.100)*. The same advantages exist when it comes to chipping. Hovering the club promotes an unimpeded takeaway and also enhances the quality of your strike. If the ball is lying in rough around the green, hover the blade of the club around the ball's equator rather than nestling it in the grass. In your takeaway you will notice how freely the clubhead moves away from the ball. It does not become caught up in the grass on the way back, which can so easily upset the rhythm of your swing. Also, by hovering the clubhead behind the ball at address, you will raise the base of your swing by just a fraction. This means that you are less likely to bury the clubhead in the grass behind the ball and should instead make a better strike. This technique might require a little practice, but it is well worth becoming accustomed to, as the benefits are significant.

RAISE YOUR GAME *Hovering the clubhead behind the ball in the rough promotes a smoother takeaway, as the clubhead does not become caught.*

LEVEL THREE

THE PERFECT CHIP SHOT

NICK PRICE IS RENOWNED for his quick-fire golf swing and the tracer-bullet trajectory of his iron shots and drives, but what many people fail to realise is that his short game is every bit as special as his long game. Nick has the three key ingredients that separate the great from the merely good – a wonderful imagination (in essence, the ability to visualize the right shot at the right time), supersensitive feel in his hands, and a totally correct technique. This enviable combination enables him to play all manner of chip shots with the kind of accuracy most other golfers associate with a medium-length putt. Talent such as this is well worth studying.

Backswing
Nick retains his original weight distribution to promote a descending blow toward impact

Impact
The slight leg movement is merely the knees moving toward the target in response to the change in direction of the swing

Followthrough
Nick's body turns in harmony with the arm swing to keep the clubhead from overtaking the hands and leading to poor contact

1 ADDRESS
Earlier in this section we brought to your attention one sentence that summed up the essence of a good setup for chipping – ball back, hands and weight forward. Here you see that theory put into practice, as Nick plays an orthodox chip and run shot with a 9-iron. Nick has the ball back in his stance, opposite his right foot. The hands are ahead of the ball, the shaft angled towards the target, and the weight slightly favours the front foot. All of this is designed to encourage a descending angle of attack into impact. Also note how relaxed Nick is over the ball. He appears totally comfortable, with not an ounce of tension in his hands. This gives him maximum feel for the clubhead throughout the swing, enhancing his control over how the ball behaves.

KEYS TO PERFECT CHIPPING

CHIPPING IS A RELATIVELY straightforward business if you adhere to the important fundamentals. These four simple keys should keep you on the right track.

○ *Put the ball back in your stance, with your hands and bodyweight forward to help ensure that the clubhead travels on a descending angle of attack into impact.*

....

○ *Only use as much loft as you need. So if there are no hazards to carry, aim to land the ball on the green as near to you as possible since this helps guarantee an even first bounce, then let the ball run out from there. You will find these chip-and-run shots much easier to judge than high, lofted shots, which should only be played when you have no other option.*

....

○ *Make a length of backswing that enables you to smoothly accelerate the clubhead into impact, producing the required length of shot.*

....

○ *Think of the clubhead traveling low to the ground through impact, as this encourages a downward hit and thus helps to prevent the dreaded scooping action that is the ruin of many a chip shot.*

2 BACKSWING

The backswing is essentially a simple movement whereby the triangular relationship established at address between the arms and shoulders is maintained as the club moves away from the ball. The weight distribution does not alter, still favoring the left side to help promote a descending blow at impact. Trouble for the majority of golfers starts when the backswing is either too long or too short for the shot in question.

3 CHANGE OF DIRECTION

As the arms and body begin the transition from backward to forward motion, a softness in the hands and wrists produces a slight hinging of the wrists giving the feeling of the clubhead momentarily lagging behind the hands. This sets the hands in a position to lead the clubhead on a downward path into impact. It is a subtle move, especially on a shot as short as this, but nevertheless it is an essential ingredient of a crisply struck chip.

4 IMPACT

Nick's hands stay ahead of the clubhead to produce a slightly descending angle of attack and the perfect ball-then-turf contact. Such a strike produces the smallest of divots on soft ground and merely grazes the turf on firm. You might describe this position as back to square one, because a chip is the only shot, other than a putt, where a freeze-frame of impact is scarcely discernible from the setup, the hands and weight kept forward to strike a ball that is back in the stance.

5 FOLLOWTHROUGH

Notice how Nick's body turns in harmony with the movement of the hands, arms, and club through impact. This coordination enables him to keep his hands ahead of the clubhead through the hitting area. If the body stops moving the club tends to overtake the hands and flip at the ball in the hitting area. Look also at how the hands travel further in the followthrough compared to the backswing helping to promote the necessary acceleration through impact.

BUNKER PLAY

THERE IS LITTLE DOUBT that for most club golfers, bunker play creates more fear and problems than any other type of shot. This cannot be attributed to the degree of difficulty involved because, ironically, the standard bunker shot is one of the most forgiving strokes in golf. For one thing, you do not even have to hit the ball. With a sound technique you can hit the sand between 1 in (2.5 cm) and 2½ in (6 cm) behind the ball and still produce an acceptable result. You cannot get away with anything like this margin for error with other clubs.

If this does not comfort you, the even better news is that in no other department of the game can you go from poor to good, or from good to excellent, in such a short time.

DEVELOPING NEW SKILLS

As you work your way through this section, your fear of bunker play will evaporate. Praying to get the ball out of the sand the first time will

LEVEL ONE

LEVEL TWO

LEVEL THREE

soon become a distant memory. You will learn that long-range bunker shots are no harder than normal iron shots, and from short range you will start expecting to finish the hole in two strokes almost every time (unless the lie is terrible). To approach bunker play in this way may seem an impossible dream, but as you perform the following drills, you will see how achievable good sand performance actually is.

THE BUNKER-PLAY TEST

etting out of the sand the first time might be the sole ambition for many of you reading this, but that does not represent a worthwhile test. As with chipping (see pp.106–7), you have to judge your performance with accuracy in mind However, because you probably find bunker shots tougher than chips psychologically at the moment, for this test the radius of the target circle is tripled.

1 Find a greenside bunker where the flag is between 6½ yd (6 m) and 8 yd (7.5 m) away. Because bunkers are uncommon at driving ranges, perform this test on a golf course at a quiet time (so that you will not be interrupted).

2 Make a circle of tees – with a 3 yd (3 m) radius – around the flag. As a rough guide, 3 yd (3 m) is approximately three times the length of your sand wedge.

3 Take your sand wedge and 15 balls into the bunker. From a good lie, try to get as many balls as possible inside the circle of tees (left). Once you have completed this exercise a total of three times, average your scores, and check your results against the performance chart (below).

○ Fear of bunker shots can cause you to aim away from bunkers (rather than at the flag) and to take too many shots every time you are in the sand. It is easy to imagine, then, what a difference good bunker play can make.

PERFORMANCE CHART

○ ○ ○ ○ ○
1–5 = Level One
(pp.134–41)

○ ○ ○ ○ ○
6–10 = Level Two
(pp.142–9)

○ ○ ○ ○ ○
11–15 = Level Three
(pp.150–55)

DRILL 1: Open your feet, hips, shoulders, and the clubface

IN GOLF THERE IS NOTHING more futile than trying to hit good shots from a poor address position, and this is never more so than when you are playing from sand. Next time you practice your bunker play, use the following drill to rehearse and become familiar with the perfect setup for a greenside bunker shot.

12 o'clock
(target line)

10 o'clock
(feet
alignment)

2 o'clock
(clubface
alignment)

1 *Stand in a greenside bunker, and address a ball as you would any ordinary iron shot, with your stance parallel to the ball-to-target line, and the clubface square to the flag. The ball should be opposite your left heel.*

2 *Take your right hand off the club, and loosen your left hand grip. Hold the bottom of the club's grip with your right hand, and turn the club clockwise (so that the clubface opens). Imagine that the flag is at 12 o'clock on a clockface, and stop turning when the clubface is aiming at 2 o'clock. Reapply your left hand, and place your right hand back on the grip.*

3 *Now move into an open stance, so that the alignment of your feet, hips, and shoulders aims at 10 o'clock (to the left of the flag). Make sure that the clubface remains open, however (aiming right of the target).*

4 *Shuffle your feet down into the sand. This not only gives you a secure footing on an insecure surface but also gives you a feel for the sand's texture.*

○ If you perform badly in bunkers, the simple process of organizing your setup is probably the single most significant step forward you can take. It will promote the correct shape of swing and allow the bounce on the sand wedge (see the Key Checkpoint on p.135) to work to maximum efficiency.

DRILL 2: Make right handed swings to feel the splash

AS NOTED in the Key Checkpoint on the opposite page, one of the most important things to understand about bunker play is that the bounce on your sand wedge is designed to help you but can only do so if your technique is correct. Drill 3 *(right)* helps you appreciate how the sand wedge moves through the sand. The following practice drill has a similar theme and also introduces some freedom into your technique.

1 *Step into a bunker with your sand wedge. For now, do not worry about a ball.*

2 *Assume a good address position (see Drill 1, above), but hold the club with your right hand only.*

3 *Make one-handed swings, and almost "throw" the clubhead into the sand. Allow your right*

arm to straighten, and your wrist to unhinge. Try to make the clubhead slide through the sand (utilizing the bounce on the club), rather than letting it dig too deep. You should be left with a shallow cut of sand, about 12 in (30 cm) long.

○ None of the early drills in the "Bunker Play" section involves hitting a ball. This is because these drills lay the foundations that promote the correct swing shape. It is a case of learning to walk before you can run.

DRILL 3: Listen to the sound of good bunker play

IF YOU STRUGGLE to escape from a bunker in one shot, then you have to go right back to basics. This exercise, which is performed as much by sound as by feel, does just that by examining the correct and incorrect clubface positions for greenside bunker shots.

1 *Take up your normal address position (see Drill 1, left), but without a ball. To begin with, do not open the face of your sand wedge.*

2 *Make some practice swings, and strike the sand as if you were playing a shot. With the clubface square to the target, you should find that it buries itself with a muffled thump. This moves mountains of sand, but if you were playing a proper shot, very little energy would be passed on to the ball, and you would end up leaving the ball in the bunker.*

3 *Now swing with the clubface open. The broad flange at the back of the sand wedge makes a quite different sound as it hits the surface of the sand. The clubhead moves freely through the sand, courtesy of the bounce effect (see the Key Checkpoint on this page), leaving a shallow trough. When you play a shot, more energy is passed on to the ball, and it should come out every time.*

◯ Rehearse this exercise several times, alternating between an open clubface (which is ideal) and a square clubface (which is not). Listen to and feel the difference, which is more significant than you might have thought. When you can make the correct sound every time, you are ready to become a better bunker player.

✔ Clubface open to the target

✘ Clubface square to the target

KEY CHECKPOINT

THE "BOUNCE" IS ALL-IMPORTANT

UP UNTIL the early 1930s, golf clubs were not designed to cope well with shots from sand. The sole of the club was too thin, like the 3-iron in your bag today, which meant that the clubhead cut deeply into the sand at impact. This made bunker play much harder than it is now – a sobering thought if you already struggle in the sand. But Gene Sarazen (the first man to win all four of golf's majors), who thought bunker play was more difficult than it should be, filed the sole of his sand wedge. This made the sole more rounded, introducing a wide flange (as seen on today's sand wedges). His invention completely transformed bunker play.

When the rounded sole of the clubhead (the "bounce") makes contact with the sand, it does not bury itself like the clubs of old but instead bounces back up leaving a shallow trough of sand where the ball was. This is known as the bounce effect. The rounded sole acts in the same way as a tennis ball, for example, thrown on a low trajectory into a bunker. The ball does not bury itself in the sand, but instead skims off the surface at the same angle it came in. The sand wedge only reacts in this way, however, if your technique is sound.

THE BOUNCE *The wide, rounded sole of a sand wedge, known as the bounce, encourages the clubhead to travel more easily through the sand.*

DRILL 4: Draw a line in the sand to guide your path

IT IS NOW TIME to hit some proper greenside bunker shots. This practice drill involves drawing a line in the sand to indicate the ideal swing path through impact. Remember that you cannot do this during a round of golf because touching the sand with your club before playing the shot is against the rules *(see the Key Checkpoint on p.145)*.

1 *Place a ball in the sand and address it* (see Drill 1, p.134).

2 *Use the butt end of the club to draw a line in the sand along the line of your toes. Then draw another line that extends about 8 in (20 cm) either side of the ball, parallel to the first line.*

3 *Swing the clubhead back along the second line, hinging your wrists a little earlier than you would for a chip shot. This will set the club on a slightly more upright swing plane. Do not forget to turn your body as you swing the club upward.*

4 *Splash the clubhead into the sand behind the ball (see Drill 5, p.137), again swinging the clubhead along the line in the sand through impact. This means that in essence you are swinging the club along the line of your toes, to the left of the target, with the clubface open. This will help you propel the ball out of the sand and toward the flag.*

❍ Drill 22 in the "Off the Tee" section *(see p.46)* discusses the importance of releasing the clubhead. However, for greenside bunker shots, you should not release the clubhead. As you swing to the left of the target through impact it is vital that the clubface stays open: do not let your right hand cross over your left. This will stop the clubface closing, and insure that the ball does not fly left of the target.

DRILL 5: Draw a line in the sand to focus your strike

JUST LIKE DRILL 4 *(left)*, this drill involves drawing a line in the sand. But rather than assisting your alignment and swing path, it helps in the development of another important element of bunker play: learning to consistently hit the right spot in the sand behind the ball.

1 *Use the butt end of your sand wedge to draw one long line in the sand, perpendicular to the ball-to-target line.*

2 *Place a row of balls 2 in (5 cm) in front of that line. Make sure that there is at least a 10-in (25-cm) gap between each ball.*

3 *Play each ball along the line in turn. As always, make sure that your stance and the clubface are open. Swing the clubhead down on the line in the sand, and accelerate through the sand under the ball. You do not have to worry about the ball because if your technique is good, it will splash out every time.*

While you have to strike the ball cleanly with your iron shots in order to be able to judge distance accurately, with sand shots you have to strike the correct point in the sand if you want to control how far the ball flies out of a bunker. This drill will give you a consistent, repeatable swing that delivers the clubhead to the same spot at impact every time.

Perfect setup
Address the first ball as you would a normal greenside bunker shot

Entry point
Aim to splash the clubhead down on the line and to swing freely through the sand

PUT THE BALL FURTHER FORWARD THAN YOU THINK

MOST GOLFERS who struggle with bunker play almost always have the ball in the middle of their stance. Although this is appropriate for pitch shots and chips, in a bunker it is too far back – the clubhead will travel down too steeply and dig deeply into the sand. This means that you will lose all the energy in your swing, and there will not be enough force to propel the ball up and out. In view of this, always have the ball forward in your stance – opposite your left instep (as you do with the driver and long irons). This ball position will allow you to swing the clubhead into the sand on a shallower angle of attack, which encourages it to slide through the sand under the ball. This creates a splash that sends the ball upward and forward over the front lip of the bunker.

As is so often the case, a small adjustment to your setup can have a major effect on your swing. Whenever you practice your sand play, make regular checks on this and the other address fundamentals.

BALL POSITION *If the ball is forward in your stance, this promotes a shallower angle of attack, which helps create a wave of sand that propels the ball outward.*

LEVEL ONE

LEVEL ONE

DRILL 6: Throw a stone to recreate the right hand action

DRILL 4 *(see p.136)* explained that you should not release the club when playing a bunker shot so as to insure that the clubface stays open through impact. Here is a practice drill that will help you become accustomed to how your right hand should work when playing a bunker shot. It involves a movement apparently unrelated to golf yet which comes naturally to almost everyone.

1 *Take a small stone, and throw it as if trying to skim it across a body of water. Notice that after drawing your throwing arm backward, your right shoulder then turns down and under your chin as your body opens up, and your right hand swings through to throw the stone on a flat trajectory. Repeat this action a few times, and be aware of how your right hand moves and your body turns.*

2 *Step into a bunker with your sand wedge, and make a practice swing. Try to imagine your right hand moving as it did to throw the stone. In your downswing, your right shoulder should again turn down as your body opens up, and your right hand should swing flat so that the clubhead slides through the sand on a shallow trajectory.*

3 *Now hit some shots, recreating the sensations experienced in step 2. Let the clubhead splash freely through the sand under the ball.*

○ This practice exercise encourages not only the correct right hand action but also good acceleration of the clubhead into and through the sand. These are two factors that will stand you in good stead as you work your way through this section.

LIKE THROWING A STONE
When playing a bunker shot, the movement of your right arm should mirror the action of throwing a stone. In your followthrough, your right shoulder turns under your chin.

DRILL 7: Focus on the sand, not the ball

WALTER HAGEN, a flamboyant figure from the first half of the 20th century (and one of the greatest golfers of all time), used to say that bunker shots should be the easiest shots in the game because you do not even have to hit the ball. This thought can make playing a good bunker shot more straightforward, as this drill will illustrate.

1 *Step into the sand and set up for a regular greenside bunker shot from a good lie.*

2 *Instead of looking at the ball, which is something you* instinctively *do on every shot, focus on a spot in the sand 2 in (5 cm) behind the ball (left). Although this might seem a little strange at first, resist the temptation to look at the ball.*

3 *Keep focusing on the sand as you swing: do not even worry about the ball. If you make a good swing, and accelerate the clubhead into the right spot in the sand, the ball will naturally fly out of the bunker every time. Hit several balls using this technique.*

○ This exercise works on the same principle as Drill 5 (see p.137). But rather than drawing a line in the sand, which is against the rules, you can use this drill during a round of golf. Focusing on the sand and ignoring the ball makes sense because, as Walter Hagen noted, it is the sand, and not the ball, that you are trying to hit.

DRILL 8: Double your swing length from grass to sand

GOLF IS NOT an exact science. The way to approach a shot cannot usually be determined using special formulas. However, the following drill will show you a simple equation that will help you judge the distance of your greenside bunker shots.

1 *Find a greenside bunker that is approximately 11 yd (10 m) from the flag.*

2 *Play a chip shot with your sand wedge from beside the bunker. Select a good lie, and try to leave the ball as close as possible to the flag.*

3 *Now step into the bunker, and double the length of swing that you just made from the grass. Try to feel that your rate of acceleration through impact, and the overall tempo of your swing, is the same as for the previous shot. The cushioning effect of the sand trapped between the clubface and the ball should ensure that the ball travels the same distance as the chip.*

Swing length from grass

Swing length from sand

○ Although it is impossible to play golf by numbers, doubling the length of your swing from sand compared to a shot from the same range on grass is a useful piece of mental imagery that will promote better judgement of distance out of greenside bunkers.

LEVEL ONE

DRILL 9: Experiment with two methods of varying your distance

OPINION IS DIVIDED when it comes to recommending the ideal way to vary the distance you hit a bunker shot. Most golf instructors say it is best to take the same amount of sand every time and vary the length of swing to generate more or less distance. The previous drills in this section have been based on this theory. A few experts, however, say you should make the same length swing every time and vary the amount of sand you take at impact: not much sand for longer shots; more sand for short shots. That was the way the great Bobby Jones used to play bunker shots. Because each method has its merits, the best way to decide which you prefer is to rehearse this drill, and then make up your mind.

1 *Push three tee at random into any green that features a bunker.*

2 *Select your sand wedge, step into the bunker, and separate six balls into two batches of three.*

3 *Firstly, hit one ball to each of the three tees using the method whereby you take the same amount of sand every time. Vary the length of your swing to control distance. Start with the tee closest to you, and make progressively longer swings to send the remaining two balls further each time.*

4 *Now, hit the remaining three balls using the technique whereby you make the same length swing every time and vary the amount of sand you take at impact to control distance. Take lots of sand to send the first ball to the nearest tee, slightly less sand to make the next ball fly to the middle tee, and even less sand still to reach the furthest tee. Experimentation is the key here.*

A shorter swing means less distance

A longer swing means more distance

Further behind the ball
Hit 3¼ in (8 cm) behind the ball, and see how far it flies

Close to the ball
Hit ⅜ in (1 cm) behind the ball, and see how far it flies

○ **Repeat this exercise several times to see which method gives you the best distance control. Once you have made your decision, it should form the basis of your approach to bunker play, and you should practice accordingly.**

DRILL 10: Match your backswing and followthrough

W HEN PLAYING a greenside bunker shot you must accelerate the clubhead through impact to insure that there is sufficient energy to create a wave of sand big enough to propel the ball from the bunker. This drill will help you accelerate the club through the sand every time.

1 *Find a greenside bunker approximately 20 yd (18 m) from the flag.*

2 *Rehearse a backswing, and note how far back your hands and arms go. There is no need for a ball at this stage.*

3 *Splash the clubhead into the sand, accelerating the club so that it ends up in a position which is further through than you went back. This means that your followthrough will be longer than your backswing.*

4 *Place a ball on a good lie in the sand, then hit a shot, concentrating on making your followthrough longer than your backswing.*

○ It is worth stressing again that decelerating the clubhead in the downswing is a serious mistake in bunker play. The sand easily soaks up what little speed is left in your swing, virtually guaranteeing that the ball will stay in the bunker. Making sure that your followthrough is longer than your backswing means that every bunker shot you play will be a positive strike.

Backswing
Note the position your hands reach in your backswing

Followthrough
Swing the club so that your followthrough is longer than your backswing

RETEST YOURSELF

Before moving to Level Two, take the test on pp.132–3 again. If you have not improved, it is worth revisiting the Level One drills. However, if the performance chart shows that your bunker play has progressed sufficiently, then you are ready to tackle the more advanced drills in Level Two.

THESE ARE TOUCH SHOTS: CHOKE DOWN ON THE GRIP

CHOKING DOWN on the grip is recommended for almost every short shot, and bunker shots are no exception. By all means experiment to see what suits you best, but, as a rule, about 2 in (5 cm) down the grip is ideal. This change is helpful because the closer your hands are to the clubhead, the more control you will have. If you were to hold the top end of a pen, for example, you would find it difficult to write neatly and would grip the pen nearer to the nib for extra control. The same applies when playing a bunker shot. Choking down on the grip gives you better feel for, and increased control over, what the clubhead is doing in your swing.

The only time it is not a good idea to choke down is when the ball is well below the level of your feet. In this situation you need all the length of your sand wedge just to reach the ball at the moment of impact (see Drill 18, p.149).

HANDS DOWN *Choking down on the grip enhances your touch from close range, and bunker shots are certainly no exception to this rule.*

DRILL 11: Build a cleaner strike for long-range bunker shots

THE FOLLOWING PRACTICE drill is designed to improve your long-range bunker shots. The exercise will teach you how to strike the ball cleanly, with no interference from sand between the clubface and the ball, which – unlike in the case of greenside bunker shots – is exactly what you should do in fairway bunkers. The benefits gained from this drill are just as great for your general iron play, too.

1 *Find a fairway bunker without a major front lip, and with plenty of space to hit shots from a flat lie.*

2 *Draw a narrow line in the sand, and place as many balls as possible along that line. The back of each ball should just be touching the line.*

3 *Take your 7-iron and address the first ball in the line. Use the same setup you would for an iron shot (see pp.20–23).*

4 *Shuffle your feet into the sand to secure your footing. As this lowers the base of your swing, choke down on the grip by about 1 in (2.5 cm) to compensate.*

5 *Now hit shots with a full swing. Do not worry about a target – the object of the exercise is to strike the ball cleanly. To do this you need to strike the ball first, then the sand, which requires a descending blow. The principles are the same as for producing a good iron shot (see the Key Checkpoint on p.61). If you are playing the shot correctly, there will be a small mark in the sand after the spot where the ball was, indicating ball-then-sand contact. If the clubhead touches the sand before the line, you will know you have hit the shot "heavy." Try placing the ball a fraction further back in your stance to promote clean contact. Do not try to scoop the ball out of the sand.*

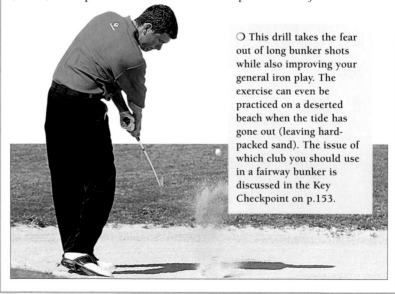

○ **This drill takes the fear out of long bunker shots while also improving your general iron play. The exercise can even be practiced on a deserted beach when the tide has gone out (leaving hard-packed sand). The issue of which club you should use in a fairway bunker is discussed in the Key Checkpoint on p.153.**

Drill 12: Make light of the intermediate bunker shot

THIS DRILL answers one of the most commonly asked questions about bunker play: should you strike intermediate length bunker shots – those in the 44–55 yd (40–50 m) range – cleanly or with a bit of sand at impact? As these bunkers are neither truly greenside bunkers nor fairway bunkers, most golfers become caught in two minds and make a mess of the shot. The following exercise will eliminate all confusion.

1 Find a bunker 44–55 yd (40–50 m) from a flag. Give yourself a good lie in the sand.

2 Use your pitching wedge rather than your sand wedge. Imagine that the flag is at 12 o'clock on a clockface (see Drill 1, p.134), and stand slightly open, with your feet, hips, and shoulders aligned to 11 o'clock (left of the flag). Open the clubface so that it is aiming between 12 and 1 o'clock (right of the flag).

3 Take less sand than you would from a greenside bunker – aim to strike the sand about ⅜ in (1 cm)

behind the ball. Remember that for most greenside bunker shots you should strike the sand 2 in (5 cm) behind the ball (see Drill 5, p.137), and for fairway bunker shots you should strike the ball then the sand (see Drill 11, left).

4 Now imagine that your head is at 12 o'clock and that the ball is at 6 o'clock (see Drill 23 in the "Pitching" section, p.101). Swing your hands back to 10 o'clock and aim to strike the sand in the spot identified in step 3. Your open stance will produce an out-to-in swing path (see pp.26–7) through impact, which, combined with

an open clubface, produces a shot with a touch of sidespin. You can therefore anticipate some left-to-right movement through the air and a kick to the right when the ball pitches on the green.

○ Another way to deal with intermediate length bunker shots involves taking a shorter swing and playing a cleanly struck shot with a pitching wedge, a technique that will be explored toward the end of Level Three (see Drill 25, p.154). For the meantime, the current drill will give you a method that is easier to use and is simple to repeat.

LEVEL TWO

Drill 13: Take a pitching wedge on hard-packed sand

THE BOUNCE ON YOUR SAND WEDGE *(see the Key Checkpoint on p.135)* is what enables you to play good greenside bunker shots: the clubhead slides freely through the sand under the ball, rather than digging down too deep. When the sand is hard-packed, however (perhaps after a prolonged spell of rain), bounce is the last thing you want because the sand wedge will tend to skid off the surface into the middle of the ball, which could send your shot into the face of the bunker or beyond the green. Next time you are in wet or hard-packed sand, try this drill to get you out of trouble.

1 *Instead of your sand wedge, select your pitching wedge, which has a sharper leading edge. This will help the clubhead cut into the hard-packed surface of the sand, slide underneath the ball, and create the all-important "splash" that makes a good bunker shot.*

2 *Stand a little squarer to the target than you would for a normal bunker shot (instead of opening your stance), and have the clubface only slightly open.*

3 *As you swing, hinge your wrists a little earlier in your backswing to create a slightly steeper arc. Aim to hit a spot in the sand about 1 in (2.5 cm) behind the ball. As always, accelerate the clubhead down and through impact.*

○ As you practice this shot you will notice distinct differences between this and a regular greenside bunker shot. Because you are taking a less-lofted club, and not opening the face as much as you would normally, the ball will come out a bit lower than it would with a sand wedge and will therefore have more run. Bear this in mind when you are selecting a landing spot on the green.

DIFFICULT SHOT
When the ball is on hard-packed sand, you should use your pitching wedge, which will cut through the sand more easily.

Shallow mark
Aim to take a little less sand than you would when playing a regular bunker shot, therefore leaving a shallower mark in the sand

DRILL 14: Stagger your targets to improve your range

SEVERAL OF THE LEVEL ONE drills concentrated on the important subject of judging distance out of sand. The following exercise continues this theme and takes it a stage further, training you to make an even better job of different length greenside bunker shots.

1 *Armed with at least 12 balls, set yourself up in a greenside bunker. The bigger the putting green, the more value you will gain from this drill.*

2 *Hit your first shot on to the green with the object of making it land as near to you as possible. Try to strike the shot so that the ball lands only 6½–7½ yd (6–7 m) away.*

3 *Aim to hit your second ball a little further up the green, perhaps 2–3 yd (2–3 m) beyond the first.*

4 *Try to hit your third ball 2–3 yd (2–3 m) further still, and so on*

until you run out of room on the green. The more balls you can land in a line before you run out of putting green, the better your bunker play and judgement of distance will become.

○ With this drill it is important that you give yourself a good lie with each ball, as this provides continuity. When you are becoming proficient at the exercise, try to land each ball only, for example, 1 yd (1 m) apart. Constantly challenging yourself in this way is an excellent way to build your confidence and your skill.

KEY CHECKPOINT

HOVER THE CLUBHEAD TO AVOID BREAKING THE RULES

ALTHOUGH THERE IS a section dedicated solely to the rules of golf later in the book (*see pp.242–9*), it is relevant now to examine the rule that represents the biggest difference between bunker play and other areas of the game. The benefits of hovering the clubhead at address were discussed in the "Pitching" (*see Drill 21, p.100*) and "Chipping" (*see the Key Checkpoint on p.129*) sections. However, in a bunker this is essential: you *must* hover the clubhead above the sand as you address the ball. If you allow the clubhead to touch the sand, either at address or in your backswing, you incur a one-stroke penalty. Always be aware of this when you are playing bunker shots.

Be particularly vigilant if your ball comes to rest on a severe downslope, as it is all to easy for the clubhead to touch the sand during your takeaway. How to play bunker shots from a downslope is discussed in Drill 16 (*see p.147*).

BE CAREFUL IN SAND *It is an essential requirement in bunkers to hover the clubhead at address so that it does not touch the sand. A one-stroke penalty results if the club comes into contact with the sand.*

LEVEL TWO

DRILL 15: Be bolder on an upslope

MORE OFTEN THAN NOT your ball settles into a reasonably flat lie in bunkers. But there are occasions, especially on courses that use soft, powdery sand, where your ball will cling to a slope. At times, your normal bunker technique will not suffice: you have to be creative with your setup, and adapt your swing in order to counteract the effects of the slope. This drill will show you how to do this.

1 *Place a ball on the upslope at the front of a greenside bunker.*

2 *Take your sand wedge from your bag, and address the ball.*

3 *Although your first instinct will be to lean into the slope, absorb the majority of your weight on your lower foot, which in this case is your right. Flex your knees to anchor your weight in place – this will provide a stable foundation from which to swing. Once you have effected this weight distribution change, your shoulders will be more level with the slope, as they would be on a flat lie in the sand. This position enables you to swing the clubhead through the sand on the ideal angle of attack.*

4 *In your backswing, it is important to focus on keeping your knees flexed and your head steady. Do not sway backward or forward because this will upset your balance, making it extremely difficult to strike the correct spot in the sand.*

5 *As you change direction from backswing to downswing, keep your weight on your right foot, and focus on swinging the club up the slope through impact. If you let your weight shift toward the target in the downswing, you will bury the clubhead too steeply into the face of the bunker and the ball will not receive enough energy.*

○ Because an upslope adds loft to the clubface (*see Drill 14 in the "Chipping" section, p.118*), the ball may pop out with too much upward momentum and too little forward flight, which means you end up leaving the ball well short of the flag. To avoid this, be much more positive. Aim to land the ball on top of the flag. You can be comforted in the knowledge that the ball will land softly and not run too far. One final note on playing from an upslope: if the ball is resting right under the front lip of the bunker, you may want to consider playing the ball out to the side, rather than aiming for the flag.

Balance
Settle about 60 percent of your weight over your right foot

40%
60%

Backswing
Maintain your original weight distribution during your backswing

40%
60%

Impact
Feel that you swing the clubhead up the slope through the hitting zone

DRILL 16: Chase the ball down a downslope

THE PREVIOUS DRILL *(left)* covered one of the least demanding sloping-lie shots. This drill covers a more difficult option – when the ball comes to rest on a downslope. You cannot afford to ignore practicing these shots – however difficult they might seem. If you do, a potential nightmare awaits you on the course.

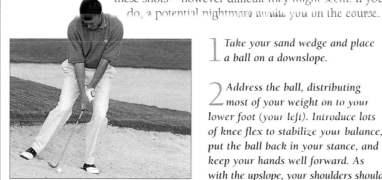

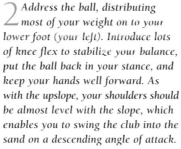

1 *Take your sand wedge and place a ball on a downslope.*

2 *Address the ball, distributing most of your weight on to your lower foot (your left). Introduce lots of knee flex to stabilize your balance, put the ball back in your stance, and keep your hands well forward. As with the upslope, your shoulders should be almost level with the slope, which enables you to swing the club into the sand on a descending angle of attack.*

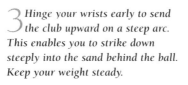

3 *Hinge your wrists early to send the club upward on a steep arc. This enables you to strike down steeply into the sand behind the ball. Keep your weight steady.*

4 *Keep your hands ahead of the clubhead, and hit down into the sand behind the ball. You need to feel as if the clubhead is chasing the ball down the slope so that it stays low to the surface well into the followthrough.*

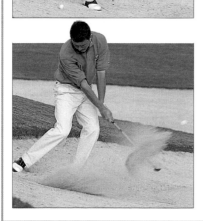

○ While the ball will emerge on a high trajectory from an upslope, it comes out much lower from a downslope, which creates plenty of run on landing. In view of this, be sensible with your target area. You may need to go for the main part of the green, rather than aiming at the flag, just to make sure your next shot is a putt. This is a good result from a downslope lie in a bunker.

KEY CHECKPOINT

HIT FROM THE HIGH FOOT

HERE IS A USEFUL rule of thumb that takes some of the mystery out of playing from sloping lies in the sand: always play the ball towards your higher foot. The reason for this comes down to basic impact mechanics. On a downslope, the clubhead comes into contact with the sand earlier in the downswing, which means that you need the ball back in your stance in order to obtain the correct contact. On an upslope, the clubhead meets the sand much later in its downswing arc, which means that you need the ball further forward in your stance to insure a good strike.

SIMPLIFY SLOPING LIES *Always remember to address the ball toward your high foot: your right on a downslope (top); your left on an upslope (above).*

LEVEL TWO

DRILL 17: Aim right to play a ball above your feet

IN ADDITION to the slopes dealt with in drills 15 and 16 (*see pp.146–7*) you may also encounter sideslope lies in bunkers. These shots are just as intimidating to the uninformed but equally manageable if you adapt your stance and swing to suit the slope. This drill will examine the situation in which the ball comes to rest well above the level of your feet.

1 *Place a ball in the right edge of a greenside bunker so that it is above your feet. Then take your sand wedge from your bag.*

2 *Adopt a square stance, with the clubface aiming a little right of the target. These changes to your normal greenside bunker setup compensate for the fact that in this situation the ball will fly left of where you aim.*

3 *Choke down on the grip so that your right hand almost touches the metal (or graphite) of the club's shaft. This means that you will be able to stand normally, even though* the ball is effectively higher off the ground than usual.

4 *Make a rounded backswing, taking an inside path that is more behind you than upward.*

5 *Swing down on the same path you went back on, moving the clubhead from inside the target line to right of this line through impact. This is referred to as an in-to-out swing path (see pp.26–7). As always with greenside bunker play, identify a spot behind the ball, and splash the clubhead down into the sand at that point (see Drill 5, p.137).*

○ Judging distance and direction is not an easy task when the ball is above your feet because the ball not only comes out of the bunker left of where you aim but also tends to run a bit further than in a regular bunker shot. At least there is no real problem keeping your balance, though, which is more than can be said about the more difficult shot covered in the following drill (*see Drill 18, right*).

Clubface alignment   Target line   Stance

DRILL 18: Steady yourself when the ball is below your feet

ARGUABLY THE TOUGHEST bunker shot is when the ball is below your feet – if the ball is close to the edge of the bunker, you will not even be able to stand in the sand. (This situation calls for serious innovation, where you might have to play the shot on your knees.) Even assuming you can stand in the sand, it is still difficult to maintain your balance. The following drill will help you play this demanding shot.

1 Take a sand wedge and place a ball in the left edge of a bunker, so that it sits below the level of your feet as you take your stance.

2 Because you have to reach down to the ball, hold the club so that your left hand is at the top of the grip.

3 Since balance is such a major concern when playing this stroke, spread your feet further apart than you would for a normal bunker shot. This stabilizes your weight and lowers your upper body, so that you are a little closer to the ball and do not have to reach down so far. Bend over more from your waist if necessary. Also, if you settle your weight towards your heels, this will counter the tendency to topple forwards as you swing.

4 Open your stance so that it is aligned even further left than for a regular greenside bunker shot. This allows for the fact that the ball will fly right of where you aim when it is below your feet.

5 Swing your hands and arms back, and use your wrists to hinge the club steeply upwards. Keep your head at the same level throughout, as this will help you maintain your height as you swing the clubhead down into the sand.

○ This is probably the toughest of all the greenside bunker shots, mainly because your address position feels so uncomfortable that you wonder how you can make a swing without falling over, let alone controlling where the ball flies. Like all sloping-lie shots, though, you have to practise the shot so that you are not in trouble when the situation arises in a round. If you find yourself in a situation where the ball is below your feet in a bunker, remember to think of "balance and arm swing". You need to swing your hands and arms more, and use your body less. This will help you keep your balance.

RE-TEST YOURSELF

Before moving to Level Three, take the test on pp.132–3 again. If you have not improved, it is worth revisiting the Level Two drills. However, if the performance chart shows that your bunker play has progressed sufficiently, then you are ready to tackle the more advanced drills in Level Three.

LEVEL TWO

Drill 22: Take a shallow cut for extra spin out of sand

THIS DRILL introduces another method designed to produce a delicate bunker shot from very close range. This is a difficult shot, but the rewards are in direct proportion to the difficulty. When played correctly, this technique generates impressive levels of backspin, which is essential for short bunker shots.

1 *Open your stance and the clubface – a little more than you would for a standard greenside bunker shot.*

2 *Focus on a spot only ¾ in (2 cm) behind the ball. The key to the success of this shot is taking less sand than normal (see Drill 5, p.137) at impact.*

3 *Now make your swing, and try to hit the spot identified in step 2. Take a shallow cut of sand from under the ball: the shallower the cut, the more the ball will spin (a thin layer of sand acts like sandpaper when it is trapped between the clubface and the ball). Keep your weight evenly spread throughout the stroke, as this promotes the desired (shallow) angle of attack.*

○ You will probably hit the first few shots too far, due to the fact that less sand means less resistance, and therefore more force is imparted to the ball. Experiment with clubface positions and the relationship between swing length and acceleration through impact to see how much spin you can apply to the ball. This shot requires lots of practice.

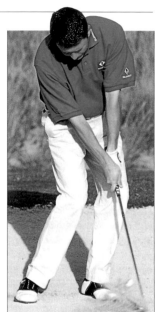

Drill 23: Cup your left wrist to open the clubface

WHEN PLAYING sand shots, if the clubface is open, the flange on the sand wedge's sole can bounce and slide through the sand under the ball, promoting a high flight and a soft landing.

Drills 20, 21, and 22 (*see pp.151–2*) suggested ways of increasing the height and spin of a bunker shot. Here is a more advanced method, which involves "cupping" your left wrist in your backswing.

1 *Take your sand wedge, and address a ball as you would normally for a greenside bunker shot (see Drill 1, p.134).*

2 *As you move the club away from the ball, rotate your forearms to the right to open the clubface even more. Also hinge your wrists so that when you reach the top of your backswing (with your hands at about 9 o'clock), the back of your left hand almost arches back on itself – you should be able to see creases in your skin where your thumb meets your wrist. This is described as a "cupped" left wrist. Pause at this point, and look at your hands and the clubface, which will be wide open. Rehearse this backswing a few times to become familiar with the movements and feelings.*

3 *Now hit some shots. Having set the clubface into a very open position in the backswing, it will stay that way through impact.*

○ If the clubface is wide open through impact, it will slide easily through the sand and cause the ball to climb steeply. You will soon find that you can make a very aggressive swing and generate lots of height but little distance.

DRILL 24: Try putting from sand

Y OU MIGHT THINK that putting from a bunker is a cowardly last resort for golfers who are terrified of "proper" bunker play. However, if there is no front lip to speak of, and the lie is good, then a putt might be a sensible option. You should never be afraid to play an unconventional shot if it suits the situation.

1 *Take your putter from your bag, and find a shallow bunker with a low front lip. Place a ball in the sand on a good lie.*

2 *Position the ball in the middle of your stance, and stand with your feet and shoulders parallel to the ball-to-target line, as you would for a normal iron shot on the fairway. Do not forget to hover the putterhead above the surface of the sand, otherwise you will incur a one-stroke penalty (see the Key Checkpoint on p.145).*

3 *Make a stroke that is controlled by your shoulders and arms, allowing for a little softness in your hands and wrists. Make a positive stroke, and aim to strike the middle of the ball. The putterface should meet the ball cleanly with a slightly*

descending blow. If you strike the ball correctly, there should be a shallow trough in the sand after impact.

4 *The ball should then skip along the surface of the sand, hop over the insubstantial front lip, run on to the green, and roll like a normal putt.*

❍ There is no question that this is unorthodox. But if you have never attempted the shot before you may be surprised how easy it is to play and how effective it can be. If the sand is firmly packed, a putt is even more appropriate because the ball will run over the surface with less resistance. However, it is essential that the front lip of the bunker is low enough to act as a ramp for the ball to roll up. If the lip is not sufficiently low, do not even contemplate playing this shot.

"CLUB UP" FROM A FAIRWAY BUNKER

W HEN THE BALL lands in a fairway bunker, use a slightly less lofted club than you would otherwise from the same distance on the fairway. If, for example, the ball were to land 165 yd (150 m) from the flag, you would probably use a 6-iron if you were on the fairway. But from a similar distance in sand, "club up" to a 5-iron (assuming, of course, that the lie is good). The main reason for this concerns the swing arc when playing from a bunker.

Drill 11 (*see p.142*) explained that for a long bunker shot you should choke down the club an inch or so to allow for the fact that your feet shuffle into the sand, effectively lowering the base of your swing. Therefore, if you do not choke down on the grip you can easily hit the shot heavy. However, choking down, even by as little as 1 in (2.5 cm), reduces your swing arc and, therefore contributes to a shorter ball flight. Also, with your feet buried in the sand, your leg action will be slightly restricted, which leads to a less powerful swing. This again takes some distance off the shot.

However, before you finally commit to playing the shot, you must be certain you have sufficient loft on the club to clear the front lip of the bunker. If there is any doubt in your mind, it is as well to remember that your first priority is to get out of the sand and on to the grass in one shot. There is nothing worse than hitting the ball into the face of the bunker having tried for too much distance and not allowed enough loft. In this situation, the ball usually stays in the sand, leaving you with yet another bunker shot. Remember this important saying: "if in doubt, just get it out."

LEVEL THREE

KEY CHECKPOINT

MATCH BOUNCE TO THE TEXTURE OF THE SAND

THE KEY CHECKPOINT on page 135 describes how Gene Sarazen reinvented the sand wedge by introducing bounce into the sole of the club. Things have moved on considerably since the 1930s, and you can now buy sand wedges with a variety of degrees of bounce. This is something you need to be aware of when making a purchase, as your requirements will depend on the type of sand used on the course at which you play most often. As a rule, the softer the sand the more bounce you need on the sole of the sand wedge; on heavier sand you need less bounce. Equipment requirements are looked at in greater detail in the reference section (*see pp.230–35*), but this is a point worth making before leaving the bunker and moving on to the putting green.

MORE OR LESS BOUNCE *The bounce on your sand wedge should suit the sand in the bunkers on your home course: less bounce (left) suits heavier sand; more bounce (right) is best for soft sand.*

DRILL 25: Try playing the "punch-and-spin" bunker shot

THE FOLLOWING EXERCISE is one of the last of the featured drills on bunker play because you need skill and confidence in equal proportions to pull off this shot. It is an intermediate length bunker shot (*see Drill 12, p.143*), which involves striking the ball first, not the sand.

1 *Give yourself a good lie in a bunker that is approximately 44–55 yd (40–50 m) from the flag. Instead of using a sand wedge, reach for your pitching wedge.*

2 *Position the ball in the middle of your stance, rather than opposite your left foot. Then place your hands well ahead of the ball, so that the shaft of the club leans toward the target. Now aim the clubface straight at the flag, rather than opening it.*

3 *Make an arms-and-shoulders swing, keeping leg action to a minimum. You also need to keep your weight slightly favoring your left side throughout the swing, as this promotes a ball-first strike. Keep your hands ahead of the clubhead as you*

swing into impact, and focus on the back of the ball. The aim of this shot is to strike the ball cleanly with a descending blow, leaving a shallow trough in the sand after the point of impact. If you play the shot just right, the ball will fly half the height of a normal bunker shot, then will bounce once or twice across the green before backspin checks its progress.

○ This shot is fun to try out in a practice session. However, during a round you need to be sure that the conditions are right for playing the shot: the front lip of the bunker must be relatively insubstantial (because the ball flies on a low trajectory), and you need lots of green to work with.

DRILL 26: Experiment with different clubs from sand

THE SAND WEDGE did not get its name by accident: it is designed to make bunker play as easy as possible. But it is not the only club you can use from sand around the green. With a little skill and know-how, using other clubs can increase your options and flexibility in the bunker. Practicing this drill will enhance your repertoire of shots and make your short game more complete.

1 *Step into a greenside bunker with a sand wedge, a pitching wedge, a 9-iron, and 12 or so balls.*

2 *Start with your sand wedge, and hit a couple of normal greenside bunker shots. Observe the way the ball flies and how far it runs.*

3 *Now switch to your pitching wedge. Remember, every club other than a sand wedge has a relatively thin sole, which in sand is not* necessarily what you want. Therefore, make sure that you use the same technique as when using your sand wedge. Open the clubface, which will help it slide through the sand, and commit to making a positive swing to stop the clubhead becoming buried. You will find that the ball flies from the bunker on a lower trajectory than a shot with a sand wedge and also runs more.

4 *Finally, take your 9-iron. Open your stance and the clubface again.* You will find that the same swing produces an even flatter trajectory with even more run on landing.

○ Obviously the lower flying shots do not work when the front lip of the bunker is high. But a 9-iron or pitching wedge is a useful tool when you need to play a running bunker shot across a long green – a situation where a high-floated sand wedge often leaves the ball short.

DRILL 27: Practice in preparation for the worst

THE DRILLS IN THIS SECTION have covered the skills required to make you a better bunker player. Now for the ultimate practice drill – one that enables you to apply your imagination and technique to a variety of different shots.

1 *Take 10 balls, and place them in a bunker. Position the first ball at the left edge of the bunker, below the level of your feet, and the tenth ball at the right edge of the bunker, above the level of your feet. Give each of the other balls a different lie. Make sure some have a good lie, while others are either partially buried, completely plugged, or stuck on upslopes or downslopes.*

2 *Work your way along the line, playing each ball in turn. You will find that the sand wedge is best for most shots, but have other clubs, such*

as a pitching wedge and a 9-iron, within easy reach should you wish to experiment as you go along.

3 *Size up each lie, visualize how the ball will come out of the sand, and try to match your technique and club selection to suit the shot.*

○ The object of this exercise is to land as many of the 10 balls as possible within 2 yd (2 m) of the hole, a distance that makes for an easily sinkable putt. You may also wish to aim at different targets to add further variety to the exercise.

LEVEL THREE

THE PERFECT BUNKER SHOT

THERE WAS A TIME WHEN a couple of names stood out from the crowd when it came to bunker play. These days, however, almost all top tour professionals display exceptional skills from the sand. Lee Westwood – arguably the finest player to come out of England since the emergence of Nick Faldo in the late 1970s – is in this category. To him, a greenside bunker shot is no more difficult than a chip from light rough. From anything but the nastiest of lies he can accurately predict how the ball will come out of the sand and what it will do when it lands on the green. Like all experts in their chosen sport, Westwood makes this shot look easy. Having worked through the "Bunker Play" drills, and now seeing a master at work, you too should find yourself starting to believe that these shots are easy.

Swing length
The backswing is approximately twice the length of a pitch shot from similar range on grass

Downswing
The uncocking of the wrists is delayed in the downswing to produce the necessary descending angle of attack into the sand

1 ADDRESS
Westwood has adopted perfect alignment for a greenside bunker shot: his feet, hips, and shoulders are aligned left of the target, while the clubface aims right. The open stance promotes the desired out-to-in swing path; the open clubface helps the wide flange at the base of the sand wedge slide through the sand. These two elements combine to produce a straight shot.

2 TOP OF BACKSWING
As Westwood's hands and arms swing the club up, his body continues to turn: an essential combination even on short shots such as this. The club points to the left of the flag, and this position (which is described as "across the line") makes it easy for Westwood to swing the club down and through on an out-to-in path. This is essential for a greenside splash shot.

3 DOWNSWING

In the downswing, the basic swing fundamentals are again at work – Westwood's hands and arms are swinging the club down as his body unwinds. The club appears to be outside the line, but this is the ideal path for a short bunker shot. Note that Westwood's wrists are yet to fully unhinge, which keeps his hands ahead of the clubhead as it approaches the hitting zone.

4 IMPACT

Notice how Westwood swings the clubhead freely through the sand under the ball. This image again highlights the importance of the correct address position. The open stance facilitates the vital out-to-in path, while the open clubface ensures that the club slides through the sand and "splashes" the ball out of the bunker and toward the flag.

5 FOLLOWTHROUGH

Despite the delicacy of this shot – the ball is almost floating toward the target, where it will land softly and roll gently towards the flag – the firmness in Westwood's swing is confirmed by the length of his followthrough. Westwood has positively accelerated the clubhead through the sand, which you must always do in bunkers.

Impact

The clubhead momentarily overtakes the ball as it accelerates down and through the sand, creating a "splash" effect

KEYS TO BETTER BUNKER PLAY

SUCCESSFUL sand play, which is not as difficult to achieve as as many golfers think, makes a big difference to your scoring potential. The following keys form the core of a good bunker technique.

○ *Open your stance so that your feet, hips, and shoulders aim at least 11 yd (10 m) left of the target. Open the clubface so that it aims at least 11 yd (10 m) right of the target.*

○ *Place the ball opposite your left heel so that you can swing the clubhead into the sand on a shallow angle of attack.*

○ *Take the clubhead back parallel to the line of your feet, to establish an out-to-in shaped swing path. Swing left through impact with the clubface open (aiming right).*

○ *Except when the ball is plugged, always follow through in sand to ensure that you achieve the proper acceleration in the hitting zone.*

PUTTING

ALTHOUGH the putting stroke is very short in comparison to the full swing, it is open to greater personal interpretation than any other shot. You only have to watch the green play in a professional event to appreciate the variety of styles that are used. One characteristic that all great putters share, however, is a consistent, repeatable stroke where all the moving parts complement one another perfectly. With this type of stroke, the ball will travel along the chosen line at the required speed relative to the length of the putt.

As putting accounts for about 40 percent of the total shots played in a round, it would be a terrible mistake to neglect this department of the game. The following section will give you a thorough understanding of the mechanics of putting, which will enable you to incorporate the essential ingredients of an effective stroke into your personal style. You will also develop the two vital attributes of touch and confidence.

THE PUTTING TEST

To assess fully your putting ability, this test is split into two parts: short-range holing-out skills (steps 1–4) and long-range putting (steps 5–6).

1 Find a green that does not feature significant slopes: the flatter the better.

2 Place seven tees in the ground to form a circle around the hole. Each tee should be about one putter-length from the hole – approximately 1 yd (1 m).

3 Place a ball next to each of the seven tees. Then work your way around each of the balls, trying to hole each one (right). Empty the hole whenever necessary to make room for other falling balls.

4 Make a note of your score out of seven, and leave the tees where they are, since these form an integral part of the long-range putting test.

LEVEL ONE

LEVEL TWO

LEVEL THREE

5 Now move about 11 yd (10 m) away from the hole. Place a batch of eight balls on the ground.

6 Putt as many of the eight balls as possible into the circle of tees (above). If any drop in the hole, so much the better, but for the purposes of this exercise a holed putt counts the same as a putt that finishes inside the circle. You may find that a ball occasionally strikes a tee, in which case you must be honest with yourself and assess whether or not it would have finished in the circle.

○ Successful putting is about balancing two crucial ingredients: pace and line. One without the other is no use to you on the greens.

7 Total your short- and long-range results to give you a score out of 15. Then repeat steps 3–6 another two times, and calculate an average score out of 15.

PERFORMANCE CHART

○ ○ ○ ○ ○
1–5 = Level One
(pp.160–67)

○ ○ ○ ○ ○
6–10 = Level Two
(pp.168–75)

○ ○ ○ ○ ○
11–15 = Level Three
(pp.176–81)

LEVEL ONE

DRILL 1: Form your putting grip

W HILE THERE ARE THREE main types of recommended grip for the full swing *(see p.19)*, with putting there is much more choice. That said, however, conventional wisdom suggests that using the grip known as the "reverse overlap" is the best way to control the putter as you swing. Use this drill to form the reverse overlap.

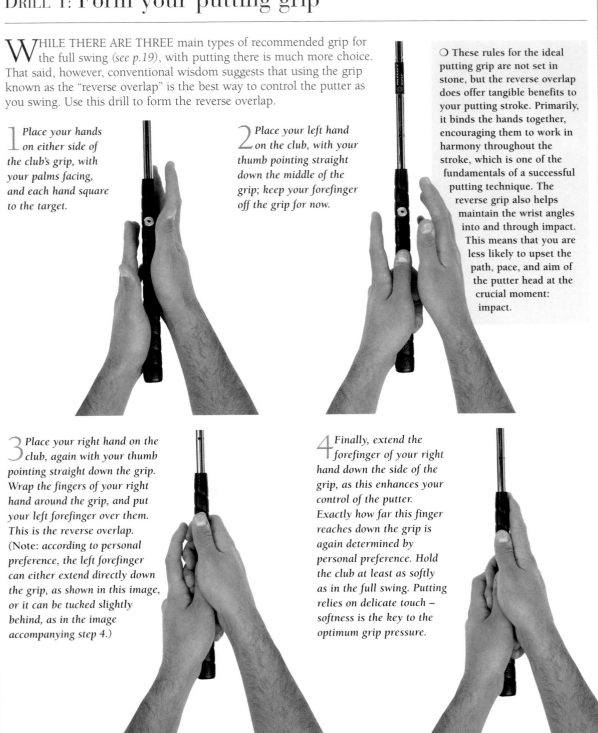

1 *Place your hands on either side of the club's grip, with your palms facing, and each hand square to the target.*

2 *Place your left hand on the club, with your thumb pointing straight down the middle of the grip; keep your forefinger off the grip for now.*

○ These rules for the ideal putting grip are not set in stone, but the reverse overlap does offer tangible benefits to your putting stroke. Primarily, it binds the hands together, encouraging them to work in harmony throughout the stroke, which is one of the fundamentals of a successful putting technique. The reverse grip also helps maintain the wrist angles into and through impact. This means that you are less likely to upset the path, pace, and aim of the putter head at the crucial moment: impact.

3 *Place your right hand on the club, again with your thumb pointing straight down the grip. Wrap the fingers of your right hand around the grip, and put your left forefinger over them. This is the reverse overlap. (Note: according to personal preference, the left forefinger can either extend directly down the grip, as shown in this image, or it can be tucked slightly behind, as in the image accompanying step 4.)*

4 *Finally, extend the forefinger of your right hand down the side of the grip, as this enhances your control of the putter. Exactly how far this finger reaches down the grip is again determined by personal preference. Hold the club at least as softly as in the full swing. Putting relies on delicate touch – softness is the key to the optimum grip pressure.*

DRILL 2: Take up the ideal putting posture

GOOD POSTURE is very important if you are about to make a full swing. But it is critical to the success of your putting stroke, too. Ideally, you should adopt a posture at address that allows your arms to hang down – not totally straight, but free from tension to promote a smooth action back and forth. This simple routine will help you establish a good putting posture.

1 *Stand up straight with the putter resting against your left leg.*

2 *Flex your knees a little and bend from your hips so that your arms hang limp from your shoulders. Jiggle your hands to relax your arms.*

3 *Form your putting grip in the normal way (see Drill 1, left).*

4 *Now take a minute or two to take note of the key elements of this posture. There should be a slight bend in your arms, with your elbows pointing in toward your ribcage. If you think of your arms and shoulders as a triangle (see Drill 5, p.163), it will help you to produce the correct stroke. You should also feel comfortable and relaxed, with your weight evenly balanced between both feet.*

○ This drill shows you how to assume excellent posture for putting. Your alignment, on the other hand, is more a matter of personal taste. However, most experts recommend that your shoulders be parallel to the ball-to-target line, whereas your feet can be slightly open to the target.

KEY CHECKPOINT

THE GEOMETRY OF A GOOD PUTT

FROM A WORM'S eye view, the putting stroke is saucer-shaped. The putterhead sweeps away from the ball on a very gradual upward curve and comes down on the same angle. At the bottom of its arc, the putterhead travels horizontally before following an upward curve through impact. One of the secrets to a good putting stroke is making sure that ball contact occurs just after the putter has reached the bottom

of its swing arc (use a mirror to identify the exact position of the flat spot at the bottom of your putting stroke). This means that the putter is traveling slightly on the up when it meets the ball, which helps give the ball a smooth roll. The followthrough, which mirrors the backswing in shape, should be slightly longer than the backswing. This promotes the correct amout of acceleration through impact.

As for the path of the putter, it should be straight back and through impact for close-range putts – up to about 2 yd (2 m). As the stroke becomes progressively longer, the putterhead should follow this path: inside on the way back, square at impact, then inside again on the followthrough. This swing path is just the same as for the full swing (*see* pp.26–7) but on a much smaller scale.

PERFECT SWING *In all the best putting strokes, the putter works in much the same way as a pendulum, swinging freely back and forth. The ball should merely get in the way of the putter as it swings through.*

DRILL 3: Check your ball position

PUTTING ALLOWS YOU more individuality than any other aspect of the game. But, whatever method you decide to employ, you should always insure that your eyes are directly over the ball while you are in your address position. The following exercise enables you to fulfill this key requirement.

1 *Assume your putting posture (see Drill 2, p.161), but do not place a ball on the ground.*

2 *Take your right hand off the club, and hold a golf ball against the top of your nose, right between your eyes.*

3 *Let the ball drop (you might have to move the club slightly). Take careful note of where the ball first strikes the ground. This spot is where you should position the ball in your putting stance.*

○ With your eyes over the ball, you have the best possible view down the line of the putt. If your eyes are either side of this line, your view is distorted, which can upset your aim. Try to find time to monitor ball position on a regular basis. In fact, it is a good idea to go through this routine each time you start a practice putting session, whether it is before a round or not. If you play the ball from the correct position, bad habits are less likely to infiltrate your technique.

DRILL 4: Check your putterface alignment at address

DRILL 5 *(right)* touches on aiming the putter correctly, which is not as easily done as you might imagine. A test carried out at a tour event produced some startling results: from a distance of 3½ yd (3 m), over half the professionals failed to aim the putterface within a 1 in (2.5 cm) margin either side of the hole. This drill will insure that you are always aiming at the target.

1 *Crouch down about 3½–4½ yd (3–4 m) away from the hole on a green.*

2 *Line up the face of your putter so that it is square with the hole.*

3 *Stand up very slowly and take up your address position. Make very sure that you do not allow the putter to twist at all.*

4 *Study the position of the putterface in relation to the hole. Look back and forth from the putter to the hole several*

times. Try to memorize the position of the putter in relation to the hole.

5 *Hit a putt. If the ball does not travel straight to the hole, you know it is not a problem with your aim and must, therefore, be caused by a crooked stroke. If this is the case, work through Drill 5 (right) to get your stroke back on track.*

○ Try to practise this drill before every round. Striking your putts with a correctly aimed putter is one of the secrets to developing a consistent, non-compensating stroke (where you do not have to twist the putterface during the stroke to get the ball to run straight).

DRILL 5: Find the correct alignment to develop good stroke repetition

IN A PROFESSIONAL TOURNAMENT, you will notice that those at the top of the leaderboard will seem to be sinking every putt within 2 yd (2 m) of the hole. Similarly at club level, in your best rounds, you are likely to have holed your putts like a professional. The following drill focuses your attention on the three key elements of successful short-range putting: putterface alignment at address, swing path, and putterface alignment at impact.

1 *Find a straight putt on the green no more than 2 yd (2 m) from the hole.*

2 *Place two clubs on the green on a straight path to the hole, with about 1 in (2.5 cm) to spare either side of the heel and toe of the putterhead. These two clubs will give you an invaluable visual reference to help you aim the putterface squarely at the hole and will also allow you to monitor the putter's swing path.*

3 *Place a ball directly between the two clubs, and take up your address position. If the putterface is at 90 degrees to the two parallel clubs, as it should be, you will be aiming straight at the hole.*

4 *Make sure that the putter tracks a neat path between the rails in your backswing.*

5 *Swing the putter into the back of the ball, again making sure that it stays within the rails. If the putterface is square at impact, the ball will roll into the hole. Your shoulders, arms, hands, and the club should all be moving together. Try to maintain the triangle formed by your arms and shoulders at address, and adopt a soft grip pressure. Also, try to feel some "lag" (softness in the wrists) as you change direction from backswing to downswing.*

○ Repeat this drill as often as you can: it allows you to see the correct alignment of the putter and trains you to produce the ideal swing path. If you can, set up two clubs on the carpet at home, both pointing towards a target 24 in (60 cm) away. Then, whenever you have a spare 10 minutes, stroke some putts between the rails to develop a repeatable and well-honed stroke.

THE ART OF READING GREENS

TO READ A GREEN proficiently means taking into account a number of factors.

Study the green as you approach it to establish the predominant slope: this will give you a clue as to which way the ball will break. Once on the green, look from behind the ball down the line of the putt. If you crouch down, you will see subtle slopes more easily.

A good place to obtain another reading is from the low side of the hole. Stand a few paces back, midway between the ball and the hole. From this position you can assess how the ball will break as it rolls down the slope. Also look for unevenness close to the hole. The ball will be most affected by undulations when it is rolling at its slowest speed (when it is close to the hole).

Finally, bear in mind that the ball will break more on a fast green than on a slow green: you should generally read more break into your putts in summer, when the greens are most closely mown.

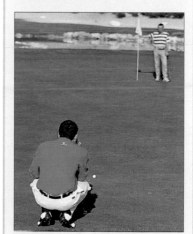

READING THE SLOPE *There are many areas on the green where you can read a putt. Crouching behind the ball is one of the most effective positions.*

KEY CHECKPOINT

TELL YOURSELF: "THIS PUTT TO WIN THE OPEN"

IT IS EASY to lose concentration when you practice your putting. The best way to stop this happening is to try to recreate some pressure by simulating a "real life" situation. To do this, tell yourself that the next putt you hit is to win the next competition at your club. Many of today's top professionals have told stories about when they were younger and dreamed of holing a putt "for the Open Championship". A few of them, such as Nick Faldo (in 1987, 1990, and 1992), had the opportunity to do it for real.

As you practise, if you imagine playing an important putt in a major tournament, the pressure is greater, and there is more satisfaction when you hole it. And, if in a competition you are on the last hole with a putt for victory, you have more chance of making it because you will have mentally rehearsed just such a shot.

OPEN WIN *Nick Faldo used to practice his putting telling himself: "this putt to win the Open." In 1990, he put the theory into practice (for the second time).*

DRILL 6: Match your backswing to the distance

WHEN YOU WATCH good putters in action, it is almost as if there is no "hit" as such; instead, the ball simply gets in the way of the swinging putterhead. This is a useful way to think of a putt, but you can only achieve such a smooth strike if your backswing is of a length appropriate to the length of putt. This drill will help you match the correct length of backswing to whatever putt you are faced with.

1 *Stand about 6½ yd (6 m) away from a hole, drop three balls, and address the first.*

2 *Make a very short backswing: no more than 4 in (10 cm) from the ball. To hole the ball from this position, you will have to jab the putter into the ball with an abrupt movement.*

3 *With the second ball, make an exaggerated backswing of approximately 20 in (50 cm). To hit the ball the correct distance you will find you have to slow down in the hitting area.*

4 *With the final ball, split the difference between the two backswing lengths employed in steps 2 and 3. You should find that you are able to accelerate the putter smoothly through the hitting area and send the ball the required distance. This movement should feel like a swing, rather than a hit.*

✔ Correct backswing

✘ Backswing too long

✘ Backswing too short

○ The backswing lengths suggested in this drill relate only to a putt of about 6½ yd (6 m). Try this exercise from various distances around the green, using backswings that are too short, too long, then perfect. In doing so you will learn to recognize the correct backswing length.

LEVEL ONE

DRILL 7: Learn to hit the sweet spot consistently

THIS DRILL, like Drill 8 (*below*) examines the importance of striking the ball consistently out of the sweet spot on the face of your putter. The theory is just the same as in, for example, tennis: if you do not hit the ball out of the center of the racket, performance is impaired.

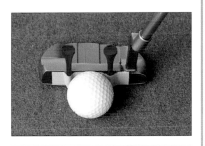

1 Take two tees and use sticky tape to attach them vertically to the face of the putter, so that each is about ¾ in (2 cm) either side of the sweet spot. This spot is clearly marked on almost all modern putters, either by a dot or a line on the top edge of the putterhead.

However, if one of the two tees becomes trapped between the ball and the putterface, the ball will shoot off at a strange angle (you should feel and hear that something is wrong with the strike, too). Such indications mean that you have hit the putt out of the toe- or heel-end of the putterhead.

2 Hit some putts of no more than 2 yd (2 m), trying to strike the ball without making contact with the tees. If you can do that, you have successfully hit the sweet spot.

3 As you become proficient from short range, gradually increase the length of your stroke, with the sole aim of striking the ball out of the sweet spot – right between the tees.

○ The longer your stroke becomes, the harder it is to avoid hitting the tees. However, if you can consistently strike the sweet spot, this will have a dramatic effect on your judgement of distance because you can more accurately predict the pace at which the ball will come off the putterface.

DRILL 8: Keep your eyes down for a perfect strike

THE OLD SAYING "keep your head down" has caused more faults in golfers' full swings than any other piece of advice because it prevents a good body pivot and free swing of the arms through impact. But with putting, keeping your head down is an excellent idea. It insures that your body is steady, which helps keep the putter on a true path back and forth; this in turn promotes a controlled, confident strike. The following practice drill will help you keep your head down as you putt.

1 Place a coin under a golf ball, and take up your address position.

2 Make a comfortable-length backswing (the length of putt you hit is not important), keeping your eyes firmly fixed on the top of the ball.

3 As you strike the ball, focus on the coin. Doing so will insure that your head remains still until the ball has started its journey toward the hole.

○ Although this drill is great for the practice ground, you cannot place a coin under the ball during a round (it is against the rules). But that does not mean you cannot benefit from the principle learned. When you are on the course, try to think in terms of keeping your head down as you swing the putter through the ball. If you can discipline yourself to do this on every putt, you will strike more putts out of the sweet spot and will send the ball off on the correct line more consistently. Drill 12 in Level Two (*see p.168*) shows you another way to help keep your head down when you putt.

DRILL 9: Stand against a wall to practice your stroke

IF THERE ARE LONG INTERVALS between each round you play, your game can become a little rusty. Often it is the short game, especially your putting, that is worst affected. This need not be the case, however.

Between games, perform this simple indoor exercise based on the key subjects covered so far in this section: five minutes per day will be of enormous benefit to your game. You will soon notice a difference on the green.

1 *Take your putter and adopt your normal address position, with your head resting gently against any of the interior walls in your home.*

2 *Drop a ball from the bridge of your nose. Wherever it lands is where you should position the ball in your stance (see Drill 3, p.162).*

3 *Now hit some medium-length – about 4½ yd (4 m) – putts along the wall. Keep an eye on the path of the putter relative to the straight line of the wall or skirting board. The putterhead should initially travel straight back, gradually arcing inside as the backswing becomes longer. It should then return to square at impact,*

before again tracking an inside path as the putter swings through. If the path of the putterhead is correct, and if the putterface is square at impact, the ball should set off on a line parallel with the wall. If it does not, you know there is something wrong with either the path of your stroke or the alignment of the putterface.

Head
Practicing against a wall trains you to keep your head steady during the stroke

○ By regularly rehearsing this exercise between games, your eyes become accustomed to seeing an online stroke, and your muscles will remember how to produce such a shot. When you do eventually return to the course, you will not spend the first 10 holes struggling to recover your putting stroke.

Ball's path
The ball should travel parallel to the wall

Drill 10: Hit a bull's-eye at the back of the hole

ROLLING THE BALL in very slowly from short range is a risky business because even the slightest imperfection or subtle slope on the putting surface will knock the ball off course. For putts up to 1 yd (1 m), a firm strike, hitting the ball into the back of the hole, is often the best option. This will help stop the ball from breaking left or right, enabling you to treat most short putts as straight putts, which saves a lot of trouble. The following drill will give you the confidence to hole-out from short range with authority.

1 *Find a relatively straight short putt on the practice putting green.*

2 *Stick a tee into the back of the hole. Angle it upward slightly so that the cup of the tee faces you, like a miniature bull's-eye, as you address the ball.*

3 *Hit a putt, and try to strike the ball with sufficient force to make*

it hit the tee before dropping into the hole. Imagine you are using the ball to hammer the tee further into the back of the hole.

4 *Repeat step 3 with at least 10 balls, so that you become accustomed to hitting your short putts firmly. If you previously "dribbled" short putts into the hole, you should now be striking the ball more firmly.*

○ When you are on the course, faced with a tricky short putt, imagine that there is a tee in the back of the hole. Focus on that mental image, and try to hit the imagined tee. On all but the most severe downhill slopes, this positive approach will usually work far better than trying to dribble the ball softly into the hole. A bolder strike is almost always better.

KEY CHECKPOINT

THE HOLE IS WIDER THAN YOU THINK

WHEN YOUR confidence on the greens is low, the hole can seem half its actual size. You may feel that no putt is short enough to be an easy tap in. In desperate situations, try to find a new perspective. If you examine the photograph of a standard size hole shown below you will see that the hole is almost three balls in width (no trick photography is involved). If you visualize the hole in this way, it eases the pressure because you know that there is a margin for error.

HOLE SIZE *When you are putting, it is worth remembering that the hole is much bigger than you might think – almost three ball widths, in fact.*

RETEST YOURSELF

Before moving to Level Two, take the test on pp.158–9 again. If you have not improved, it is worth revisiting the Level One drills. However, if the performance chart shows that your putting has progressed sufficiently, then you are ready to tackle the more advanced drills in Level Two.

DRILL 11: Become accustomed to holing putts

IF YOUR PUTTING is a little shaky from 1½–2 yd (1.5–2 m), the worst possible way to start your practice routine is by trying to hole putts of this length. This is because you will most likely miss more than you hole, which only serves to lower your confidence. Therefore, before you play your next round, make sure that you work on holing putts, not missing them. The following drill will help you achieve this aim.

1 Start at a distance from which you feel absolutely confident about holing every putt. Although this distance will vary from one golfer to the next, you will probably want to start about 12 in (30 cm) from the hole.

○ Initially, it may seem that this exercise is too easy. However, the progressive nature of the drill is the secret to its effectiveness. By starting from close range and seeing the ball hit the back of the hole (rather than putting from further back and becoming accustomed to the ball slipping past the hole), you will start to believe that you are a solid putter.

2 Hit five or six balls into the back of the hole (see Drill 10, p.167). Build a strong mental image of the ball going into the center of the hole, and let your confidence grow.

3 Move back another 6 in (15 cm). Use the same number of balls and work on repeating a positive stroke.

4 Repeat step 3 until you are about 1 yd (1 m) from the hole. Any further back and you run the risk of missing too many putts.

DRILL 12: Listen, but do not look

DRILL 8 (*see p.165*) suggests one way to help you keep your head down when you putt. This can be quite easy in practice, but psychologically it is very different during a proper round. Anxiety over a short putt (a frame of mind which simply does not occur in practice) can cause you to look up too soon to see if the ball is going in the hole. But your desperation to see the path of the ball can upset your stroke and usually results in a missed putt. Here is a method guaranteed to stop you looking up too soon.

1 Set up a short, straight putt of approximately 2 yd (2 m).

2 Make a stroke, and insure that you do not look up until you hear the sound of the ball dropping into the hole (or the ominous silence of a miss).

3 Work your way through as many balls as time allows. If you are putting well, you will find that you have to empty the hole regularly to make room for more balls to drop in.

○ You can use this putting technique throughout a round – from the first to the last green. By listening, rather than looking, your head and body will be still as you swing, and the path of your stroke will remain true. You might be surprised what a difference this small adjustment makes. When you finally do look up, there is a much better chance that the ball will have disappeared down the hole.

DRILL 13: Putt with a mirror for better results

HAVING YOUR EYES directly over the ball at address is one of the most important aspects of a good putting action (see Drill 3, p.162). From this position you can swivel your head for the perfect view down the intended line of the putt. If you can see down this line, you will more easily hit along it. This practice drill will not only insure that your eyes are directly over the ball when you putt but will also give you visual feedback on the alignment of the putter and its path as you swing.

1 *Use a thick, black marker pen (or black tape) to draw two lines on a small mirror: one vertical and one horizontal, so that they form a cross in the center.*

2 *Place the mirror on a flat portion of a green (or on the carpet at your home). The horizontal line should point directly at the target.*

3 *Position a ball on the mirror, in the center of the cross.*

4 *Address the ball, and check your reflection in the mirror. Your eyes should be hidden by the ball.*

5 *Line the putterface up with the vertical line, which will be square to the target.*

6 *Use the horizontal line to guide the putter on the correct path back and forth.*

7 *As you swing, make sure that your head stays perfectly still throughout.*

○ Keep this mirror somewhere easily accessible when you are practicing – perhaps in your locker at the golf club or in the trunk of your car. Like all forms of practice, repetition is the key to perfection. If you putt with a mirror in your free time, you will see the results reflected in your lower scores on the course.

Eye position
As you look down at the ball, you should not be able to see your eyes in the mirror

DRILL 14: Work your way around the compass

THIS IS A MORE ADVANCED variation on Drill 11 (*see p.168*), and is also designed to improve your holing-out skills. As this exercise incorporates a variety of different breaking putts, it is one of the best ways to improve your short-range putting skills.

1 *Choose a putting green with a slope, so that you can hit a variety of putts: uphill and downhill, as well as left-to-right and right-to-left breaking putts.*

2 *Place four balls 12 in (30 cm) from the hole, each at one of the four compass points (north, south, east, and west).*

3 *Putt each ball into the hole. Having started at such close range, you will immediately develop the confidence that comes*

with hitting the ball into the back of the hole every time.

4 *Complete one "set," move back 6 in (15 cm), place four balls at the compass points around the hole, and again try to hole each putt. If you succeed, move another 6 in (15 cm) further from the hole, and repeat the process.*

○ You can add a competitive edge to this drill by keeping track of the number of consecutively holed putts, and striving to beat your record. If you can get into the mid-teens without missing you are doing well. Any number in the 20s is exceptional.

DRILL 15: Give yourself a decent break

THE MOST COMMON PROBLEM with putts on slopes is not so much reading the amount of break, which is a talent within everyone's grasp (*see the Key Checkpoint on p.163*), but in actually trusting what

you see and committing yourself to striking the ball along your chosen line. The following exercise addresses both of these problems, and will give you extra confidence when tackling breaking putts.

1 *Take eight or nine balls and your putter to a green with a slope.*

2 *Place the balls at regular intervals in a gentle arc away from the hole. Start from about 2 yd (2 m) and go back as far as the edge of the green.*

3 *Beginning with the ball closest to the hole, carefully read each putt before hitting the ball. As the ball rolls toward the hole, take note how much the putt breaks. Because you are always working along an extension of the same line, as you hit the balls, you will start to see the break more clearly in your mind's-eye.*

○ This practice exercise improves your ability to judge the pace and line of a breaking putt by encouraging you to form a clear mental picture of the slope and its effect upon the ball. This means that your confidence will grow, and you will become accustomed to making a committed stroke that sets the ball off along your chosen line. Although you may not hole every putt you look at, if you trust your judgement you will at least make a good, positive stroke. This in itself will significantly improve your performance on the greens.

DRILL 16: Treat every putt as a straight putt

DRILL 15 explained that missing a breaking putt often results from not committing yourself to the line you chose. The slightest doubt or indecision usually manifests itself in a tentative stroke. The following drill should help avoid this tendency. It is based on the principle of treating every putt as a straight putt.

1 *With your putter in hand, find a green with obvious slopes on it.*

2 *Set yourself up with a putt about 5½ yd (5 m) from the hole.*

3 *Read the green to see how much break there is on the putt (see the Key Checkpoint on p.163).*

4 *Decide on the line along which you want the ball to start. Visualize a secondary target on an extension of that line. Therefore, on a putt where*

you see 12 in (30 cm) of right-to-left break, imagine that there is a target 12 in (30 cm) to the right of the hole.

5 *Make a few practice putting strokes, and focus on the imaginary target.*

6 *Hit the putt at that target: the hole becomes of secondary importance.*

○ When you practice this drill, you are effectively treating every putt as a straight putt, allowing the contours of the green to sweep the ball toward the hole. This simplifies the whole business of break putting.

DRILL 17: Brush forward to check your aim and stroke

THE FOLLOWING EXERCISE will reveal two key pieces of information about your putting stroke: whether the face of the putter is aimed correctly, and if the path of your stroke is on the correct line. Many of

the world's leading tour professionals have been known to rehearse this exercise – Nick Faldo went so far as to credit it as one of the secrets behind his 1992 Open Championship victory.

1 *Locate a green, and set up a straight putt about 1 yd (1 m) from the hole.*

2 *Address the ball as you would normally, with the putterface sitting behind the ball, square to the hole.*

3 *Now brush the ball toward the hole with a smooth forward motion. Do not make any backswing at all.*

○ Where the ball goes when you brush it forward will tell you much about your putting action. If the ball travels into the middle of the hole, you know that the putterface was square at address and that your stroke was on line in the through swing – two key elements in a successful putt. If the ball goes to the left of the hole, either the putterface was closed at address, or you pulled the shot by swinging the putter to the left in the through swing. If the ball finishes right, the face was open at address or you swung the putter to the right.

DRILL 18: Putt one ball past the next

MOST GOLFERS are quick to blame their short putting when they frequently three-putt, but, more often than not, the real problem lies in not getting the long-range approach putt close enough to the hole. The following drill will help solve this irritating problem, training you to be a better judge of the running speed of the ball across a green.

1 *Take 12 or so balls and putt the first one about 5½ yd (5 m) across the green.*

2 *Putt the second ball past the first by a distance of 1 yd (1 m).*

3 *Try to putt each subsequent ball the same distance past the previous one.*

○ You can never be too good for this drill: all you have to do to enhance the challenge is reduce the space between each ball. A variation on this exercise is to reverse the process: hit the first ball to the far end of the putting green, and leave each subsequent ball just short of the previous one. Good distance judgement has two benefits: it takes the pressure off your short putts, and more of your long putts are likely to drop in the hole.

DRILL 19: Try a "dress rehearsal" of the ideal stroke

FOR TOO MANY GOLFERS, the practice putting stroke is little more than a casual, almost aimless, waft of the putter back and forth. Often it has no purpose or resemblance to the actual stroke. Make your practice putting stroke really count by rehearsing the following exercise and making it a permanent fixture in your putting routine.

1 *Drop a ball anywhere on the green, and go through your usual process of reading which way the putt is likely to break (see the Key Checkpoint on p.163).*

2 *Once you have decided on a line, assume your normal posture, but do not address the ball just yet.*

3 *Make a few practice swings while all the time looking at the hole. Try to match what you feel will be the ideal length of stroke with the visual messages received from your view of the hole. Your backswing should be of a length that enables you to smoothly accelerate the putter through the hitting zone (see Drill 6, p.164).*

4 *When you are happy with your practice swing, address the ball, repeat the stroke you were rehearsing, and let the ball get in the way of the swinging putter (you should be looking at the ball now, not the hole).*

5 *Repeat this routine several times, but for each putt, drop the ball at a different distance from the hole.*

○ As you work on this drill you should develop a much better feel for distance. If you think of your practice strokes as "dress rehearsals" for the actual stroke, you are more likely to putt well when it matters most.

DRILL 20: Hit up-and-down putts to improve your speed

A S WAS INDICATED in Drill 18 *(left)*, the main reason for three-putting is a poorly judged approach putt from long range. This is exacerbated when slopes come into play because golfers often struggle to adjust their stroke accordingly. The following exercise is designed to improve your judgement of speed but, unlike Drill 18, it has the added difficulty of uphill and downhill putts.

1 *Find a green with a pronounced slope right across the putting surface. You will need only three balls, your putter, and two tees.*

2 *Place one of the tees in the green 1 yd (1 m) short of the top of the slope and the other the same distance from the bottom of the slope. To make this exercise truly effective, there should be at least a 13 yd (12 m) gap between the tees (otherwise the drill is not demanding enough).*

3 *Place three balls at whichever end you wish to start from, and putt towards the tee at the opposite end of the green. Take your time over each putt, and try to leave the balls as close as possible to the target.*

4 *Now putt the balls back toward the opposite tee.*

5 *Go backward and forward, putting the balls uphill and downhill, for as long as time permits.*

○ As you perform this exercise, you will find that your judgement of speed rapidly improves. This shows that you are adjusting your stroke well to cope with opposing slopes. If you want an added challenge, try this drill with just one ball. It is much harder when you have only one attempt at getting the speed right. This drill recreates the kind of challenge you face during a round.

SPEED IS EVERYTHING

T O GIVE YOUR BALL the optimum chance of dropping into the hole, irrespective of the putting distance, scientific research has shown that the ball should be moving fast enough to travel 17½–24 in (45–60 cm) past the hole. This ideal "running speed" insures that the ball holds its line as it approaches the hole, when subtle breaks can all too easily knock the putt off line. Bear this in mind next time you size up a putt. It is a good idea to visualize an imaginary hole beyond the actual hole. This technique will encourage you to get the ball running at the perfect speed.

RUNNING SPEED *The ideal pace for holing a putt is such that if the ball did miss, it would travel 17½–24 in (45–60 cm) beyond the hole.*

DRILL 21: Avoid excess wrist action in your putting stroke

THE CONVENTIONAL putting method involves a stroke controlled primarily by the shoulders and arms, with a small amount of wrist action – referred to as "lag" (see Drill 5, p.163). This wrist movement is desirable because it promotes good rhythm and a smooth acceleration of the putter through the hitting zone. However, excessive wrist action is sometimes the cause of erratic putting, as it can upset the alignment of the putterface and disrupt your ability to control the distance of your putts. This exercise will help keep your wrist action within sensible limits.

1 *Address a ball as normal, and trap another ball between your right wrist and the top of the grip on your putter.*

2 *Hit some putts of about 8½ yd (8 m), making sure that the ball remains in place throughout the stroke. This prevents excessive wrist movement, which should promote a smooth, direct stroke. If the ball falls to the ground, there is too much wrist action in your putting stroke.*

○ Remember that the putting stroke is open to personal interpretation: the advice given in this drill is only a recommendation; but it is, nevertheless, a strong recommendation. Even though there have been some wonderful "wristy" putters in golfing history, such as multiple major winners Gary Player and Arnold Palmer, for most people this method is much less reliable than the more conventional technique advocated throughout this section. A wristy action is more difficult to repeat and increases the likelihood of inconsistent strikes and poor judgement of pace (especially in a pressure situation).

DRILL 22: Try this long-range test

THIS SECTION has already introduced two exercises devoted to improving your long-range putting: Drill 18 (see p.172) and Drill 20 (see p.173). As this part of your game is so important, here is another, in the form of a mini-test. The results will give you an honest assessment of your long-range putting skills.

1 *Place any club 26 in (65 cm) behind a hole, and retreat to a distance from which you feel confident that you will not three-putt.*

2 *From this position, putt five balls toward the hole.*

3 *Award yourself points for each putt based on the following scoring system:*
- *In the hole: 3 points*
- *Short of the hole: minus 3 points*
- *Beyond the hole but short of the shaft: 1 point*
- *Hitting the club: minus 2 points*

The idea is to complete one "set" of balls and finish with a positive score. If you manage this, move a few paces further away, and repeat the exercise. Remember that you can only move back when you achieve a positive score.

○ This drill trains you to impart the correct pace to the ball, which gives you the best chance of not three-putting – your first priority when you are a long way from the hole. You will also stand a better chance of holing the occasional long-range putt.

DRILL 23: Hit to a smaller target to put the hole into perspective

VISUALIZATION CAN HAVE a wonderful effect on your game, as the following practice drill will illustrate. The exercise, which will give you a new perspective on holing-out, has maximum benefit if it is performed just before you start a round.

1 *Place a coin anywhere on the green.*

2 *Putt three or four balls toward the coin from a distance of 2 yd (2 m). The idea is to make each ball hit the coin.*

3 *If you are feeling very confident, move to a distance of 3 yd (3 m) or more, and repeat the drill.*

Perception
By focusing on a coin, when you play a round, the hole will seem bigger and easier to hit

Control
Keep your grip pressure light, and your stroke smooth

○ This drill challenges your putting stroke and concentrates your practice time. When you face your first putt, the hole will seem much bigger and considerably easier to find. One cautionary note, however: if you do try this exercise over a distance of more than 3 yd (3 m), you risk missing the coin so often that your confidence lowers, and you end up doing yourself more harm than good. Therefore, keep your putts within an achievable distance.

KEY CHECKPOINT

"TUNNEL VISION" PROVIDES A CLEARER FOCUS

SEEING THINGS in your peripheral vision can distract you when you are trying to focus on reading the line of a putt – a time when you want to be completely concentrated. To rectify this problem, shield your eyes by placing your hands around your face to create a "tunnel vision" effect. This will help you read the green and will lessen the danger of distractions upsetting your concentration. If you find that your mind is wandering, try narrowing your field of vision: many professionals do just the same.

FOCUS
If you blinker your eyes when you are reading a putt, it will help block out unwanted distractions. This green-reading technique will also aid your concentration.

RETEST YOURSELF

Before moving to Level Three, take the test on pp.158–9 again. If you have not improved, it is worth revisiting the Level Two drills. However, if the performance chart shows that your putting has progressed sufficiently, then you are ready to tackle the more advanced drills in Level Three.

LEVEL TWO

KEY CHECKPOINT

HOW TO COPE WITH FAST PUTTS

ON FAST GREENS or with downhill putts, you cannot afford to make an abrupt or jerky stroke. Every move has to be smooth in order to maximize your control and to improve your chances of trickling the ball into or near the hole. (For fast downhill putts, it is not advisable to give the ball enough force to travel beyond the hole, as with a normal putt.)

Although it would be unwise to remodel your stroke just to play one type of putt, there is a change you can introduce to your technique that will help with fast putts, without making your stroke feel strange. The alteration involves striking the ball from nearer the toe of the putter, rather than from the center. This means that you can make your regular stroke (as if the green was flat) but, because you are not striking the ball from the sweet spot, less energy is produced at impact, and the ball leaves the face at a slower speed. If you try hitting the ball towards the toe, you will be better equipped to tackle fast putts.

LESS SPEED *On very quick putts, striking the ball toward the toe of the putter deadens the blow so that the ball does not race past the hole.*

DRILL 24: Make your stroke flow

HERE IS ONE OF THE BEST ways to promote a free swing of the putter in your stroke: a prerequisite for good judgement of distance. Although this exercise relates to one of the fundamental putting issues, because it requires you to putt with one hand only, a reasonable level of skill is needed.

1 *Grip the putter with your right hand, and let your left hand hang down by your side (or put it in your pocket).*

2 *Stroke some balls across the green. Keep your grip pressure light, make a free swing with your right arm, and let your wrist hinge slightly in response to the momentum of the putter changing direction from backswing to followthrough. This softness in your wrist encourages the putter to flow back and forth, whereas a stiff-wristed action tends to lack fluidity and makes it difficult to control the pace of the putt.*

3 *Think about pace rather than concentrating on a specific target. Have in mind an approximate distance, and try to group four or five balls as close together as possible.*

○ After a few attempts you will be pleasantly surprised at the quality of your strike and how well you are judging distance – all using only your right hand. When you reintroduce your left hand and putt as normal, you will find that your stroke is less inhibited and not restricted by the tendency to guide the putter back and forth (which is a very damaging fault).

DRILL 25: For close-range putts be very precise

DRILL 11 IN THE "Pitching" section (*see p.90*) stressed the need for accurate approach shots. The same principle applies to close-range putts. Just as for pitch shots, where you need to aim for the flag rather than just the green, with short putts it can help to focus on a single point, not just the hole. This drill will teach you to narrow your focus to a very specific target.

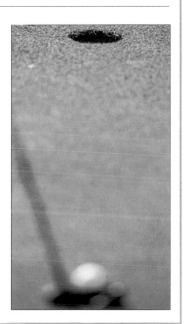

1 *Set yourself up with a straight putt no more than 2 yd (2 m) from the hole.*

2 *Address the ball. But rather than focusing merely on the hole, set your sights on a smaller detail within the hole, such as a slight imperfection on the rim of the cup.*

3 *With the specific target identified in step 2 fresh in your mind, switch your attention back to the ball and, without delay, make a stroke. Do not raise your head early to watch the run of the ball. Instead trust your stroke, and look up only to see if the ball has found your specific target.*

○ Although the Key Checkpoint on p.167 showed that there is a margin for error when putting, accomplished golfers might want to aim for a smaller target. The break on a putt will, however, affect the target. It may be inside the hole, but equally, if the putt breaks severely, the target may be on the surface of the green either side of the hole.

DRILL 26: Hover your putter to promote a smooth stroke

WHENEVER YOU ARE under pressure or feeling nervous, it is extremely easy to lose the smoothness and rhythm of your putting stroke, which can be disastrous. Try the following exercise on the practice putting green, then use it on the course whenever you feel especially in need of a steady hand and a sure stroke.

1 *Assume your putting posture, but without a ball on the ground.*

2 *Raise the putterhead off the ground so that it hovers fractionally above the putting surface. Focus on maintaining a soft grip pressure.*

3 *Make a couple of practice putting strokes. Do not let the putter come into contact with the ground at any time.*

4 *Without altering your grip pressure, hover the putter behind the ball, and make a stroke from this position. Repeat this procedure – hover, practice stroke, hover, proper stroke – several times.*

○ You will notice that hovering the putter above the green promotes a smooth first move away from the ball, whereby your hands, arms, shoulders, and putter all work in harmony. There is no jerkiness or sudden independent movement. By then addressing the ball and again hovering the putter off the ground, you will enjoy the same benefits in your proper stroke, which will be of enormous benefit to your putting.

LEVEL THREE

DRILL 27: Watch your hands, not the ball

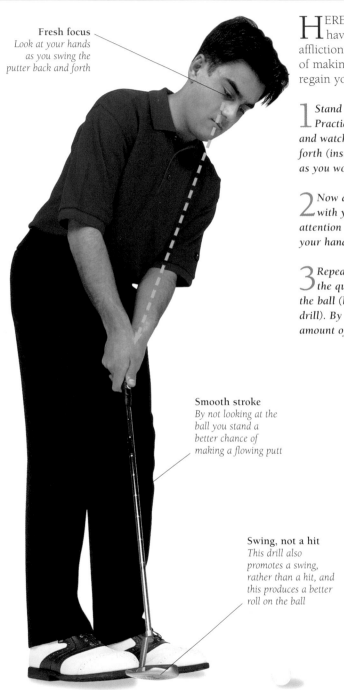

Fresh focus
Look at your hands as you swing the putter back and forth

Smooth stroke
By not looking at the ball you stand a better chance of making a flowing putt

Swing, not a hit
This drill also promotes a swing, rather than a hit, and this produces a better roll on the ball

HERE IS A GREAT DRILL that will help if you have a tendency to freeze over short putts – an affliction caused by anxiety, which ruins any chance of making a smooth, direct stroke. Try this exercise to regain your confidence and composure.

1 *Stand on a green 3–4½ yd (3–4 m) from the hole. Practice your putting stroke before addressing the ball, and watch your hands as they swing smoothly back and forth (instead of looking at the putterhead or the ground as you would ordinarily).*

2 *Now address the ball, and when you are satisfied with your aim, posture, and alignment, switch your attention back to your hands. As in step 1, keep an eye on your hands as they swing back and forth in your stroke.*

3 *Repeat step 2 several times. Try to concentrate only on the quality of your swing, rather than thinking about the ball (holing the putt is not the principal aim of this drill). By not looking at the ball, it is easier to control the amount of force and acceleration in your stroke.*

○ As a practice routine, this drill can be incredibly beneficial. It completely removes the tendency to hit at the ball, which is often at the root of short putt problems. Instead, concentrating on your hands promotes a smooth, controlled stroke. It also has the added benefit of stopping you from looking up too soon, which is a sure-fire way to miss a short putt – see drills 8 (p.165) and 12 (p.168). But if you keep your eyes fixed firmly on your hands, you will regain your confidence and your stroke. You may even want to try this technique out on the course to help you during a round.

DRILL 28: Make a century on the green

THE FOLLOWING DRILL is one that Colin Montgomerie used to practice every day without fail when he was at university in the US in the mid 1980s. It requires application, dedication, and concentration, but the rewards are tremendous.

1 *Set yourself up with a putt you feel confident of holing. Just less than one club-length is a good distance for an accomplished player. If you lack confidence on the greens, place the ball a little closer to the hole.*

2 *Knock in one putt after another from the same spot, emptying the hole when necessary. Keep count as you go, and try to hole 100 consecutive putts. The twist is, if you miss a putt, you have to start again from one. The pressure intensifies greatly as you near the 100 mark.*

○ The first 10 putts will seem easy, as there is no pressure. So might the next 10, and even the 10 after that. But the reason you do this exercise is for the last 20 or so balls. They are difficult because you know that if you miss one, you have to start again. This pressure makes you concentrate at least as hard as you would on the course. Next time you face a short putt in a proper round, you will be far more confident of knocking it in. After all, you will be able to say to yourself: "I have done this hundreds of times before."

THE LONG PUTTER IS MORE THAN JUST A GIMMICK

IF YOU DECIDE to try a long putter – a club that caused a furore among traditionalists when it first came to prominence in the late 1980s – your level of success will depend on your address position. Firstly, anchor the butt end of the putter either under your chin or against your chest. Then grip the club lightly between the thumb and forefinger of your right hand, which acts as the guiding hand. Many professionals work on the basis that the position of the right palm should mirror the putterface. This makes it easier to keep the stroke on line and also establishes a relationship between your hand and the putter – where your right hand goes the putterface follows. Your left hand should form a loose, "fist-like" grip at the top of the club's grip. Think of a grandfather clock, and imagine your left hand as the hinge and the shaft as the pendulum.

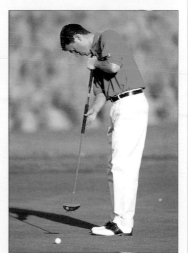

FREE SWING *When using a long putter, your right hand should guide the club back and forth like the pendulum on a grandfather clock.*

DRILL 29: Cross your hands if your stroke is not working

IF YOU ARE UNHAPPY with your putting performance, do not be afraid to experiment with a less conventional stroke. The following exercise involves one of the most popular "alternative" methods of putting. Tour professionals such as Denmark's Thomas Bjorn and Jim Furyk of the US have putted like this from an early age, and many other players have enjoyed success on the green using this method.

1 *Place your right hand above your left on the putting grip. The palms should still face one another, with each thumb pointing down the center of the shaft. The reverse overlap (see Drill 1, p.160) is also still apparent, only with this grip the forefinger of the right hand rests on the fingers of the left hand, rather than the other way around.*

2 *Start with a medium length putt of approximately 6½–7½ yd (6–7 m). Rock your shoulders to move the putter back and forth. A soft grip is essential because, as you take the club back and then change direction into the downswing, you will experience that all-important "lag" (see Drill 5, p.163). This softness in your wrists*

heightens the sensation of smooth acceleration into the ball and helps maintain the correct relationship between your hands and the putter as the club swings through the hitting area.

3 *Continue to hit putts, and you should start to notice that your left wrist is more inclined to maintain its original angle through the hitting zone, which in turn helps maintain the alignment of the putterface. The putter is therefore less likely to open or close at impact, which means more of your putts will start on the desired line.*

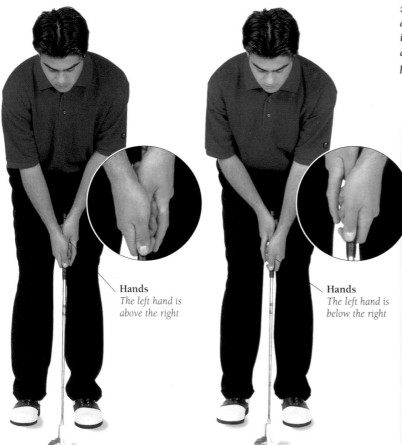

Hands
The left hand is above the right

Conventional method

Hands
The left hand is below the right

Crossed hands method

○ In a sense, this technique involves more of a "pulling through" motion than the "swinging through" action of a conventional stroke.

Although this grip will feel strange at first (your hands are in the opposite positions to every other golf stroke you play), it should not adversely affect the quality of your stroke. Indeed, many proponents of this method claim it is easier to rock your shoulders more naturally, which aids a consistent stroke. Also, the fact that this technique is very much arms-and-shoulders dominated, with the wrists moving barely at all throughout the stroke, means that it is simple to repeat. Although this technique will not be to everyone's taste, if you struggle on the green you might find that, with a little practice, it works better for you than the conventional method. It is certainly worth trying.

Drill 30: Experiment with pace and line

DRILLS 15 AND 16 *(see pp.170–71)*, as well as the Key Checkpoint on p.163, suggested that judging breaking putts is not an exact science. There is always more than one line into the hole, and which route you choose depends entirely on the amount of speed you apply to the ball (a softly struck putt breaks more than a putt struck firmly). Here is a useful exercise that will reveal the relationship between pace and line, enhancing your visualization and touch on breaking putts.

1 *Find a 4½-yd (4-m) putt, where there is an obvious break from left to right or right to left.*

2 *Try to hole 3 or 4 putts from the same spot, hitting each ball on a different line and varying the speed of the stroke. For example, with the first ball, try to "straighten" the putt by striking it firmly so that there will be very little break. And with the next putt, stroke the ball so as to just trickle it into the hole, allowing for much more break than with the previous shot.*

3 *Continue in this fashion for as long as time permits. As you practice, keep trying to hole putts while always experimenting with different paces and lines.*

○ This exercise will teach you what you can and cannot do with breaking putts, and will give you more confidence when dealing with breaking putts during a round. When faced with a breaking putt, use your imagination to pick whichever line you feel most comfortable with, and match that line with the right pace.

THE PERFECT PUTT

THERE ARE NO POOR PUTTERS at the top level of the game, but there are some exceptional putters and David Duval is one of them. His putting stroke contains the three essential ingredients for success. The putter-face is square at impact, swinging on a path which corresponds with the intended line of the putt and at the absolute perfect speed. On top of that, David reads greens as well as any other golfer which means not only does he produce one of the best strokes in the world, he invariably starts the ball on the perfect line. It is a formidable combination and when he gets in a position to win a tournament, no one holes out better than him. There is as much to learn from this sequence of David striking a 25-foot putt, during practice for the 2000 Open Championship at St Andrews, as there is from the full-blooded swing of the driver.

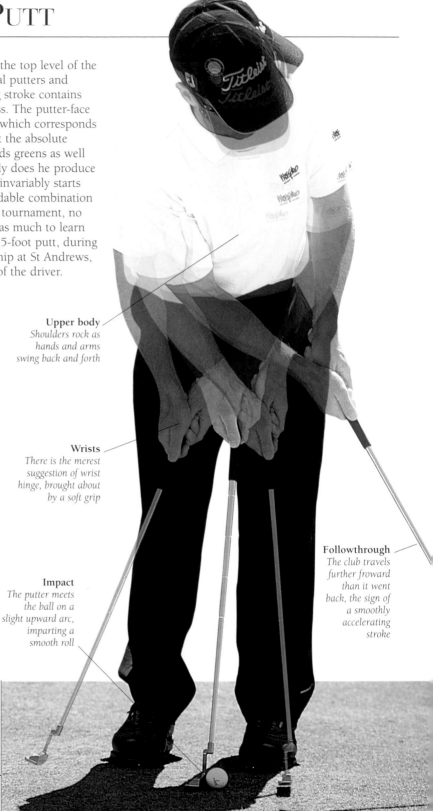

Upper body
Shoulders rock as hands and arms swing back and forth

Wrists
There is the merest suggestion of wrist hinge, brought about by a soft grip

Followthrough
The club travels further froward than it went back, the sign of a smoothly accelerating stroke

Impact
The putter meets the ball on a slight upward arc, imparting a smooth roll

1 ADDRESS
David's address position is quite distinctive, stamped with his own personal touch, but there is nothing unorthodox about it. The grip is neutral, the palms facing one another and both thumbs pointing down the center of the shaft. The stance is narrow, with the ball forward allowing the putter to deliver a slightly upward blow. And David positions his eyes directly over the ball. Finally, take note of how comfortable and relaxed he is at address. There is no sign of tension for this, the ultimate feel shot.

2 BACKSWING

The shoulders, arms, hands, and club all move away together to produce a smooth and synchronized backswing. The wrists do not hinge independently, but the hands stay relaxed to ensure that when David makes the transition from backswing to downswing, there is a softness and pliability in the wrists which causes the putter to momentarily lag behind the hands, rather like a miniversion of a chip. This ensures that the putter does not overtake his hands at impact, which would cause the face to close and the ball to go left.

3 IMPACT

In putting the impact position should be identical to the setup. Study this image and compare it with David's setup. It is hard to see the difference, save for the movement of the ball leaving the putter-face. The putter-head has actually just traveled beyond the bottom of its swing arc at the moment of impact, which produces an upward stroke and helps impart top spin on the ball for a smooth roll. His head is steady as a rock, aiding a precision strike and ensuring that no unwanted upper body movement can upset the intended path of the putter.

4 FOLLOWTHROUGH

You can see that the putter-head finishes much higher in the followthrough than it ever reached in the backswing, which is a product of smooth acceleration and an upward strike. Only now does David's head come up affording his eyes a view of the ball heading inexorably towards its destination five inches below ground. Unfortunately, one thing these pictures cannot convey is the wonderful rhythm of a great putter's stroke. The putter flows smoothly back and forth. There is no hit as such, just smooth acceleration letting the ball get in the way – a wonderful final thought.

KEYS TO BETTER PUTTING

AS WE'VE SAID BEFORE in this section, putting is an individual thing. However, these final thoughts will help irrespective of your style.

○ *Make sure your eyes are directly over the ball in your address position, offering the purest view down the line of the putt.*

○ *Put the ball far enough forward in your stance to ensure that the putter-head meets it on a slightly upward curve imparting a smooth roll.*

○ *Keep independent wrist action to a minimum and feel that your stroke is controlled predominantly by a synchronized shoulders-and-arms movement.*

○ *Always try to produce a length of backswing that allows smooth and natural acceleration of the putter through the hitting area. Do not hit at the ball.*

○ *Keep your head still and resist the temptation to look up until the ball is well on its way to the hole.*

Chapter Two
FAULTS
AND FIXES

THE PREVIOUS CHAPTER encompassed just about every conceivable aspect of developing a repeatable, effective golf swing and a purposeful short game. However, no matter how hard you work on your technique, there are times when faults creep in, resulting in wayward shots. Such is the nature of the game at every level, from the bottom to the very top. Consequently, this chapter offers "trouble-shooting" advice that will provide useful fixes for those irritating faults. All the prime suspects come under the spotlight – essentially, ten of the most common problems. This chapter explains how and why such faults occur and, crucially, demonstrates a swift and effective way to cure them.

FAULT FIXING
Here Mitchell Spearman, one of Nick Faldo's former coaches, is examining Faldo's game. Even the best players occasionally experience faults in their swing.

THE SLICE

THIS IS THE MOST COMMON fault of all – the bête noire of thousands of golfers the world over. A slice is a shot where the ball starts on a course to the left of the target and swerves, often quite dramatically, from left to right through the air. Because the problem is made more acute by a lack of loft, the biggest slices are hit with straight-faced clubs such as the driver, 3-wood, and long irons.

✔ FIX: TRAIN AN ON LINE ATTACK

To cure a slice you must start by straightening your address position. Stand square to the target line, with your shoulders and feet in parallel alignment. This will promote a more correct path in your backswing. Then attempt to strike the ball so that it starts on a course to the right of the target line, encouraging an inside path of attack into impact. Also feel that you rotate your forearms through impact to promote an aggressive release of the club. Together, these measures will help to eradicate a slice.

○ An open clubface at impact is often the result of not releasing the club properly (*see p.27*). Soften the pressure in your grip to promote a free-flowing "swish" of the clubhead. This helps square the face at impact. But, if this does not work for you, an alternative is suggested in the "Off the Tee" section (*see Drill 10, p.36*).

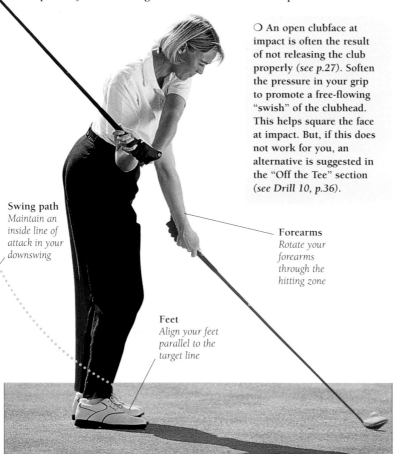

Swing path
Maintain an inside line of attack in your downswing

Forearms
Rotate your forearms through the hitting zone

Feet
Align your feet parallel to the target line

✘ FAULT: POORLY ALIGNED SETUP

It is hard to say which fault comes first – an open clubface or an out-to-in swing path. One thing is certain, however: these problems arise from a poor address position. The typical slicer is aligned to the left of the target, and the swing path simply follows the lines established at address.

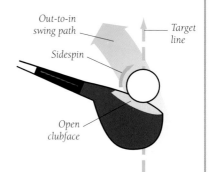

Out-to-in swing path

Sidespin

Target line

Open clubface

WHAT CAUSES A SLICE?

The cause of a slice is an open clubface combined with an out-to-in swing path (see pp.26–7), whereby the club travels across the target line through the hitting area. This swing path causes the ball to travel left initially, and the open clubface delivers a glancing blow that imparts sidespin, which causes the ball to swerve to the right through the air.

THE HOOK

THIS SHOT IS SOMETIMES DESCRIBED as the "good player's bad shot" because the hands are very active through the hitting area. This is generally desirable, yet an incorrect swing path and closed clubface leave the ball flying well off line. With a hooked shot, the ball begins on a path to the right of the target and then moves right-to-left through the air. As with the slice, the problem is exaggerated by a lack of loft on the clubface, hence the biggest hooks occur with the driver

✔ FIX: CORRECT YOUR SWING PATH

To eliminate the excessive inside-the-line attack and to train a more on line swing path through impact, practice with an obstruction, such as a headcover, on the ground behind the ball *and 6 in (15cm) inside the target line. The obstruction blocks the path on which the clubhead swings into impact for a hook, forcing you to deliver the club to the ball on the correct path. While reestablishing a better swing path, concentrate on unwinding your hips, clearing them out of the way in your downswing, rather than sliding them toward the target.*

○ **If, once you have aligned your swing path correctly, you see your first shots flying to the left, the clubface is still closed. Check your left-hand grip and make sure that you can see only two knuckles (*see Drill 11, p.37*). This should work the clubface into a more neutral position at impact, culminating in a straighter ball-flight.**

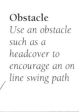

Obstacle
Use an obstacle such as a headcover to encourage an on line swing path

✘ FAULT: TRAPPED ON THE INSIDE

Typically with a hooked shot, the tendency is to slide your hips (instead of unwinding them) toward the target in your downswing. This leaves your hands, arms, and the club trapped too much on the inside. Instinctively, this feels as if the swing path will cause the ball to fly to the right; in an attempt to recover the situation, your hands become over active, causing the clubface to close and the shot to hook.

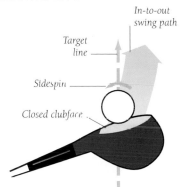

In-to-out swing path

Target line

Sidespin

Closed clubface

WHAT CAUSES A HOOK?

The ball-flight for a hook is the opposite of a slice, as are the impact conditions The club approaches the ball from too far inside the target line, producing an in-to-out swing path combined with a closed clubface. The hooked ball tends to fly lower than it would normally and also runs a long way.

THE "HEAVY-CONTACT" CHIP

THERE IS NOTHING IN GOLF that matches the ignominy of making a complete mess of a short shot, and the heavy-contact chip – a stroke in which heavy contact is made with the ground instead of the ball – ranks high in the embarrassment stakes. Somehow it is worse than missing a short putt and seemingly much harder to correct. However, the changes required to eliminate this shot are simple to apply.

✔ FIX: KEEP YOUR HANDS AHEAD OF THE CLUB

The desired ball-then-turf contact (see Drill 5, p.111) can only be achieved if you keep your hands in front of the clubhead into and through impact. To do this, as you start your downswing, maintain the angle in your right wrist – it should remain constant through the hitting zone. The bottom of the swing arc should now coincide with the ball (see Drill 4, p.110), producing a clean strike and the smallest of divots after impact (instead of before).

○ Make sure the ball is not too far forward in your stance, as this is often the cause of a poor strike. The ball should be opposite your right foot, with your hands forward. There should be a straight line formed by your left arm and the shaft of the club *(see Drill 1, p.108).*

Wrists
Make sure your hands lead, and stay ahead of, the clubhead through the hitting zone

✘ FAULT: CLUB HITS THE GROUND BEFORE THE BALL

Heavy contact is the result of trying to help the ball into the air rather than letting the loft on the clubface do the work. Employing a scooping action causes the clubhead to pass the hands prior to impact and to strike the ground before the ball – hence, a "heavy-contact" chip. Generally, a divot is taken behind the ball, although this will not be the case if the ground is very hard.

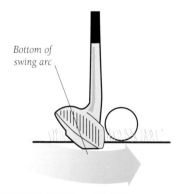

Bottom of swing arc

WHAT CAUSES A HEAVY-CONTACT CHIP?

The cause of this shot lies in the clubhead's angle of attack into impact. The crux of the problem is that the bottom of the swing arc occurs before the ball. Therefore, the clubhead buries itself in the ground, which absorbs most of the power in the shot. This means that hardly any energy is passed on to the ball.

THE SHANKED IRON SHOT

T HE SHANK IS PROBABLY the most destructive shot you can hit. The ball shoots off the club at an angle of at least 45 degrees to the target, often never to be seen again. You can hit a shank with any iron, but, whatever the club, once the damage is done it cannot be easily remedied.

✔ FIX: BLOCK THE PATH TO A SHANK

Curing a shank relies on eliminating the destructive path of attack into impact. Place a headcover or an empty ball-box just behind the ball, 3 in (8 cm) outside the target line. Then hit a shot with a short iron. The obstruction makes it necessary for you to swing the club toward the ball on the correct path, leading to solid contact between the center of the clubface and the ball. If your old swing fault reappears, the club will hit the obstacle before it reaches the ball.

○ *Ironically, taking the club back too far on the inside often causes you to loop the club outside the target line in your downswing. Slowly rehearse your backswing and make sure that the club travels inside but also upward, as this promotes the correct downswing path (see Drill 16, p.95).*

✘ FAULT: POOR LINE OF ATTACK

With a shanked shot, the ball is hit from the hosel instead of the middle of the clubface. For that to happen, the clubhead must be further away from your body at impact than at address. This is caused by "throwing" the clubhead away from your body at the start of your downswing, so that it swings through the hitting zone on an out-to-in path.

Clubface
With the club on the correct path, solid contact is made between the center of the clubface and the ball

Obstacle
Place a ball-box just outside the ball-to-target line to prevent an out-to-in swing path

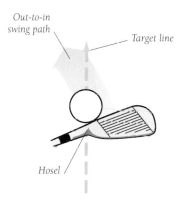

Out-to-in swing path

Target line

Hosel

WHAT CAUSES A SHANK?

The shank occurs when the the hosel of the club (the point where the shaft joins the clubhead), rather than the clubface, strikes the ball. This happens when the clubhead travels into impact from way outside the ideal swing path. Because of the shape of the hosel, the ball flies almost sideways to the line of play – a highly destructive fault.

THE SKIED DRIVE

THE SKIED DRIVE is not the most damaging of shots – indeed, the ball tends to fly reasonably straight, which means you rarely lose a ball. You do, however, lose as much as 70 percent of the normal distance for any given club. A skied drive occurs when the clubhead chops down steeply under a ball that is teed up (occasionally too high). The result is a ball-flight more reminiscent of a lofted pitch than a solid drive.

✘ FAULT: STEEP DOWNSWING ATTACK
A skied drive is usually caused by an excessively upright backswing. This is the result of picking the club up too steeply with your hands in your takeaway – in essence, too much lift and not enough width. This establishes a narrow swing arc, and your downswing becomes a product of your poor backswing.

✔ FIX: START YOUR TAKEAWAY LOW AND SLOW
To promote a shallower angle of attack, widen your backswing arc. Concentrate on sweeping the club away "low and slow," turning your back on the target (see Drill 19, p.44), and swinging your arms and the club around your body

❍ Hitting lots of skied drives is almost certainly a result of poor technique, but it is also worth checking the height at which you set the ball on the tee. Make sure that only half of the ball is showing above the top edge of the driver (*see the Key Checkpoint on p.31*).

more (see Drill 15, p.40). This promotes a backswing that is full and wide. In your downswing, try to focus on sweeping the ball away rather than hitting down on it. Create a longer flat spot at the bottom of your swing – the arc should be more saucer-shaped than cup-shaped.

Body motion
Turn your shoulders and swing your arms around your body to promote a rounded swing

Steep angle of attack

Steep ball trajectory

Wide backswing
A wide backswing arc in your takeaway promotes a shallow angle of attack in your downswing

Saucer-shaped arc
Think of the club traveling back on a saucer-shaped arc

WHAT CAUSES A SKIED DRIVE?
A skied drive occurs when the top-edge of the clubhead makes contact with the bottom portion of the ball. The ball then shoots up into the air quickly but with very little forward momentum. The shot is the result of a very steep angle of attack into impact, combined with the ball being teed up (sometimes too high), allowing the clubhead to make contact with the underside of the ball. The shot is most common with the driver and 3-wood.

THE TOP

THE TOP IS GENERALLY looked upon as a beginner's fault, but it also afflicts experienced players. In fact, even professionals have been known to hit this shot – a rarity, admittedly, but true nevertheless. Whatever your standard, it is an embarrassing shot because the outcome looks so pathetic. The clubhead just clips the top of the ball, sending it scuttling along the ground. The top occurs most with either a drive or a fairway-wood shot.

✔ FIX: MONITOR YOUR POSTURE FROM ADDRESS TO IMPACT

Whichever fault is causing you to top the ball, the conclusion is the same. You have to make sure you maintain good posture from address until the point of impact. Adopt a good posture (see pp.24–5) and address a tee with your driver. Now take practice swings, trying to clip the tee out of the ground while maintaining your spine angle

○ If you have a tendency to top your fairway wood shots, check that the ball is not too far back in your stance (*see pp.22–3*). This is sometimes the cause of a topped shot. Position yourself so that the ball is opposite your left heel. This setup allows you to sweep the ball away in your downswing and followthrough.

throughout your backswing and through the hitting zone. Then tee up a ball and hit some drives, working on the same principles. Concentrate on solid contact rather than distance.

✘ FAULT: GAINING HEIGHT DURING YOUR SWING

If you top a shot, you are raising your posture in your swing, which brings up the bottom of your swing arc to the point whereby the clubhead is close to missing the ball altogether. This comes about because you fail to maintain the posture you established at address: you are either straightening your legs or lifting your upper body during your downswing.

Posture
Maintain your spine angle from address until impact

Impact
If you maintain your original height in the swing, you are more likely to generate solid contact

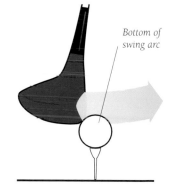

Bottom of swing arc

WHAT CAUSES A TOP?

With a top, the ball's behavior painfully reveals what happens at impact. The bottom edge of the clubhead strikes the top third of the ball. This means that the ball ends up shooting along the ground. Although you will rarely lose a topped ball, neither will you progress very far down the fairway.

LOSS OF POWER

A TOWERING DRIVE is almost certainly the most admired shot in the game. Unless your name is Tiger Woods, you no doubt aspire to hit the ball further off the tee. Lack of power off the tee, which results in poor carry with the driver, is basically down to the ball spending too much time on the ground and not enough in the air.

✗ FAULT: REVERSE PIVOT WRECKS YOUR SWING

The most likely explanation for loss of power is an incorrect weight transfer during your swing, a move often called a reverse pivot. Instead of your weight shifting on to your right side in your backswing, then transferring to your left side during your downswing and through impact, the reverse happens. Your weight shifts toward the target in your backswing (above) and away from the target in your downswing.

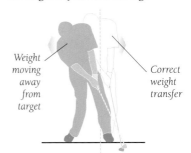

Weight moving away from target

Correct weight transfer

WHAT CAUSES LOSS OF POWER?

Insufficient power off the tee comes down to a lack of clubhead speed through the hitting area and is often caused by a reverse pivot. In this situation your weight shifts on to your front foot in the backswing and on to your back foot in the downswing and hitting zone (above). Therefore, the shift in weight that helps provide power is moving the wrong way.

Backswing
Your body should move away from the target in your backswing

Body turn
Turning your body in sympathy with the club promotes a good position at the top of your backswing

Weight transfer
As the club is swung back, transfer your weight to your back foot

70%   30%

✔ FIX: SHIFT YOUR WEIGHT TO PACK A PUNCH

To fulfill your potential power, transfer your weight in sympathy with the swinging club. Give yourself a head start by setting up with about 60 percent of your weight on your right side. Shift at least another 10 percent to your right side during your backswing, then transfer your weight on to your left foot in your downswing to maximize the force applied to the ball. Think of a boxer throwing a big punch: the weight briefly shifts to the back foot, then moves forward rapidly as the punch is thrown (see Drill 7, p.34).

○ **Remember, at the top of your backswing, there should be a 90-degree angle between your right forearm and the shaft of the club. Any wider than that and there is insufficient wrist hinge, which will result in less power (*see Drill 24, p.48*).**

WEAK SHOT FROM ROUGH

IT DOES NOT TAKE a terrible tee shot to find yourself in the rough; it could be that you have strayed from the fairway by only a few paces. The penalty is disproportionately severe, however, if you cannot produce a powerful strike and a decent ball-flight to put you back on track.

✔ FIX: POINT THE BUTT OF THE CLUB AT THE BALL

To hit strong iron shots from the rough, you have to create a steep angle of attack into impact. Use a mid-iron, and stick a tee in the hole at the butt-end of the grip. *As you make your backswing, try to point the tee at the ball by the time your hands reach hip height. This presets a more upright swing, which leads to a steeper angle of attack into impact. This means less interference from the grass around the ball, generating a more powerful strike.*

✘ FAULT: SHALLOW ATTACK TRAPS TOO MUCH GRASS

Unless your lie is horrendous, you should be able to hit a good shot with all but the long irons. If you cannot, the clubhead's angle of attack into the ball is probably too shallow, which is often the result of an overly wide takeaway with insufficient wrist hinge (above). While a shallow attack is desirable with the driver, from thick grass a steeper angle is required.

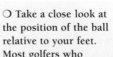

POINT THE TEE
The tee stuck in the grip of the club should point toward the ball when your hands reach waist height.

○ Take a close look at the position of the ball relative to your feet. Most golfers who struggle to hit short and mid-irons out of thick rough tend to have the ball too near their front foot at address, instead of further back as it should be (see pp.22–3).

Upright backswing
An upright backswing promotes a steep angle of attack

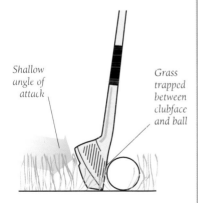

Shallow angle of attack

Grass trapped between clubface and ball

WHAT CAUSES A WEAK SHOT FROM ROUGH?

A poor strike out of the rough is often caused by too much grass being trapped between the clubface and the ball. The result is a weak, cushioned blow, which takes the "sting" out of the strike and lessens the shot's distance.

THE PUSH SHOT

THE END RESULT OF A PUSH shot is much the same as a slice: the ball finishing way off to the right. But the cause is a different story. Whereas the slice begins on a leftward path and swerves from left to right through the air, the push shot starts on a path to the right and stays right. This can happen with any club from a driver to a wedge, and it is not necessarily caused by a poorly struck shot, either. Often, contact is solid.

✔ FIX: TRAIN AN ON LINE ATTACK

The key to curing a push is to eliminate the excessive inside path of attack. Address the ball with your left toe in line with your right heel. Because your left side is already cleared out of the way (due to the very open stance), you have room to swing the club more to the left through impact. Once you have played a shot this way, try to recreate that swing from a normal stance. You should find that the ball sets off straight at the target, the sign of an online swing path.

○ Although a push can happen with any club, if you are pushing your tee shots, it is probably because the ball is too far back in your stance. This means that the club fails to reach the online portion of its arc. Put the ball opposite your left heel to help ensure that the club is traveling on the correct path at impact (*see the Key Checkpoint on p.33*).

Swing path
With your left side out of the way, it is easier to correct an in-to-out swing path

Normal feet alignment

Open stance
Hit practice shots from a very open stance to encourage an online swing of the club through impact

✗ FAULT: HITTING FROM IN-TO-OUT

The fault at the heart of a push is, in one respect, the same as for a hook (see p.187): the clubhead approaching the ball from inside the optimum swing path, and therefore traveling in-to-out through impact. The difference between the hook and the push is in the position of the clubface – for a hook, the clubface is closed to the in-to-out swing path, whereas for a push, the face is square to that same path. Hence the contrasting ball-flights.

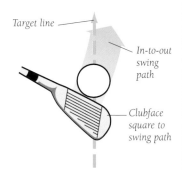

Target line

In-to-out swing path

Clubface square to swing path

WHAT CAUSES A PUSH SHOT?

A push is the result of the clubhead swinging into the ball on an exaggerated in-to-out path, with the clubface square to that (incorrect) path. These factors cause the ball to fly in a direct line, albeit one that is off course. (Note: if the clubface is open to this path, a push-slice results, whereby the ball starts right and swerves further to the right in the air.)

THE PULL SHOT

A PULL IS THE OPPOSITE of a push. The ball starts on a leftward path, because of an out-to-in swing path. It then continues on that path because the clubface is square to the out-to-in line of attack. As with the push, it can happen with any club, from a driver down to a wedge.

✔ FIX: DEVELOP AN INSIDE ATTACK

In curing a pull, it is important to appreciate the sensation of the clubhead approaching the ball from inside the target line. Draw your right foot back from this line so that your right toe is level with your left heel (make sure that your shoulders stay square, though). This stance promotes a fuller body turn and, more importantly, creates space for the club to travel on an inside path during your downswing. Try to recreate the sensation of this stroke from a normal stance. This should promote an online swing path.

○ If you are persistently pulling shots, check the alignment of your clubface at address (*see pp.20–21*). If it is closed (aiming left of target), this could be the reason for the fault.

✘ FAULT: "THROWING" THE CLUBHEAD OUTSIDE THE CORRECT LINE

A pulled shot means that your hands and arms are moving too far away from your body at the start of your downswing. You are "throwing" the club outside the ideal swing path, so that it meets the ball on an out-to-in path at impact. If the ball-flight were not evidence enough, another clue (at least with iron play) is the divot-mark, which will point to the left of the target (see Drill 9, pp.88–9).

Shoulders
Your shoulders should be parallel to the target line at address

Closed stance
Hit practice shots with your right toes aligned with your left foot's heel to promote an inside attack

Normal feet alignment

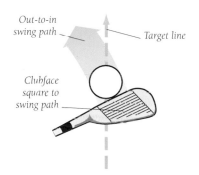

Out-to-in swing path

Target line

Clubface square to swing path

WHAT CAUSES A PULL SHOT?

As with a slice, a pull shot is the product of an out-to-in swing path. But, whereas a slice occurs if the clubface is open, a pull occurs if the clubface is square to the out-to-in path (Note: if the clubface is closed to this path, the result is what is known as a pull-hook. This shot starts left of the target and curves even further to the left in the air – a wild shot indeed.)

Chapter Three
THE ART OF SHOTMAKING

SHOTMAKING ENCOMPASSES two distinct areas of the game. There is the shot played out of necessity, as a result of a bad or unlucky previous stroke. The first part of the chapter *(see pp.198–205)* covers a number of ways to cope with these problem shots (particularly bad and awkward lies). And there is the shot played out of choice, where you call upon your golfing knowledge and powers of imagination and improvisation to shape your shots to suit the hole you are playing. The second part of the chapter *(see pp.208–11)* teaches you how to produce these shots, by altering either the ball's trajectory or direction. Sandwiched between the problem shots and the more creative shots is a section on wind play *(see pp.206–7)*, an area of the game that combines both elements of shotmaking.

RECOVERY SHOT
Every player needs good shotmaking skills –
sometimes just to escape from trouble. Here
Jack Nicklaus is playing out of a tricky situation
in the 1996 Open Championship.

SLOPING LIES

THE ONLY PLACE on a course where you can guarantee a totally level lie is on the teeing ground. Once off that manicured turf, you have to accept that the ball may well come to rest on a sloping lie, whether it be an upslope, a downslope, or a sideslope lie (where the ball is awkwardly positioned either above or below your feet).

An upslope effectively creates more loft on the club, generating additional height. This makes it a relatively easy lie to deal with. The downslope, on the other hand, deprives the club of loft and places greater demands on your ability to strike the ball cleanly. It is a trickier prospect than an upslope lie, both psychologically and technically.

Up- and downslopes each produce different flight paths. From an upslope, there is a tendency for the ball to move from right-to-left, whereas a downslope has the opposite effect, causing a left-to-right ball-flight. But do not be perturbed by such apparent difficulties. Once you have knowledge of the techniques outlined on these two pages, you

PLAYING FROM A DOWNSLOPE

This is the tougher of the up- and downslope shots because the slope deprives the club of its normal loft (see p.199). Also, because the ground is effectively higher behind the ball than from a flat lie, it is easy to strike the turf before hitting the ball ("heavy" contact). Your first consideration is club selection. On even the slightest downslope you need to "club-down": use a more lofted club, which decreases distance and gives a higher trajectory. Change from a 6-iron to a 7-iron, for example, to make up for the lack of loft caused by the slope (on a severe slope you might find there is a two-club difference). The ball tends to fly low off a downslope, running further than usual on landing. Therefore, pitch the ball short of the target to avoid overshooting.

Left side
Put more of your weight on your left side

CHASE THE BALL DOWN THE SLOPE
When the ball is on a downslope, the natural inclination is to lean back, in an effort to help the ball into the air. Resist this temptation. In your backswing, keep your weight distribution as it was at address. Then swing down the slope so that the clubhead chases after the ball through impact. Let your bodyweight go with the clubhead's flow. These factors encourage a steeper angle of attack, so that you can strike the ball cleanly (rather than leaning back and taking a large divot).

Ball position
Position yourself so that the ball is further back in your stance

KEEP THE BALL BACK
Position the ball 2–4 in (5–10 cm) farther back in your stance than it would be from a flat lie, to lessen the likelihood of heavy contact. Put slightly more weight on your front foot, and try to feel that your left shoulder is slightly lower than for a regular shot. This posture promotes a steeper swing, which will help you strike the ball cleanly.

45% 55%

Impact
There should be a descending blow into impact

45% 55%

will soon become accustomed to making informed club selections and allowances for the differences in ball-flight. Downslopes and upslopes will then hold no fear for you.

Now consider sideslope lies (see pp.200–201). In these situations, the ball will be either above or below the level of your feet, and each case places unique demands on your technique. Unless the slope is severe, having the ball above the level of your feet is not overly challenging. Indeed, your setup should feel quite comfortable at address. However, when the ball is below the level of your feet, your setup will probably feel very awkward at address and even more so in the swing – maintaining a balanced stance becomes a problem.

Coping with sloping lies is, in essence, a two-part strategy. First, you must identify what you need to do to strike the ball correctly; and second, you need to understand and make allowances for what the ball will do after impact.

PLAYING FROM AN UPSLOPE

This is considered the easier of these two up- and downslope lies. You can strike the ball cleanly without difficulty, and loft is added to the club (right), which means that the ball will fly higher and shorter than from a flat lie. Again, club selection is important: you need to "club-up." For example, if the shot would call for a 6-iron from a flat lie, club-up to a 5-iron to regain the distance that is lost when playing from an upslope. Experience will teach you to match the right club to the degree of slope.

PREPARE FOR LAUNCH

Put the ball forward in your stance (exactly how far will depend on the severity of the slope). Settle your weight on your lower foot, with a little more flex than normal in your left leg to align your hips with the ground – as they are when playing from a flat lie. The ball will tend to fly right-to-left from an upslope – aim slightly right to compensate.

REMAIN STEADY

As with the shot off a downslope, any lateral shift of your body in your backswing makes it difficult to strike the ball correctly. Therefore, keep your weight firmly anchored over your right knee as you take your backswing – do not sway any further down the slope. Your head should be steady in your downswing and you should feel that you swing the club up the slope, almost sweeping the ball away.

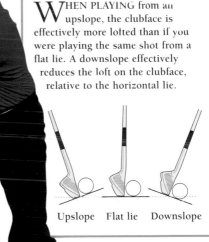

Impact
There should be a sweeping blow into impact

BALL BELOW YOUR FEET

This is the toughest of the sloping lies because it necessitates a swing from such an uncomfortable address position. The keys to success are establishing a balanced address position, and then maintaining your height through the hitting area. If you can do these two things, you should strike the ball solidly. However, you will not be able to make as powerful a swing as from a flat lie, therefore use a less-lofted club to make up the extra distance.

KEEP THE WEIGHT ON YOUR HEELS

When the ball is below your feet, adjust your posture to facilitate a solid strike. "Sit down" a little at address by flexing your knees, and widen your stance to further enhance your sense of balance. Because the ball is lower than usual, stand a fraction closer to it so that you are not overstretching. Because the ball will fly from left-to-right off this type of lie, aim left of the target to compensate.

SWING SMOOTHLY TO PROMOTE GOOD BALANCE

With sloping lies it is important that you swing smoothly and do not overextend yourself – this is certainly the case when the ball is below your feet. Keep your knees flexed and make an "arms-dominated" swing to help you keep your balance. The slope tends to force your weight downhill, which can produce a shank (see p.189). To counter this problem, keep your weight back on your heels as you swing.

(see p.189)

KEY CHECKPOINT

ADJUST THE CLUBFACE AIM

ONE OF THE EFFECTS of playing from above or below your feet is that the ball tends to deviate to the right or left through the air. As discussed, you can allow for this by altering your alignment. But an alternative is to change the aim of the clubface. When the ball is above your feet, open the clubface to counter the ball's right-to-left flight. And when the ball is below your feet, close the clubface to fight the left-to-right flight path.

Arms
Let your arms do the majority of the work in your swing

Legs
Flex your legs and stand a little closer to the ball to avoid overstretching

BALL ABOVE YOUR FEET

This is probably the easiest of all four sloping-lie shots, partly because the address position will feel comfortable but also because the slope does not hinder your ball-striking. What you do need to be wary of is the ball flight, which can be quite "hot" (less backspin and lots of forward momentum) from this type of lie. The ball also travels on a powerful right-to-left flight path. Therefore, it is always wise to club down to decrease distance and to aim right of the target.

STAND TALL; CHOKE DOWN
With this sort of shot, the ball is effectively raised Therefore, on a severe slope, shorten the club by choking down on the grip and standing more erect at address. To maintain your balance as you swing, settle your weight a little more toward your toes.

ALLOW FOR A ROUNDED SWING
From this kind of setup and from this type of slope, your swing will be a little more rounded than usual. This means that your hands will not rise as high above your shoulders as with a regular swing. Other than that, there is nothing to worry about with this shot. Just take a smooth swing, maintaining your height and balance to produce a solid strike.

Stance
Stand more upright than for a flat lie, with your weight more on your toes

Grip
Choke down on the grip to effectively reduce the length of the club

TACKLING PROBLEM SHOTS

IN GOLF'S EARLY days, when the only greenskeepers were the sheep grazing on the land, virtually every shot – bar the drive and putt – might have been considered problem shots. Nowadays, modern greenskeeping equipment produces nicely manicured playing surfaces, and bad lies are less frequent. But inevitably they still occur, and it is important to be able to deal with these tricky situations. The process of playing a successful shot from a problem spot can be separated into three stages.

First, assess the lie of the ball and decide what effect it might have on your club selection. For example, some lies in the rough are so bad that – in order to obtain the loft necessary to dig the ball out of thick grass – all but the short irons are ruled out. In such cases you have to forget distance and play for position instead. Ultimately, the shot you choose to play must reflect the limitations of the lie.

Secondly, picture the shot in your mind's eye. If the target is within range, think where you want to pitch the ball, and try to envisage how the ball will react on landing. Or, if you are playing a lay-up shot (in which you want to find a position for a simple chip or pitch onto the green), focus on a spot that should give you a good lie for your next shot.

Thirdly, commit yourself to the shot you have elected to play, and trust the club you have chosen. Do not let doubt creep into your mind. Here are three of the most common bad lies. But if you apply this three-part strategy, you should, with practice, find that such lies need not cost you dearly.

SHOT FROM A BARE LIE

This is one of the toughest shots in golf, and the closer you are to the green, the more difficult the task. Even the slightest mishit can be heavily punished from a bare lie. For this reason, the challenge is to produce a perfectly clean strike, trapping the ball between the clubface and the ground.

PRESET A CLEAN STRIKE
Never use a sand wedge from a bare lie, as the rounded sole tends to bounce off the ground into the middle of the ball. All other clubs have a sharper leading edge, which sits flush to the ground. To further promote a clean strike, position the ball roughly 1 in (2.5 cm) further back in your stance than for a normal fairway shot.

STEADY INTO IMPACT
As you take the shot, trust your setup and swing to deliver the leading edge of the clubhead into the bottom of the ball. This should create a low trajectory but plenty of backspin because there is less interference between the clubface and ball at impact. This means that the ball will stop quickly on landing.

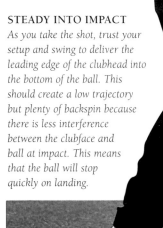

Rhythm
Maintain good balance by taking a smooth swing with good rhythm

Clean strike
Do not try to help the ball into the air, but rather trust the loft on the club to do the job for which it was designed

PLAYING OUT OF A DIVOT-MARK

When your ball lands in an old divot-mark, the chances are it is when you have just hit a nice shot down the middle of the fairway – such is the nature of the game. But unless the divot mark is very deep, this is by no means a hopeless situation. Start by taking out a more-lofted club than if you were playing from the same distance with a good lie.

BALL BACK; HANDS FORWARD
Position the ball almost opposite your right heel and align your hands with your left thigh. This will promote an almost V-shaped swing, where the clubhead travels steeply into impact.

IT IS ALL IN THE WRISTS
To promote the necessary angle of attack in your downswing, hinge your wrists abruptly in your takeaway so that the club travels steeply upward. Then hit down hard into the back of the ball. Imagine that you are trying to drive the ball down even deeper into the ground. You will need to keep a firm hold of the club, as the force of impact is severe. (The followthrough is kept short with this shot.) Expect a low trajectory with lots of run on landing. Because of this, be aware of trouble spots beyond the back of the green. Because the ball will tend to have a left-to-right flight path, aim a little left of the target to accommodate the swerving ball flight.

IRON SHOT FROM THICK ROUGH

Light rough presents the accomplished golfer with very few problems, as all you need to do is allow for less backspin (as you cannot strike the ball cleanly) and, therefore, a little more run on landing. Thick rough, however, severely limits your options. Determine the longest club you can hit, and if you can reach the green with that, fine. But if you cannot, accept your fate and play a well placed lay-up shot instead. Either way, you should apply the following principles of successful deep-rough play.

ORGANIZE YOUR SETUP
If your setup is not correct, no amount of muscle will pull you out of trouble. Put the ball in the middle of your stance. Then aim the clubface at the target. Keep your weight evenly balanced, maybe even slightly favoring your left foot if the lie is terrible. Align your feet about 15–20 degrees left of the target (at 11 o'clock if you imagine the target at 12 o'clock). This type of stance goes some way to presetting a steep downswing attack, which is essential for decent contact.

PUNCH DOWN AND THROUGH
To further promote a steep attack, swing your hands up a little higher in your backswing. Then swing the clubhead steeply into the back of the ball. However, even if you achieve a perfect technique, you will still need to put a little bit more effort into this shot at impact – use a powerful strike and try to shift a sizable chunk of grass from around the ball.

CONJURING EFFECTIVE ESCAPE SHOTS

HAVING HIT a ball into trouble, all too often the tendency is to opt for an inappropriate recovery shot, sometimes attempting wildly ambitious escapes that even a tour professional would think twice about playing. The result usually turns the situation from bad to worse. When in doubt, it is usually best to play safe.

However, there are occasions when it is necessary to take a *calculated* risk and play an attacking escape shot. You might, for example, be in a matchplay situation (*see pp.236–7*) in which taking a penalty drop would probably cost you the

hole and maybe the match. Or you might be playing a friendly game and testing the limits of your ability.

Here are three great escape shots for when you have a difficult lie close to a tree or near a cluster of bushes or trees. This is a common problem, and one that most golfers can, with a little practice, negotiate successfully. (Whereas playing from, for example, ditches or water are tasks best left to the professionals.) Even these three shots may seem tricky at first, but, if you follow the advice outlined on these two pages, you should soon become proficient.

A STRAIGHT-ARMED SWING
Swing your right arm back and through like a pendulum, and accelerate the clubhead into the back of the ball. The shot calls for a straight-armed swing, and wrist action should be virtually nonexistent as it increases the likelihood of a miss. Do not swing your hand above waist height, and settle for a maximum range of 38–49 yd (35–45 m).

AWKWARD OBSTRUCTION

This shot is handy when the ball comes to rest at the base of a tree-trunk in a position that makes it impossible for you to take up your usual stance – the tree is precisely where you would normally stand. A penalty drop may seem like the only option, but not if you learn how to play the back-handed chop.

ADDRESS POSITION
Select one of your more lofted clubs, as they have a broader hitting area than a long iron. Turn your back on the target, and stand with the ball 6 in (15 cm) outside your right foot. Hold the grip with your right hand only, and twist the club around so that it sits on its toe-end, the clubface still looking at the target. Your arm should be relatively straight, hanging by your side.

Impact
Make sure that you accelerate the clubhead into the ball at impact

RESTRICTED BACKSWING

It is quite common on heavily wooded courses for a wayward ball to come to rest in a spot where your backswing is restricted by branches. Making a normal swing is out of the question as the club would become tangled, which often results in an air shot (where you miss the ball entirely). The following technique shows you how to avoid the branches and how to generate sufficient power, so that you will hit the ball well up the fairway.

A LOW ADDRESS POSITION

This shot revolves around the principle of dramatically lowering and reducing your swing arc. Start by taking a severely wide stance, spreading your feet at least double the distance of your normal setup. Then choke down on the grip so that your right hand touches the metal of the shaft. These two factors ensure that the club will not be anywhere near as high as normal at the top of your backswing.

TAKE A NARROW SWING

To reduce your swing arc, use maximum wrist hinge. At the top of your backswing, your hands should be around chest height so that the clubhead does not rise too far. This enables you to make an unimpeded downswing. More lofted clubs, which have short shafts, are ideal for this shot.

IN THE TREES

If the ball has come to rest among a cluster of trees or in the clear behind a large thicket, making a normal swing is usually not a problem. The difficulty you face is having to thread the ball through the tangle of branches in your path. As you eye the gaps, there are several factors to bear in mind.

USE A STANDARD TRAJECTORY

First and foremost, you should always try to find an approach that allows you to play a normal shot. Look for gaps that suit the natural loft of a particular club, rather than manufacturing a punchy low shot or a fantastically high lofted shot, which is riskier.

FRAME YOUR GAP

Take a moment to frame a gap in your mind's eye, and pick the club that will produce the required trajectory (see Drill 26, p.77). Try to avoid tiny openings, and select a patch of fairway or green in the distance that does not place extra demands on the bounce and run of the ball. If you can take as normal a swing as possible, you stand a better chance of success.

BETTER WIND PLAY

A ROUND OF GOLF in the wind presents a greater challenge than playing on a calm day, but breezy conditions need not blow you completely off course. Assessing the conditions – knowing which way the wind is blowing – is something you will need to recheck as you work your way around the turns and contours of the course. There are many clues all around you: glance up at the sky to see which way the clouds are moving; look at the treetops and note which way they are swaying; maybe even check the flag on an adjacent hole. Some tour professionals take a miniature map of the course, such as the one on the back of the scorecard, and draw an arrow across it indicating the wind direction. This gives them a broad reference throughout the round.

Assessing the conditions is all very well, but hitting the right shots for the conditions is ultimately what counts. That is the area focused on here. Contained on this spread are a handful of ideas that will improve your performance when the wind blows.

Wind

Wide stance
When hitting into the wind, widen your stance for greater stability

SWINGING SMOOTHLY OFF THE TEE

The temptation when you are hitting a driver into the wind is to swing harder than normal. This will probably cause you to lose your balance, leading to a poor ball-strike and loss of distance and accuracy. To achieve good balance, widen your stance, moving your feet 5 in (13 cm) farther apart than normal. This also helps shorten your swing slightly, promoting a more compact movement and a solid strike. Do not tee the ball too low, as this often causes you to swing down more steeply into impact, causing the ball to balloon upward into the wind. However, you should tee the ball a fraction lower than normal to promote a slightly lower flight (although it is important that you continue to focus on sweeping the ball away).

Hitting downwind, however, extends the ball flight, and you might want to select a 3-wood off the tee, as the extra loft maximizes the height of the ball and, therefore, the wind's influence on it.

SOLID FOUNDATIONS
One of the main problems when playing in a strong wind is being blown off balance. Widening your stance gives you a more stable foundation, which promotes a steadier stance.

Wind

Club selection
Take a less-lofted club so that the ball's trajectory is kept low

KEEP THE BALL LOW

There is no point in playing a high ball into a strong wind. You will struggle to judge distance, the ball is easily blown off line, and you will have little control over the outcome of your shot. For these reasons, you have to keep the ball low. This means opting for a less-lofted club than you would other- wise use. If, for example, you are 150 yd (135 m) from the flag and that represents a normal 7-iron shot, club-up to a 5-iron and swing more easily. Obviously the strength of the wind dictates how much you club-up, but experience will tell you the difference between a one-club, a two-club, or even a three-club wind.

COMPENSATING FOR WIND
When playing a shot into the wind, club-up to produce a lower ball flight, and remember the old adage: "swing with ease into the breeze."

SHAPE YOUR SHOT OR ADJUST YOUR AIM

In a crosswind you have two options. If you are proficient at shaping the ball with sidespin, work the ball into the wind. In a left-to-right breeze, for example, play a draw (see p.210), and in a right-to-left breeze go with a fade (see p.211). These measures should produce an almost straight shot, although distance is sacrificed for accuracy and control.

Alternatively, play a straight shot in which you make allowance for the crosswind by aiming left or right of the target, accordingly. The ball will carry about one club further on the wind, and will not sit down as quickly as a shot shaped into the wind.

CROSSWINDS

If, for example, the wind is blowing from right to left, you have two choices: you can play a fade, so that the ball holds its line, or you can aim right and let the wind blow the ball back toward the target.

Aim right
An alternative to the fade is to aim right and allow the wind to carry the ball leftward

Wind

Fade
A shot hit with fade fights against the wind, resulting in an almost straight ball flight

WIDEN YOUR PUTTING STANCE

The act of putting involves such a precise movement that even the slightest buffeting from the wind can upset the path and pace of your stroke. Widen your stance by up to 50 percent more than normal – this gives you a solid foundation. Also choke down on the grip so that you are more crouched over the ball. This lowers your center of gravity so that you are less susceptible to the effects of the wind. Hit a few practice putts to familiarize yourself with the new stance. Your stroke stays the same, so it should not feel too strange.

REMAIN STEADY

The main challenge when putting in a strong wind is to maintain a steady head and body position. If you are able to do this, you will be able to make a smooth, online stroke. If you widen your stance and choke down on the grip, you will find it easier to hold constant body and head positions.

WIND INFLUENCES BREAK AND SPEED

Few golfers take into account the fact that a strong wind affects the ball's journey as it moves along the green. A crosswind either exaggerates or cancels out the break on a putt; a tail wind makes a putt run faster; and a headwind slows the ball down. You have to allow for these factors when you read each putt, even from short range. This becomes a bit of a balancing act, but, if you are aware of the wind's speed and direction, you can take steps to compensate for its effects.

WIND BREAK

It is a very good idea to take into account the wind's influence when you are putting. If you do not, your shot will probably miss. This is because a strong wind makes a difference to the break and speed of a putt, especially on fast, well-manicured putting surfaces.

HOW TO HIT HIGH AND LOW SHOTS

NOW THAT PROBLEM shots have been covered, as well as the up and down world of wind play, it is time to move on to the more favorable string in a shotmaker's bow: creative shots.

While a full set of clubs offers a wide array of lofts, all designed to generate shots of various trajectories, there are occasions when it is desirable to manipulate the natural loft of a club in order to work the ball into the flag on a higher or lower flight path. Sometimes this is a better option than changing to a more- or less-lofted club. Imagination plays a large part when it comes to fine-tuning trajectory:

LOFTING THE BALL HIGH

Launching the ball high into the air toward the target is a useful skill in certain situations. One such example is when you are playing downwind and want to maximize distance with a long iron. Another scenario might be when the flag is placed close to the front of the green and is guarded by a bunker: then you would want to bring the ball down from a greater height to encourage it to sit down quickly.

Hands finish high
Finish the stroke with your hands held high to reflect the intention of sending the ball on a high trajectory

Head back
Your head should stay behind the ball for a little longer than usual through the hitting zone

SWING NORMALLY AND FINISH HIGH
You can now make what feels like a regular swing, trusting your adjusted set-up to produce the desired impact factors. As you swing the club, ensure that your head stays behind the ball for longer than normal in the downswing and hitting zone. Also, let your followthrough reflect your intentions by finishing with your hands held high.

ADD LOFT TO THE CLUB
In the situations outlined above, taking a more lofted club will not give you sufficient distance. Instead, use the club you would normally hit, and take these steps to effectively increase the loft. First, put the ball a little more forward in your stance, as this has the effect of increasing the loft on the clubface by a few degrees. Also stand a little closer to the ball, with a more erect posture. This leads to a slightly more upright swing, which generates extra height on the ball flight.

a good shotmaker can look from the ball to the target and visualize several different aerial routes, which offer up a host of attacking and defensive options. On the other hand, golfers who passively accept the constraints of the manufacturer's loft miss out on a range of shots that are fun and rewarding to play. These shots also help golfers reach the proximity of the flag or achieve a well-placed lay-up shot when a conventional stroke could not.

It is worth pointing out that the likes of Seve Ballesteros and Lee Trevino became such remarkable shotmakers and good all-around players because they started playing the game with less than a full set of clubs. Take their lead and play the occasional practice round with only three or four iron clubs in your bag. You may at first feel restricted by the lack of choice, but such an exercise teaches you a great deal about the game. It improves your imagination and skill for inventing shots, which will make you a more complete golfer. Aside from these benefits for your game, it is also great fun.

PUNCHING THE BALL LOW

*T*he *"knockdown-punch shot," as it is often called, is suited to a variety of situations. As was mentioned in the section on wind play (see pp.206–7), this type of stroke is a great weapon to have at your disposal when playing into a strong headwind, helping the ball hold its line. It is also useful when you want to pitch a ball short of the green and let it run up to the flag.*

Followthrough
Keep your followthrough low to reflect your desire to produce a low ball flight

DRIVE THE BALL AND FINISH LOW
Try to sweep the club away low to the ground and make a shorter, more compact backswing than normal. Do not forget to turn your shoulders, though. Then, in your downswing, keep your torso over the ball at impact, and swing the clubhead low to the ground through the hitting zone. Again, your followthrough should reflect the ball flight: your hands should stay low in the finish.

Torso
You should sense that your torso is over the ball as you sweep the ball away through the hitting zone

REDUCE THE LOFT ON THE CLUB
The ball needs to go back in your stance by as much as three ball widths, which has the effect of delofting the clubface by several degrees. Also push your hands even further forward than normal so that the shaft is angled toward the target. In doing so, you have to be careful that the clubface does not become open. Turn in the toe of the clubhead slightly to ensure that the face is looking at the target. Your weight at address should be evenly spread.

Two Simple Ways to Shape Your Shots

THERE ARE MANY FACETS to the shotmaker's art, and there are times when it can be helpful to shape the ball through the air. You might, for example, want to bend a ball around a dogleg fairway, avoid a tree blocking your path to the flag, or seek out a cunningly positioned flag. However, the majority of golfers view shaping shots as beyond their ability, regarding the techniques involved as for experts only. Indeed, whenever a ball moves left or right through the air, many view this as a poor shot, failing to appreciate the potential benefits of a swerving ball.

The laws of physics explain why a ball flies through the air the way it does. Basically, ball flight is determined by the clubhead's path in the swing and the aim of the clubface relative

SHAPING SHOTS WITH A DRAW

A draw is the perfect shot when the flag is located in the left corner of the green. Aiming straight at the target is risky because there is so little margin for error left of the flag. But, if you aim to the right of the flag and "draw" the ball in toward the target, the risks are less. If the ball flies straight, you hit middle of the green – no disaster there – and, if the ball draws according to plan, you are looking at a short putt. Even if you pull the shot a little left of where you were aiming, the chances are you will still find the left edge of the green.

Aim

Feet alignment

ALIGN RIGHT; FACE SQUARE
The key to playing a draw lies largely in changing your setup. If you want to swing the ball from right-to-left through the air, align your feet, hips, and shoulders right of the target. The more you want to draw the ball, the further right you stand. Then aim the clubface straight at the target. Also position the ball a little farther back in your stance than is normal for whichever club you are using.

RELEASE THE CLUB AGGRESSIVELY
A draw requires an aggressive release of the club, whereby the right hand rolls over the left. The alignment of your stance encourages an in-to-out swing path through impact, parallel to the line of your feet. And the clubface (which is closed in relation to your stance at address) will be closed to this path at impact, imparting "draw-spin" on the ball. This causes the ball to start right of the target and drift from right-to-left through the air.

to this path. These two elements combine to impart sidespin on the ball, which in turn makes the ball deviate one way or the other. Controlling these impact factors allows you to shape your shots.

So how do you exert control over a clubhead when it is swinging at speeds up to, and sometimes in excess of, 100 mph (160 kph)? Well, it largely comes down to what you do at address. Providing you introduce the necessary alterations, your swing is not that different from the norm. It does, however, take practice to reach a stage where you have the confidence to play these shots on the course. As you practice, bear in mind that the less loft there is on the club, the easier it is to shape the ball. This is because a relatively straight-faced club, which has very little loft, will always impart more sidespin than backspin on the ball, therefore making it easier to bend the flight of the ball. A lofted iron, however, creates more backspin and less sidespin, reducing the bend on the ball. Also, you need a good lie to shape a ball. Out of the rough, therefore, it is nearly impossible to make a strike clean enough to impart the necessary sidespin.

SHAPING SHOTS WITH A FADE

A fade is useful when dangers lurk on the right-hand side of the green (a bunker or water hazard, for example) or if the flag is tucked away on the right side. If the penalty for missing the green on the right side is more severe than missing it on the left, aiming to the left of the flag and playing a fade is the smart shot. If the stroke goes according to plan, you will finish close to the hole. If you stray slightly one side or other of the perfect line, you will most likely still hit the green. Even in the worst scenario, the ball will probably land to the left of the green, forcing you to make a straightforward chip onto the putting surface.

USE AN OPEN CLUBFACE
Now take what feels like a regular swing. The path of your swing through impact reflects your alignment, and so the clubhead swings along the line of your feet on an out-to-in path. The clubface will return to its position at address (open to this swing path), imparting sidespin so that the shot starts left and then fades right. This shot travels about one club less than a draw and stops quickly on landing, which is useful when the greens are firm or the landing area is small.

Aim

Feet alignment

ALIGN LEFT; FACE SQUARE
To make the ball move on a left-to-right flight path, the address position is almost opposite to that required for a draw. You do aim the clubface straight at the target (as with a draw), but you must align your feet, hips, and shoulders slightly left of the target (essentially, an open stance). Also, position the ball a touch further forward in your stance at address — just one ball-width more than normal is usually enough.

Chapter Four
PLAYING THE GAME

CONVERTING THE POTENTIAL you show on the practice ground into a low score on the course depends on many factors that go beyond the process of striking the ball. This chapter explores these fascinating areas. You will discover the key elements of successful course management, which is essentially the art of moving the ball from A to B with minimum fuss and maximum effectiveness. The chapter will also help you think more clearly on the course, which will improve your decision-making and will enable you to cope better with nerves and pressure situations. You will also learn about a host of other often overlooked ways of becoming a more consistent and competitive golfer, such as improving your psychological approach.

THE 13ᵀᴴ AT AUGUSTA
Playing golf means making decisions: on this hole you can play safely (short of the green in two shots – as Howard Clark has done here), leaving yourself a short pitch; or you can go for the green in two shots and risk landing in a hazard.

WARMING UP BEFORE A ROUND

JUST AS AN ENGINE needs to warm up before it can perform at its best, so too do your muscles, tendons, and joints. To avoid damaging these body parts, you must warm up in whatever way your schedule allows. Here are some stretching exercises and three routines of different lengths (designed to suit the time you have allowed before stepping onto the first tee). Apart from the threat of injury, walking on to the first tee cold can be bad for your score because the first two or three holes effectively become your practice range.

STRETCHING EXERCISES

The following stretches will loosen the tension in your muscles, increase the flow of blood around your body, and prepare you for the round ahead. Fit as many exercises into your warm-up as time permits, and repeat each ten times.

SWINGING WITH TWO CLUBS

When time is short, practicing with two clubs is a valuable exercise that helps prepare your muscles and joints for a proper swing.

Upper arm
Your upper arm should resist the pull of your lower – this flexes your shoulder muscles

Knees
Keep your knees flexed to imitate the feeling of a proper swing

Hips
Bend from the hips to loosen your back and hamstrings

Arms
Use your arms to help stretch the arch of your back

BODY PIVOTS
Assume a good golfing posture (see pp.24–5), and hold a club across the back of your shoulders. Pivot your body to the right to simulate a backswing and then swing back to the left to simulate a downswing and followthrough. You should feel your upper body rotating over the resistance of your lower half.

SIDE-BENDS
With your arms above your head, grasp the ends of a club in both hands. Slowly bend from your waist to the left and then to the right, in each case pulling down with your lower hand and resisting with your upper hand. This will stretch the muscles in your torso and along your spine. It will also loosen your shoulders.

TOUCHING TOES
With your arms hanging straight down, hold the shaft of a club in both hands. Bend from the waist, and gently lower the club toward the ground while keeping your legs straight. You should feel some tension in your hamstrings. Go down as far as you can manage comfortably, then slowly return to a standing position.

BACK ARCHES
Arching your back is an exercise that usefully complements touching your toes. Stand upright, hold a club above your head, and arch your spine backward. Pause for a few seconds, and return to your original position. Slow repetition of this exercise will stretch the muscles in your lower back.

THE ONE-MINUTE WARM-UP

I F YOU HAVE left yourself very little time before the start of a round, use this quick routine to minimize the chances of muscle and tendon damage. With only a minute to go, the key is to loosen-up the most injury-sensitive areas of your body. Hold a club across your shoulders and rehearse some body-pivots. This stretches your back muscles, and has the added benefit of replicating the movement required in a golf swing. Then, make some rhythmical practice swings holding two clubs. Attempt to simulate a proper swing rather than half-heartedly swishing the clubs back and forth, and try to complete a balanced followthrough. If you can do that with two clubs, you can certainly do it with one.

THE 10-MINUTE WARM-UP

A S YOU UNDOUBTEDLY know, anything can happen with the first few shots of the day; therefore, it is wise to play some settling-in strokes before you go out on the course. Start with a little stretching – body-pivots, side-bends, and touching toes – if possible. Then hit some chip shots.

The great teacher Harvey Penick believed that these were the ideal shots for a warm up if time was short. They sharpen you up mentally and put you in tune with your game. And all the while you are playing your chips, you are improving your feel for the club.

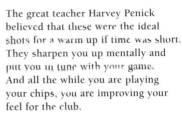

CHIPPING *If facilities allow for it, practicing your chipping is an excellent way to prepare for a round, especially if time is limited. Make sure that you vary your targets and the lie of the ball in order to promote good touch.*

THE 30-MINUTE WARM-UP

F EW GOLFERS GIVE themselves this much time for a warm-up, but 30 minutes can make a tremendous difference to your performance. Once again, start with some stretching exercises, and in this case you can work through all four laid out on the opposite page. Then hit some soft

pitch shots to fine-tune the pace of your swing, focusing solely on solid contact and a smooth rhythm.

Do not fall into the trap of thinking that being ready is all about the number of balls you hit on the range. Make your practice sessions physically undemanding but mentally focused.

Hit quality shots that mean something, thereby establishing good rhythm and boosting your confidence.

Having hit a few pitch shots, go on to play about a dozen mid-iron shots, and then turn your attention to the driver, hitting shots at about 70–80 percent power. As with the pitch shots, focus on rhythm, balance, and making solid contact out of the center of the clubface. Try to give each shot as much attention as you would during a round.

Then change down a few gears to hit some gentle chip shots. Follow that by taking three balls and hitting putts to different points around a green, developing your feel for speed. Finally, knock in a few putts from close range to bolster your confidence prior to going to the first tee (*see Drill 10, p.167*).

USE YOUR TIME WISELY *When practicing, do not hit as many balls as possible. Instead hit half as many with twice the thought and application.*

THE VALUE OF A PRE-SHOT ROUTINE

JACK NICKLAUS, perhaps the greatest golfer who ever lived, had a perfect way of summing up the importance of the address position: "If you set up correctly, there is a good chance you will hit a reasonable shot, even if you make a mediocre swing … If you set up incorrectly, you will hit a lousy shot even if you make the greatest swing in the world." The great man is, of course, absolutely right. And there is no better way to set up correctly than by developing a reliable pre-shot routine. Every tour professional uses such a ploy, whereas just about every club golfer does not.

Learning and repeating a routine gives you the best possible chance of addressing the ball correctly for every shot. Everybody's routine will vary in content and length, but the key point is to rehearse it so often that it becomes second nature to you.

The elements that follow, which are taken from the pre-shot routines of the stars, may sound like a lot to remember prior to taking a shot. But, if you develop and rehearse a routine during practice, you will be amazed how soon it becomes habit. A routine, which should take no longer than 20–30 seconds, will help you apply yourself equally to every shot, which is one of the keys to playing well under pressure.

PREPARING FOR A SHOT

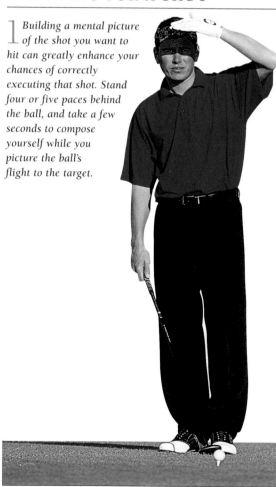

1 *Building a mental picture of the shot you want to hit can greatly enhance your chances of correctly executing that shot. Stand four or five paces behind the ball, and take a few seconds to compose yourself while you picture the ball's flight to the target.*

2 *Take one or two smooth practice swings. As you do so, concentrate on your rhythm, and try to match the physical feelings throughout your body to your mental images of the shot. This has the effect of focusing your intuitive hand-eye coordination.*

Swing rehearsal
Your practice swing should be as close as possible to the shot you intend to take

Body movement
Tune in to the physical sensations, from the turning motion of your body to the free swing of the club

3 If you are under pressure or nervous, your heart rate will quicken, and adrenaline will start to flow. One negative aspect of these natural reactions is that you inevitably hasten your movements. And if your swing becomes hurried, you can lose the rhythm necessary for a decent shot. A useful device that many good players employ is to take a couple of deep breaths before addressing the ball. This relaxes the muscles in your body, and gives you a feeling of calm.

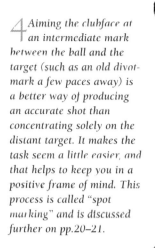

4 Aiming the clubface at an intermediate mark between the ball and the target (such as an old divot-mark a few paces away) is a better way of producing an accurate shot than concentrating solely on the distant target. It makes the task seem a little easier, and that helps to keep you in a positive frame of mind. This process is called "spot marking" and is discussed further on pp.20–21.

5 Step into your address position with your grip already formed on the club, alternately fixing your sights on the intermediate target and the target itself. Aim the clubface at your intermediate target and, assuming you want to hit a straight shot, build a stance that is parallel with the aim of the clubface. Your feet, hips, and shoulders should then be square to the ball-to-target line. Now you are ready to go.

Hands
To relieve tension in your hands, waggle the club back and forth at address

KEY CHECKPOINT

ROLE MODELS

WHEN WATCHING a tournament on television, it is easy to become caught up in the excitement of a spectacular shot – a soaring drive, a brilliant chip, or a long putt – but it is also worth paying attention to the way top golfers prepare to hit a shot. There is a great deal you can learn from them in this department of the game. Watch how the professionals approach the ball, and note how they never seem to rush. They stay calm and keep their movements smooth and unhurried. Also, if anything distracts them during their pre-shot routine, they start again. This ensures that they are always mentally ready to take on each shot.

STRATEGY OFF THE TEE

GOLF IS AS MUCH about strategy as execution. Every shot you face involves a decision of some kind, and that is as important as the swing you take. Arguably, it is the most underestimated, under-practiced aspect of the game. Yet there is no surer way to lower your average scores in a round than by exercising your gray matter before and during play.

The decision-making processes on the tee are vital to your chances of playing a good drive. Anyone who tees the ball up with little regard to placement and then merrily aims on a general path down the middle of the fairway is missing out on an opportunity to make the game easier. By adopting certain strategies and avoiding others, you can increase the average number of fairways you hit and, just as importantly, dramatically reduce destructive tee shots, which all contribute to a high score.

THE TEEING AREA

Knowing how to shape your shots (see pp.210–11) enables you to avoid danger on one side of the hole or the other. However, most golfers have a natural shape to their shots – either a slight fade or draw. If you are aware of this, you can make allowances. For example, if your natural shot is a fade, tee up on the right, and aim down the left side of the fairway. If the ball flies straight, you should still hit the fairway; if the

ball fades according to plan, you will be right in the middle of the fairway. Even if the ball fades more than you planned, you should hit the fairway, or the light rough at worst. Similarly, if your natural shape is a draw, tee up on the left, and aim down the right side of the fairway. Smart thinking on the tee effectively widens your margin for error.

TEE-SHOT STRATEGY
When playing a hole with a dogleg to the right (as shown here), hitting your drive with a small amount of fade is a good idea. Also, consider your placement of the ball on the tee so that you can utilize the full width of the teeing area. This will effectively widen your target area and increase the margin for error.

MAKE A GOOD
FIRST IMPRESSION

Hitting the first tee shot of the day safely down the middle of the fairway is important for your mental well-being, and it also lets your opponent know that you will be a tough competitor. Try to select a club with which you are confident

of striking a solid and straight shot. This helps you feel in control of your game. Your first priority should be keeping the ball in play, even if this means sacrificing distance. The last thing you want to begin the day is a wild drive into trouble. It is a stressful way to start a round and will almost certainly cost you a

couple of shots. Remember, you cannot win a competition on the first few holes, but you can easily ruin your score if you make a horrendous start to the game.

SHAPE YOUR DRIVES
AROUND DOGLEGS

Dogleg fairways are a common feature on many courses. A hole with a dogleg is an ideal opportunity to use your shotmaking skills to your advantage. If the fairway curves to the right, a drive hit with a hint of fade will hug the bend and run around the corner. On a hole that curves to the left, a drive hit with draw enables you to shape the ball around the opposite corner.

AVOID OUT-OF-BOUNDS

Any tee shot with an obvious threat of out-of-bounds is tough, mentally more than technically. With these tee shots you have to avoid taking risks, and should try to put your mind at ease. First, play with a club you feel comfortable using. Even if this puts the green out of range for your next shot, you can still chip and putt for par, and the worst score you might make is a bogey. Knock the ball out-of-bounds off the tee, however, and you could end up with a double bogey, or worse. Second, stick with your pre-shot routine (see pp.216–17). Remember, in golf, familiarity breeds confidence, and a pre-shot routine can put you at ease.

Finally, aim away from the trouble: if the out-of-bounds is on the left, tee-up on the left and aim right; and vice versa if the trouble spot is on the right. Commit yourself completely to the shot you have opted to play, and do not think about the out-of-bounds area. This might all sound too easy to be true, but that is often the nature of the game. Keeping things simple and playing with safety in mind can make all the difference.

ON THE FAIRWAY AND IN THE ROUGH

MAKING A GOOD decision on the tee and hitting a solid drive is an important start. But it is, nevertheless, only a start. Once the tee shot is away, you then have to turn your attention to the second shot. If you are on a par 3, your second shot should be a putt; but on the longer holes, you will be aiming to hit the green or find a good position further up the fairway with your second shot.

These two pages focus on some typical situations where using your brain can save you shots. As your game improves, you will realize more and more that shooting a low score is not about all-out attack. Indeed, a good round of golf can frequently be attributed as much to the overly ambitious shots you do not hit as to the terrific shots you do. Golf requires good judgment as well as great skill.

TURN PAR 5s INTO A THREE-PART STRATEGY

Many golfers are intimidated by long holes. But a simple change in approach will show you that par 5s are among the easiest holes on the course. The key is to separate a long hole into easily manageable sections: treat the hole as if it is in three parts. The only requirement of your tee shot is that you keep the ball in play. A length of around 195–220 yd (180–200 m) – which for most golfers is achievable with a lofted wood – is more than adequate. Approach your second shot in a similar way: put to the back of your mind all thoughts of hitting the ball as far as possible – instead, focus on position. Keep the ball

PLAN YOUR STRATEGY
Use a course planner to work out how you intend to play the hole. Rethink the challenge of a par 5 as a short series of mini-challenges. Put simply – divide and conquer.

in play and remember that, on all but the longest par 5, a controlled 195-yd (180-m) second shot will leave you with little more than a short-to-medium iron to the green. A birdie-putt is then one easy step away, and you will have reached such a position without having taken the slightest risk.

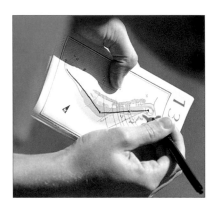

AVOID "SUCKER" PIN PLACEMENTS

A typical example of a sucker pin placement would be a pin on the right-hand edge of the green closely guarded by a deep bunker to the right. Another might be a pin at the front-edge of a green protected by water. In such situations, you only have to stray off-line by a few paces – not a terrible shot by any means – for the penalty to be severe. Do not be tempted into attacking the pin: whenever you see a sucker pin placement, aim for the center of the green, giving yourself a comfortable margin for error. If you take this theory to its logical conclusion (hitting every approach shot at the center of all 18 greens in a round), you might be surprised how well you score, as even slightly stray shots stand a better chance of finishing on the green.

AIM DEAD CENTER
If, as here, the pin is placed close to a left-hand bunker, ignore the flag and aim for the center of the green. A long putt is a better prospect than a tough bunker shot.

OBSERVE A 10-PACE RULE IN DEEP ROUGH

Most golfers are too ambitious with their shots from deep rough. As a general rule, if you cannot see the ball from 10 paces, you should think about pitching the ball safely into the middle of the fairway, where you will be back in control of your game. This reduces the chances of making a high score on the hole. If, however, you go with a longer club and try to hit the green from a terrible lie, the odds are in favor of a mishit. The ball could go anywhere: if you are lucky, you might end up on the fairway; but, since you have less control over the ball, you could end up in an even worse spot.

A BAD LIE
Consider where your ball lies and, when it is deep rough, only hit a shot that is within your capabilities. Do not risk making matters worse with an over-ambitious recovery shot from the rough. When in doubt, play the simple option.

ADD DISTANCE ON THE ANGLE

Most course planners (course maps that indicate distances between the green and various points on the fairway for each hole) are measured from the middle of the fairway to the center of the green. If you are in the rough, the angle effectively increases the distance to the center of the green (as shown on the course planner) by as much as 5 percent. A shot from 165 yd (150 m), for example, might gain an extra 8 yd (7.5 m). Also check the flag position. If it is central, you can rely on the number in the book. But if the flag is at the front or back of the green, add or subtract distance accordingly.

DO YOUR MATH
Consult the course planner, and make the necessary alterations when working out the distance to the pin. This can make the difference between a short birdie-putt and a potential three-putt.

IMPROVING YOUR MENTAL APPROACH

THERE IS NO DENYING that golf is one of the most mentally challenging games you can play. This is partly due to the fact that you have a lot of time between shots to dwell on what you have just done and what you are about to do. Professionals are acutely aware of this, which is why most tour players consult sports psychologists frequently to encourage constructive, rather than destructive, thought processes. However, most amateurs are reluctant to consider the mental aspect of the game, and this is a grave mistake. If you want better control over your game, you must learn to control your mind.

STICK TO YOUR GAME PLAN

Before a game, it is important to be prepared mentally as well as physically. Contemplate your game plan before you arrive at the course. For example, if you know the course well, you can plan your approach to different

ALL IN THE MIND
It is always wise to have a game plan in your mind, which is easily formulated if you know the course well. Decide, for example, which clubs are "middle of the green" clubs and which are "attack the flag" clubs. Stick to your plan wherever possible.

greens prior to the round. Decide when you will play defensively (by aiming for the middle of the green) and when you will attack the flag. Obviously certain factors might influence your plan – strong winds, for example, may change your tactics. However, do not let negative factors, such as a bad start, trigger a change in your game plan. Switching to a foolhardy plan of attack in an attempt to redeem a situation generally makes matters worse. Equally, if you have a great start, do not suddenly become overly defensive in your play.

TREAT EVERY SHOT THE SAME

Golfers tend to build up the importance of certain shots, most commonly the first tee shot or the last few shots in a good round. This is why you generally feel more nervous on the first tee than at any other time during a round: you have put yourself under unnecessary pressure. This is the main reason why some golfers hit poor opening drives. One of the secrets of successful play is to approach every shot in exactly the same way. If you do so, all of your shots should improve. This is because, mentally, you will not feel under extra pressure, which can lead to tension. Instead, you will feel more confident and relaxed, which all contributes to a better swing.

HAVE FUN BETWEEN SHOTS

Even with the best will in the world, you are not going to be able to maintain 100 percent concentration for the several hours it takes to play a round of golf. Indeed, it can be quite detrimental to your game if you try to do so. A far better policy is to have a chat and some fun between most shots. This is a good ploy if your last shot was good, and it is especially worthwhile if your last shot was poor because it will help you put the mistake behind you. The only shot that matters, remember, is the next one.

PLAY WITH THE BALL
Juggling the ball with a club takes the edge off the seriousness of a round and can help you forget a bad previous hole.

LOSE COUNT OF YOUR SCORE

Never add up your score when you are playing well because, subconsciously, you start thinking ahead and making predictions. "If I can make no worse than a five on each of the last four holes," you might say to yourself, "I will beat my best-ever score." That kind of attitude is rather like drafting your winner's speech while still on the 10th green. It distracts you from the shot in hand and puts undue pressure on your game. Instead of building up this extra stress, try to lose count of your score. To play consistently for the full 18 holes, you must become accustomed to taking the game one shot at a time. It takes practice, but if you focus on each shot as it comes, and stay in the present tense, the future is nearly always brighter. Save adding up your score until the last putt has dropped.

STAY IN THE PRESENT
By all means mark your card after every hole, but do not add up your score as you go and let your mind wander ahead of the game. Such thinking usually ends in disaster. Just focus on one shot, and one hole, at a time.

STAY ON AN EVEN KEEL

It can be exciting when something amazing happens in a round, such as chipping-in for a birdie. But, equally, it can be frustrating when you experience some bad luck or hit a poor shot. It is, therefore, always best to keep your emotions on an even keel. Accept the fact that you will hit bad shots and, by the same token, do not become overexcited if you chip-in or hole an impressive putt. If your emotions are under control, the chances are that your game is, too.

KEEP YOUR HEAD
Everyone reacts in a different way to good or bad luck. However, to play at your best, try to remain unaffected by changes of fortune.

SIMPLIFYING WINTER GOLF

UNLESS YOU are lucky enough to live under sunny skies all year round, there will be several occasions when you must play in adverse conditions. As well as wind and rain, you will probably encounter the inevitably inferior playing surfaces that are part of a round of golf in winter. Grim playing conditions need not ruin your chances of a good score, though:

there are certain ways you can alter your strategy and adapt your technique to suit even the roughest circumstances. And no matter how bad the weather and playing surfaces are, it is always as well to remember that the conditions are the same for everyone. Besides, compiling a good round on a nasty day is one of the most satisfying experiences in golf.

ALLOW FOR LESS BREAK ON PUTTS

Because putting surfaces tend to be less closely mown in winter, putts always travel slower than in summer. To compensate for this sluggishness, you have to hit putts more firmly. For this reason, the ball will not take as much break on its way to the hole on winter greens. Even on short putts, the "winter line" and "summer line" will be different. Be aware of this, so that you can make allowances.

JUDGING WINTER BREAK
Even on sunny winter days, because putting surfaces are generally more woolly in winter, you have to strike the ball harder than in summer. This means the ball will break less.

Winter break
Summer break

SWAP LONG IRONS FOR LOFTED WOODS

Long irons are unforgiving clubs at the best of times, but when the ground conditions are not ideal – a little soggy, perhaps – they become the most demanding clubs in the bag to hit solidly. It is wise to replace a couple of your longest irons with two lofted woods – perhaps a 4-wood and a utility-wood (see pp.231–2). Lofted woods are easier to hit from imperfect

CLUB CHANGE
In winter conditions it is a good idea to use a lofted wood rather than a long iron whenever possible.

Long iron
Lofted wood

lies (either out of the rough or on the fairway) than long irons. This is for several reasons, primarily due to the shape and design of the clubhead. First, the clubhead of a lofted wood will slide more easily through fluffy grass around the ball. Second, the sweetspot is larger than on a long iron – slightly off-center strikes produce acceptable shots. Finally, the center of gravity is much lower on a lofted wood than it is on a long iron, which makes it easier to get the ball airborne. This produces a longer carry through the air, and on soft ground, the extra "air-time" is very useful.

TAKE LESS SAND IN BUNKERS

The sand in bunkers can become much heavier in prolonged spells of wet weather, which calls for a slight change of technique. The main difference is that you should take less sand when it is wet than you would for a splash bunker shot when it is dry, as wet sand tends to offer more resistance to the swinging clubhead. As a general rule, you could perhaps halve the distance behind the ball where you would normally strike the sand (see Drill 5 in the "Bunker Play" section, p.137). That should help prevent you leaving the ball well short of the flag. As an alternative, you could experiment with a slightly longer swing. This will enable you to generate more clubhead speed through the hitting area, which will provide an effective solution when the sand is heavy. Try both of these methods in practice and see which one you like best.

STRIKE ACTION

When sand is wet it becomes much heavier and denser. To compensate, concentrate on either taking less sand at impact or swinging harder, as Cory Pavin is doing here.

BE BOLD WITH YOUR SHORT SHOTS

Unless the ground is frozen, in winter the greens will be highly receptive to a lofted shot. You can make this work to your advantage. If as you visualize your shot you imagine the ball landing on top of the pin, when you play the shot you will be amazed how often the ball travels the perfect distance. This is because the mental imagery encourages you to be bold when it is all too easy to leave the ball short.

PITCH IT UP

When the greens are soft and receptive, emulate Paul Eales (right) and pitch the ball well up to the flag, to ensure that it does not come to rest well short of the flag.

KEY CHECKPOINT

BE SMART WITH YOUR CHOICE OF BALL

IN WINTER, stopping the ball on soft greens is the least of your troubles. But these very same ground conditions make it harder to generate as much distance off the tee because there is virtually no run on landing. Therefore, if you use a high-spinning, soft-covered ball in summer, in winter it is well worth considering swapping it for a harder, two-piece ball designed more for distance (see the Key Checkpoint on p.93).

Monitor Your Performance

FOR AS LONG as you play golf, the tests featured in chapter one of this book will represent a constant and reliable barometer of your ability in every department of the game. Self-assessment is one of the keys to long-term improvement. You should, however, also keep track of your performance during competitive play. While it is easy to judge your success based on your overall score for 18 holes, a detailed breakdown of your results in each department of the game is more revealing. This is certainly also a better method of finding possible ways to lower your scores.

The key areas to examine are as follows: the number of fairways hit in a round; the number of greens hit in "regulation"; the number of successful chip-and-putt saves; the number of successful sand-saves; and your average putts per round. It is probably too time-consuming to take note of such details during a round, but once you have finished, a quick mental analysis of each hole will reveal the exact breakdown of shots. Then compare your results with the tables below. This whole operation takes only a few minutes, and is time well spent, as the data highlights your strengths and

weaknesses. Try to keep a file of this information, so that you can monitor performance trends in your game. To become a more complete golfer, you need to work on your weaknesses until there is little difference between your shortcomings and your strengths.

1. DRIVING ACCURACY

Add up the number of par 4s and par 5s on your course, and calculate a percentage figure based on the total number of fairways you hit from the tee. Remember that distance is not the main issue with driving (see p.28). Instead, keeping the ball in play – on the closely mown grass – should be your major consideration. This attitude will help keep you out of trouble.

RESULTS	
FAIRWAYS HIT	RATING
0–30 percent	Very poor
31–40 percent	Poor
41–60 percent	Adequate
61–70 percent	Good
+71 percent	Excellent

2. GREENS HIT IN REGULATION

Note how many greens you hit in "regulation" (which means that if you then take the standard two putts to complete the hole, you will achieve par). The number of strokes required to hit a green in regulation are: par 3 – one shot; par 4 – two shots; par 5 – three shots. Obviously, if you hit a green in less than the required number of shots, this also counts as a "hit in regulation."

RESULTS	
GREENS HIT	RATING
0–20 percent	Very poor
21–40 percent	Poor
41–60 percent	Adequate
61–70 percent	Good
+71 percent	Excellent

3. CHIP-AND-PUTT SAVES

Every time you miss a green with your approach shot, write down whether you make an "up-and-down" save (a chip and a single putt) or not. This is one area of the game in which good players excel. Increasing your percentage of chip-and-putt saves will have a dramatic effect on your average scores, which will in turn lead to a lower handicap.

RESULTS	
SUCCESS RATE	RATING
0–20 percent	Very poor
21–40 percent	Poor
41 60 percent	Adequate
61–75 percent	Good
+76 percent	Excellent

4. SAND-SAVES

Whenever your ball finishes in a greenside bunker, you have the opportunity of a sand-save: a single bunker shot followed by a single putt. Note how often you are successful in sand-save situations. If you have worked through the "Bunker Play" section (see pp.132–57) you should be playing out of a bunker in one shot every time, even if the lie is terrible.

RESULTS	
SUCCESS RATE	RATING
0–10 percent	Very poor
11–25 percent	Poor
26–40 percent	Adequate
41–65 percent	Good
+66 percent	Excellent

5. AVERAGE PUTTS PER ROUND

As many as 40 percent of the shots played in an average round are putts: playing well on the greens can mean a low score. Add up the total number of putts you make during a round.

(Note: Be ambitious on the greens, but do not set unrealistic goals. Take heart from the fact that from 2 yd [2 m], the world's best players hole, on average, only about half their putts.)

RESULTS	
PUTTS	RATING
+40	Very poor
39–37	Poor
36–33	Adequate
32–30	Good
-30	Excellent

ONLY PERFECT PRACTICE MAKES PERFECT

ONE WAY to improve your results is to note the old adage: "only perfect practice makes perfect." Great players know the importance of this truth, which is one reason why they can put in top performances under severe pressure. It also explains why most club golfers can hit the ball nicely at the range, but find it difficult to do the same on the course. However, if you treat every practice shot as if it is an important shot in a competition, when faced with a real pressure shot, you will be able to approach it as if it is just another practice shot. The concept of perfect practice is also explored in the "Off the Tee" section (*see Drill 1, p.30*).

Chapter Five
REFERENCE SECTION

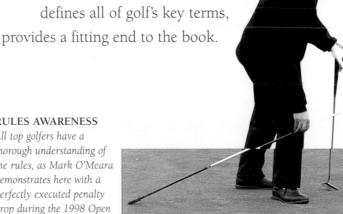

THIS FINAL SECTION of the book was conceived with the thought that many factors beyond actually striking a golf ball make a complete golfer. Within the following pages you will find an invaluable guide to buying equipment to suit your physique and level of ability. This insures that the tools in your bag help rather than hinder your performance. A description of the main forms of the game – from strokeplay to foursomes – precedes a guide to good etiquette. There is also a section on golf's most important rules, which clarifies the sometimes confusing regulations at the heart of this self-governing game. A comprehensive glossary, which defines all of golf's key terms, provides a fitting end to the book.

RULES AWARENESS
All top golfers have a thorough understanding of the rules, as Mark O'Meara demonstrates here with a perfectly executed penalty drop during the 1998 Open Championship.

BUYING THE RIGHT EQUIPMENT

ENORMOUS ADVANCES in technology over recent years have left the consumer spoiled for choice when it comes to club selection. The market has never been more exciting or more confusing. The sheer variety of clubs available, the confusing accompanying jargon, and the advanced construction materials used can sometimes conspire to make it difficult to make the right equipment-buying decisions.

As a result, some golfers stick with the same clubs for years, while others regularly splash out on the latest equipment, picking clubs off the shelf on impulse. Yet in both cases golfers are missing out on the potential benefits of using equipment that is ideally suited to them.

While no amount of modern technology can compensate for elementary faults in your swing, it is important that your clubs complement your physique and your swing. Otherwise, your clubs may be holding you back. In this section of the book you will learn how to choose the equipment best suited to you and your style of play.

DRIVERS

Selecting a driver was once a straightforward business. Virtually all were made of wood, and the only considerations were price, appearance, and loft. Nowadays metal drivers are the norm, and manufacturers use a huge variety of construction techniques and many different metals to produce clubs they claim offer the ultimate in distance, forgiveness, or both.

When purchasing a driver, it is important to consider the various elements that influence a club's playability. First, the size of the clubhead is an important issue. Big clubheads provide a larger hitting area and are more forgiving to off-center strikes than small clubheads. Despite these advantages, some golfers still find that smaller clubheads better suit their playing style. The loft on the club is also critical. Powerful ball-strikers can get away with very little loft, as little as seven degrees, whereas less accomplished golfers should not go lower than 10 degrees. Do not look at loft in isolation, however, because it is not the only factor that influences the height of your shots. Manufacturers can manipulate the center of gravity on a club so as to influence ball flight. Some clubs are designed with a low center of gravity to help the ball become airborne, which tends to suit the less-accomplished player. Other clubs

DIFFERENT DRIVERS
With so many drivers on the market, the choice can be confusing. There's always more to these clubs than meets the eye, though, so it pays to do your homework.

MAKE SURE THAT THE GRIP FITS YOUR HANDS

A CLUB'S GRIP tends to be overlooked by many golfers, yet it is the only point of contact between you and the club. Therefore, it makes sense that the grip should suit your hands. Aside from keeping grips in good condition – replacing them when they become shiny or smooth – you also need to make sure that they are the correct size. Perform this simple test. Take a club and hold it in your left hand. Ideally your middle two fingers should lightly touch the fleshy pad at the base of your thumb. If they do not touch at all, or the tips of your fingers dig into your palm, your grips need adjusting. This is a straightforward and inexpensive job that can be done by any club professional.

GRIP SIZE *The correct grip size (left) is very important. If your clubs' grips are too thin (above), it is worth having them altered.*

FACE FACTS

Most drivers and lofted woods are made of steel. But titanium, though more expensive, is also popular because it is light, which means that the clubhead can be bigger and thus even more forgiving. Titanium is also harder than steel and so propels the ball faster off the clubface, extending the ball flight, as well as reducing sidespin.

have a higher center of gravity, which is better for more advanced players and gives a more penetrating ball flight. The center of gravity can even be made bigger, so that there is more mass behind either the heel or toe of the clubhead. This makes the club more forgiving to off-center strikes. It is also important that the shaft flex is appropriate to your ability (*see "Shaft Flex, Material, and Length," above right*).

Once you have considered a club's playability, with all clubs it is important that you like their appearance, and the driver is no exception to this rule. If your driver is not pleasing to your eye, you might never pull it out of your bag. And finally, before you step into a shop, establish your spending limit and examine only clubs priced within your budget.

FAIRWAY WOODS

Over the years, lofted woods, or "fairway woods," have developed along the same lines as drivers. This means that these days, the longest clubs in your bag are easier to use, are more forgiving, and can send the ball further than ever. Essentially, you

SHAFT FLEX, MATERIAL, AND LENGTH

DO NOT FORGET that the shaft of your club is as important as the head. When deciding which shaft is best for you, flex is the first consideration. For men, there are three main flexes: regular, stiff, and extra stiff. The faster you swing and the harder you hit the ball, the stiffer the shaft you need. As a general rule, if the shafts in your set are too flexible, you will tend to hit shots high and with a hook. If the shafts are too stiff, the ball will often fly low and with a slice. The shafts in women's clubs tend to be more flexible, reflecting a generally less powerful swing. But these shafts become progressively stiffer for better players.

Also consider the shaft's material. There are two basic types: steel and graphite. These days, although drivers with steel shafts are still used, most have graphite shafts. For irons, because graphite is a light material, it is favored by players who struggle to generate speed in their swing, such as seniors. Graphite is also thought to pass on less vibration

to the hands and wrists, helping prevent injury. It is common in metal-headed drivers because the lightness means more weight can be placed in the clubhead, which provides greater force at impact. However, steel remains the most popular material for the shaft of irons because of its good all-around performance.

Finally, if you are very tall or have short arms, you might want to have the shafts of your clubs extended by ¼–1¼ in (2–3 cm) so that your posture does not suffer.

Driver with
graphite shaft

Driver with
steel shaft

WOODS: LOFT AND AVERAGE DISTANCE

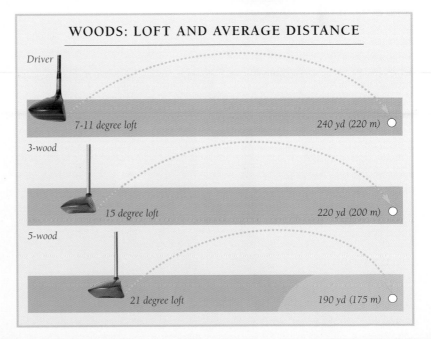

Driver

7-11 degree loft   240 yd (220 m)

3-wood

15 degree loft   220 yd (200 m)

5-wood

21 degree loft   190 yd (175 m)

should consider the same factors when buying a fairway wood that you do when purchasing a driver (see pp.230–31). However, the clubhead should be smaller than for a driver because on the fairway it is more difficult to strike the ball out of the center of the clubface with a big clubhead (this is not a problem on the tee because the ball is teed up). Your main concern when examining a fairway wood should be loft – but bear in mind that you might want to use the club off the tee as well as on the fairway. Given this proviso, a loft of between 15 and 18 degrees strikes a good balance between distance and accuracy.

It is a good idea to introduce a utility wood – a type of fairway wood – to your set. These woods come in a wide range of lofts but the most common utility woods are 5- and 7-woods, which have relatively small and compact heads. This means that utility woods are effective from a variety of lies, so that you can hit the ball from the fairway and from light rough – long irons do not offer this versatility. The other significant benefit of utility woods is that they make it very easy to get the ball into the air, which means that most golfers will hit their shots further with these clubs than with long irons.

A utility wood can fill a gap in your set. For example, some golfers will carry a 3-wood and a 3-iron, which leaves a big difference in distance between the two clubs. A utility wood with a loft of somewhere between 17 and 23 degrees will bridge the difference nicely.

UTILITY WOOD
Compact, shallow-faced clubheads offer versatility from a variety of lies.

IRONS

As with drivers, different iron clubs used to be subtle variations of what was basically the same theme. Nowadays, however, manufacturers are in a constant race with one another to come up with the latest innovation. This means that there is a phenomenal variety of iron clubhead designs on the market. However, the key issues when you come to buy are: how much forgiveness do you want, how important is it for you to be able to shape the ball through the air, and do you like the look of the club? In answering these questions you narrow your options, making the buying process that much easier. When it comes to clubhead construction, there are two main types: blades and peripherally weighted irons.

BLADE
Providing the purest feel at impact, blades make it much easier to shape shots at will through the air.

Blades

These clubs, by far the most popular irons up until the late 1970s, have a forged clubhead and a plain shape. Although relatively unforgiving to off-center strikes,

---

FINDING THE CORRECT LIE ANGLE

THE ANGLE at which the bottom edge of the club sits on the ground is described as the lie angle. If this is too upright for you, the heel will make contact with the ground first at impact. Conversely, if the lie angle is too flat the toe of the club will strike the ground first at impact. To avoid these problems, check that the bottom edge of the club is level with the ground at address. Then hit a few

shots. If the lie angle is correct, the start of the divot mark will be uniform in shape and depth and pointing straight at the target.

If the lie angle is either too flat or too upright, check your setup. If this is as it should be, the club professional can adjust the lie angle. Alternatively, you can seek out one of the manufacturers that produce clubs with a range of lie angles.

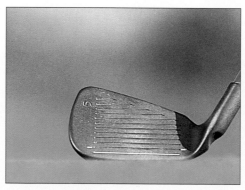

✔ Correct lie angle

✘ Lie angle too flat

✘ Lie angle too upright

PERIPHERALLY WEIGHTED IRON
Peripherally weighted irons are more forgiving to off-center strikes but do not make it so easy to shape shots.

blades produce a purer feel at impact and offer greater scope for shaping the ball through the air. Today, blades are still favored by traditionalists and some professionals and accomplished amateurs.

Peripherally weighted irons

Also known as "cavity backs," peripherally weighted irons often have cast rather than forged clubheads and are designed to offer maximum forgiveness to off-center hits. This is because they have more weight at the extremities of the clubhead. Such clubs were originally seen as game-improvement devices, and they did not offer the pure feel or shotmaking potential of blades. They were considered of most use to average golfers and were thought the antithesis of the bladed iron. That is not the case today, however. In addition to peripherally weighted cast clubs, there are now many "in-between" peripherally weighted irons available, which offer some of the benefits of bladed irons yet are still forgiving to off-center strikes. Some of these irons, especially those used by many of today's professionals, are even designed to look very much like a blade – at least from the player's-eye view.

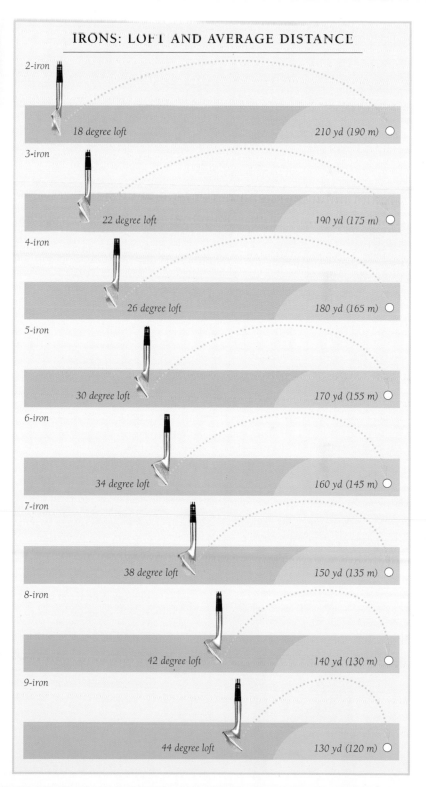

IRONS: LOFT AND AVERAGE DISTANCE

Iron	Loft	Average distance
2-iron	18 degree loft	210 yd (190 m)
3-iron	22 degree loft	190 yd (175 m)
4-iron	26 degree loft	180 yd (165 m)
5-iron	30 degree loft	170 yd (155 m)
6-iron	34 degree loft	160 yd (145 m)
7-iron	38 degree loft	150 yd (135 m)
8-iron	42 degree loft	140 yd (130 m)
9-iron	44 degree loft	130 yd (120 m)

WEDGES – LOFT AND DISTANCE

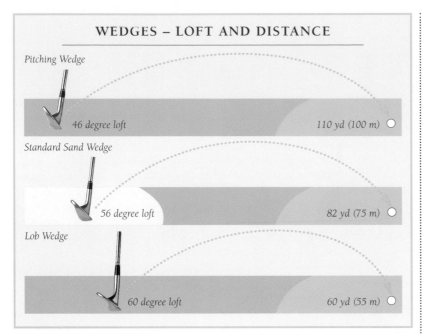

Pitching Wedge

46 degree loft   110 yd (100 m) ○

Standard Sand Wedge

56 degree loft   82 yd (75 m) ○

Lob Wedge

60 degree loft   60 yd (55 m) ○

WEDGES

There is a massive choice of wedges on offer. When buying a wedge or wedges, you should consider loft, the degree of bounce (the roundness and breadth of the flange at the bottom of the wedge), and clubhead materials.

The standard pitching wedge has 46 degrees of loft. The most lofted wedge, commonly known as a lob wedge, has 60 degrees, or even as much as 62 degrees. You should have at least three clubs within these parameters, since this offers you maximum versatility in your short game.

The bounce angle is just as important as loft. The degree of bounce you select will depend on the kind of shots you wish to play. For fairway shots, less bounce is desirable (no more than 5 degrees) because the clubhead sits almost flush to the ground behind the ball, promoting a clean strike. From most types of sand and from soft ground and rough, however, you need more bounce (somewhere between 10 and 14 degrees) to stop the clubhead from digging into the turf or sand rather than making solid contact with the back of the ball.

As for clubhead material, steel is the standard and most preferred metal for wedge clubheads. However, if you want even greater levels of control you might consider beryllium-copper, which has a softer feel at impact.

Bounce angle

SAND WEDGES

Clubs with lots of bounce (near left) work best in soft, powdery sand; less bounce (far left) is appropriate for coarser, heavier textured sand.

PUTTERS

Since as many as 40 percent of the shots played in an average round are putts, it is virtually impossible to exaggerate the importance of using a putter with which you feel confident. As with putting technique, choosing a putter is open to greater personal interpretation than any other club. Putters can have standard-length or long handles, and there are three main types of putterhead (peripherally weighted, mallet-headed, and center-shafted), but within these styles there is an unbelievable degree of variation in design, color, and feel. The best idea is simply to try out as many putters as you can, and choose one that feels right to you.

Peripherally weighted putters are constructed using the same principle employed in peripherally weighted irons (*see p.233*): the weight is positioned across the clubface to minimize performance loss caused by off-center strikes.

A mallet-headed putter has a semicircular head. This putter offers the same benefits as a peripherally weighted putter, only in a different package. This is probably the most distinctive of the three designs.

Center-shafted putters are plain in shape and, arguably, less forgiving with off-center hits than

TAKE YOUR PICK

There are literally hundreds of different putters on the market, but they all come in three basic designs; peripherally weighted, mallet-headed, or center-shafted.

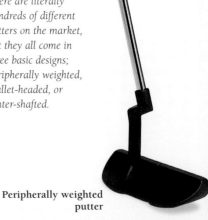

Peripherally weighted putter

INSERT PUTTER
There are many types of insert available in putters; from soft to relatively hard, but they all share one goal – to improve the feedback of the ball on the putterface on impact.

a peripherally weighted club. For this reason, center-shafted putters are best suited to accomplished golfers, who can consistently produce strikes from the center of the putterface.

Putterface inserts
Golf club manufacturers have responded to golfers' quest for maximum feel on the greens by introducing the concept of face inserts in putters. Some inserts are made from relatively soft rubber compounds, while others are built up from complex mixtures of metals.

Mallet-headed putter

Center-shafted putter

USE THE BALL TYPE THAT SUITS YOUR GAME

O NCE YOU HAVE purchased the perfect set of clubs, do not forget about balls; the type of ball you play is a reflection not only of your ability but also your priorities in the game. The following guide to the three main types of ball will help you make an informed choice.

THE CONTROL BALL
If you want maximum feel and spin when you play short shots, a control ball, which will usually have a cover made of balata (an artificial rubber compound) or a similar material with the same playing characteristics, is your best bet. This soft cover allows for good feel on and around the green. The inner construction is also designed to produce greater levels of spin, which further enhances your control for all shots. The downsides to this ball type are that you will lose some distance on long shots, the soft cover is prone to scuffing (although the covers are more durable than they were 10–15 years ago), and these balls are generally more expensive than the other types.

THE DISTANCE BALL
All manufacturers produce balls designed for maximum distance. These balls, which feel very hard off the clubface, offer the most distance of all the ball types. They are characterized by a distinctive "clicky" sound made at impact and are almost indestructible. However, distance balls offer less control: so around the green, do not expect lots of backspin on your pitch shots and chips.

THE COMPROMISE
Some balls offer a "happy medium" between control and distance. While they cannot offer the feel of a control ball or the length of a distance ball (they are not designed solely for one purpose), they do provide some of the advantages of both. Compromise balls feature an outer layer that provides some spin yet is still durable. In many respects these are the perfect balls for winter golf – giving you a decent distance for your money and, since the greens are generally soft, all the control you need from short range.

Despite the variety of colors and materials used, the idea behind these inserts is essentially the same: to promote a soft feel off the putterface in order to enhance control and give the ball a smooth roll.

The benefits of a fat grip
Some professionals have jumbo-fat grips fitted to their putters. These fill the hands more than a conventional grip and reduce excessive wrist action during the stroke. You might want to experiment with a fat grip.

LONG PUTTER
Although few amateurs currently use the long putter, the fact that several tour pros can be seen wielding it effectively may eventually make it more universally popular.

TYPES OF PLAY AND HANDICAPS

SO FAR, this book has covered almost every conceivable aspect of how to play golf and of what equipment to use. Now is an appropriate time to examine the multitude of competitive and friendly formats of the game, each of which has its own challenges and excitements. The most popular types of play seen on courses all over the world are discussed, as are a few that are sadly not played often enough. Additionally, a full and clear explanation is given of how handicaps work with each format, both in terms of playing against the course and against your opponents.

If you play the same type of game every time you set foot on a course, you risk missing out on one of golf's greatest attractions: variety. When you arrange your next round with friends, why not spice things up by trying out a new format? You will not only enjoy the change but will also learn from it.

STROKEPLAY

Most professional and amateur tournaments take place under the format known as strokeplay. In this form of the game you simply record your score for each hole, and add up the total at the end of the round. The person with the lowest score wins.

The total number of shots taken in strokeplay is known as the "gross score." In a tour event, this is the score that counts because professional players do not have a handicap. But at club level, each player's handicap is deducted from the gross figure to produce a "net score," which in most amateur events decides the winner.

STABLEFORD

This format works on the principle of awarding points for scores gained on each hole. An albatross is worth five points, an eagle four points, a birdie three points, a par two points, a bogey one point, and anything

ADAPTABLE PLAYER
For the last 20 years Bernhard Langer has been one of Europe's finest players – a master of both strokeplay and matchplay.

worse than a bogey scores no points at all. The person with the highest score at the end of the round wins.

Most stableford competitions offer competitors the full handicap allowance, so that if your handicap is 12 you are "given" a stroke on each of the holes with a stroke index of between 1 and 12. This means that you deduct one stroke from your score on each of these 12 holes: a par, for example, counts as a birdie, which gives you three points instead of two. Stroke indexes are indicated on all score cards, and, broadly speaking, reflect the degree of difficulty of each hole. The hardest hole on the course has a stroke index of 1 and the easiest has a stroke index of 18.

MATCHPLAY SINGLES

This format involves head-to-head competition, one on one. Individual holes are won, lost, or halved (whereby each player scores the same), and every hole contributes

---

HOW IS A HANDICAP CALCULATED?

HANDICAPS ALLOW golfers of different abilities to compete on equal terms. Gaining your first handicap is a straightforward process that involves playing usually three rounds on the same course. You then combine the scores and divide by three to arrive at a figure relative to the standard scratch score (SSS) of the course. For example, if you play three rounds and score 86, 91, and 84, these figures are then totalled to make 261. This number is divided by three (which makes 87). If the SSS of the course is 70, then you will be given a handicap of 17. The maximum handicap for men is 28; for women the upper limit is 36.

Your handicap is then adjusted every time you play in a strokeplay competition. There are three possible scenarios. First, you can shoot a score better than your handicap, which means your handicap will be lowered. Second, you can shoot a score the same as, or one–three strokes above, your handicap. This places you in a "buffer zone," wherein your handicap does not move up or down. This zone allows for a minor dip in form, which does not warrant an increase in your handicap. Finally, you can shoot a score more than three shots above your handicap, which places you beyond the buffer zone. In this situation, your handicap will go up.

to the state of play of the match. For example, the player who wins the first hole is "one up." If that player wins the next hole, he or she goes "two up," and if he or she loses the next, the player is back to "one up." If a hole is halved, the match score stays the same. The match is decided when a player is "up" by more holes than there are holes left to play. For example, if a player is four up with three holes to play, this is known as victory by four and three. In the event of the match being all square after 18 holes, a sudden death play-off ensues.

The golfer with the lowest handicap gives strokes to his or her opponent, based on three-quarters of the difference between the two handicaps. For example, if Player A has a handicap of 4 and Player B has a handicap of 16, three-quarters of the difference (12) is 8. Therefore, Player B receives a stroke from his or her opponent on each of the holes with a stroke index of between 1 and 8.

This means that on each of the "stroke holes," one shot will be deducted from Player B's score. Therefore, a four will count as a three, a five will count as a four, and so on.

FOURBALL BETTERBALL

This is similar to matchplay singles, only the game is played in pairs. Each player in the two pairings plays his or her own ball and the lowest score from each pair on each hole is the one that counts. The method of keeping score, and how the handicaps work, is the same as in matchplay singles. Fourball betterball can also be applied to the stableford format but seldom to strokeplay.

FOURSOMES

This is another game played in pairs, but in this format each pairing shares just one ball. One player in each pair tees off on the odd-numbered holes, the other on the even-numbered holes. Thereafter, alternate shots are played with the same ball until the hole is completed. This format can be applied to matchplay, strokeplay, or stableford.

In matchplay foursomes, the pair with the lowest combined handicap give shots to the other two players based on three-eighths of the difference. For example, if Team A has a combined handicap of 10 and Team B has a combined handicap of 26, the difference is 16. Since three-eighths of 16 is 6, Team B receives a stroke on holes with a stroke index between 1 and 6.

GREENSOMES

This is a great variation on the foursomes format, the difference being that both golfers in each

MATCHPLAY CHAMPIONSHIP
The World Matchplay Championship is one of the few professional tournaments not played in a strokeplay format. Here, Colin Montgomerie is playing Brad Faxon.

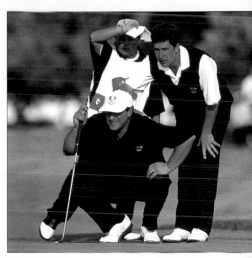

RYDER CUP
The Ryder Cup is one of the few professional tournaments played in the foursome format. Here, Costantino Rocca and Jose-Maria Olazabal are reading a putt.

pair tee off and then select the more favorable of the two drives. Then, alternate shots are played as in foursomes.

The handicap calculations work in exactly the same way as with foursomes. Greensomes is also a popular stableford format.

BOGEY

This almost-forgotten format is essentially a game against par. The course is your opponent, and the scoring system is based on holes won, lost, or halved (as in matchplay). The only difference is that the game is not over until the last hole has been completed. The ultimate aim when playing the bogey format is to finish as many holes "up" on the course as possible.

As you play, you receive shots from the course, most commonly based on three-quarters of your handicap allowance. If you play with a handicap of 8, for example, the course gives you six shots. You receive these shots on the holes that have a stroke index between 1 and 6.

THE IMPORTANCE OF GOOD ETIQUETTE

THE TERM "etiquette" can bring to mind images of stuffiness and an overly regimented code of behavior. This is a misconception, however, because following good etiquette helps insure that everyone on the course enjoys their round.

This section highlights the main principles of good etiquette. These are as easy to understand as they are to perform and in time should become second nature. It is good to remember that in striving to become a more complete golfer, good etiquette is just as relevant as the very act of striking the ball. In the eyes of many golfers, it may even be the more important half of the equation. There are two key areas of etiquette: how to look after the course and behavior on the course.

LOOKING AFTER THE COURSE
Even the finest courses are less enjoyable to play if they are in poor condition. You can play your part by ensuring that your impact on the

course is as minimal as possible. The following guidelines will insure that you always look after the playing surfaces in the correct way.

Leave the tee in good shape
While you will not usually take a divot on par-4 or par-5 tees (where you will most likely be using a wood), if you take a divot on a par-3 tee, use the sand-and-soil mix provided to fill the divot mark. If there is no sand-and-soil mix, simply place the divot back in its hole.

Replace divots in the fairway
It is extremely frustrating when your ball comes to rest in an old

DIVOT MARKS
If you take a divot, always place the turf back in its hole and tread it down. If you do this, the grass should recover quickly, and the damage to the course will be negligible.

COVER YOUR TRACKS
If you do not rake up your marks in the sand, there is a chance that someone in a group behind could have to play out of one of your footprints. This annoying situation makes the bunker shot much more difficult.

divot mark after a perfectly good shot (*see p.203*). To avoid such misfortune is not the only reason you should replace divots, however. A divot that is immediately placed back in its hole soon repairs itself because the roots usually find their way back into the ground. But if a divot is not replaced, it leaves an ugly scar, making the course look scrappy, and it is harder for the greenkeeper to repair the divot mark. Therefore, before leaving the scene of every fairway shot, place the divot back in its hole, and tread it down firmly with the sole of your shoe.

Leave no trace in the sand
In the section on bunker play, there is a discussion of the importance of raking over your footprints in the

REPAIR JOB

On receptive greens, the ball often leaves a pitch mark when it lands. Make sure that you repair these indentations immediately, either using a wooden tee, or a pitch mark repairer (above).

sand after you have played a shot *(see the Key Checkpoint on p.141).* It is worth reiterating this point because there is scarcely a more depressing moment in a round than when you walk up to a bunker only to find your ball resting in a deep footprint. No one deserves this fate, no matter how awful the stroke was that put the ball there in the first place. Therefore, once you have played your bunker shot, use the rake provided to smooth the sand. If there is no rake, use the back of your sand wedge and do the best you can. Remember to cover your footprints as well as the trough left by the clubhead splashing through the sand. Raking a bunker only takes a few moments, yet this act of consideration can make all the difference to those playing behind you.

Repair pitch marks on the green
Pitch marks on the green are unsightly and can deflect a ball on its way to the hole. Not every shot played onto a green will leave a pitch mark, but those that do should be repaired the moment you set foot on the green. You can use a pitch mark repairer, which is designed specifically for the job, or alternatively a wooden tee will suffice (plastic ones bend). The procedure is simple and takes only a few seconds. Stick the pointed end of your tee, or the fork of your pitch mark repairer, into the ground and gently ease the turf up. This will level the indentation. The pitch mark will then "heal" within 24 hours, whereas an untended pitch mark can take weeks to recover completely. A green dotted with pitch marks is no fun to putt on.

Be careful with the flag
It is amazing how many golfers are careless when it comes to placing the flag on the green. Do not throw it across the green, since this is likely to cause serious damage to the putting surface. Instead, lower it gently to the ground. It is also worth noting that if you hit a putt and the ball strikes a flag lying on the green, you receive a two-shot penalty. Therefore, it makes sense to place the flag well out of harm's way, ideally on the apron of the green. What you can and cannot do on the green is covered in more detail on pp.246–7.

GENTLY DOES IT
Never hurl the flag across the green; this can damage the putting surface. Instead, place it carefully on the ground, well away from the line of play.

HOW TO BEHAVE ON THE COURSE

While looking after the course is an essential requirement of good etiquette, your on-course behavior is equally important. Inconsiderate conduct during a round can take the shine off even the sunniest of days. However, if you adhere to the advice given below, you will not be guilty of ruining other players' enjoyment.

Wait your turn

Honor on the tee – who plays first – is secured by the golfer with the lowest score on the previous hole. On the first tee, honor is decided by lots or the toss of a coin. Elsewhere on the hole, the golfer furthest from the hole plays first. Only on the green might this order change. For example, in a strokeplay event you can elect to continue to putt out after your initial approach putt, but you must first make your intentions clear to your playing partners. This option will almost certainly not be open to you in a matchplay competition. You can ask, but as there is rarely anything for your opponent to gain by letting you hole-out, your request will probably be denied.

Out of sight, out of mind

It is very easy to be distracted by movement in your peripheral vision when you are about to play a shot. After being distracted in this way, it is sometimes difficult to regain concentration. Therefore, when your opponent is about to play, make sure that you stay out of the player's line of vision as much as possible. On the tee, the best place to stand while you are waiting is 45 degrees behind and to the right of the golfer; and remain at least four or five paces away. Do not make practice swings or talk: stand still and be quiet. On the fairway, be mindful of a player's line of sight to the target, and try to stay out of the

HOLDING UP PLAY
If you need to search for a ball, promptly call through golfers in the group behind waiting to play. Do not wait until the five-minute searching time has expired.

way. On the green, never stand on an extension of another player's putt (that is, right behind the hole) – this can be extremely distracting.

Be a good timekeeper

While golf need not be a race, neither should it be a crawl. Slow play is incredibly tiresome – do your best to keep play moving along without undue delay. There are several measures you should adopt. To begin with, if you fear your ball might be lost, play a provisional ball (*see p.243*). This way, if the original

DANGER ZONE
Before you play a shot, be aware of the positions of your fellow golfers. While they should know the correct place to stand, some players, especially beginners, might be unaware of the correct etiquette. This is a potentially dangerous situation: a quick check all around you will help avoid nasty accidents.

ball is in fact lost, you do not have to waste time walking all the way back to the site of the stroke that resulted in the lost ball to play another ball. If the ball you feared lost is not sighted right away and there is a group behind you, immediately call them through (rather than waiting until the obligatory five minutes' searching time is up).

If your ball disappears into the rough, watch where it comes to rest and try to "spot mark" it with a distinguishing feature, such as a tree that is along the same line. On the green, before you begin putting, leave your golf bag on the side of the green closest to the next tee, so that you can easily collect it on your way to the next hole. Do not mark your card on the green, since this can hold up the players behind you. Instead, it is better to do this on the next tee while waiting your turn to play. Also, always keep an eye on the group in front. If you start falling behind, take steps to catch up. And finally, walk briskly between shots.

Get ready while you are waiting

It is shocking how much time is wasted by golfers unprepared to play when it is their turn. To insure that you are not caught out, always be aware of the order of play, and go through some of your preparations while others are playing their shots (providing you do not distract them). For example, make up your mind which club you are going to hit, and start picturing the shot in your mind's eye. On the green, if you are not the first to putt, set about reading your line as you are waiting your turn (but be careful not to walk over the line of another golfer's putt). Although these measures probably only save 10 or 20 seconds on each occasion, this really does add up to a significant amount of time over the duration of an entire round.

Always shout "fore!"

Tragically, people have been killed and seriously injured as a result of being struck by a golf ball. With this in mind, if you hit a wayward shot that you think might endanger others, shout "fore!" loudly and without hesitation. Do not be shy – it is better to be safe than sorry. Also, be certain that the group ahead of you is out of range before you hit your shot. Again, err on the side of caution.

Be a good searcher

Anyone who has played golf will know how grim it can be searching for a ball; you may also be familiar with the anxiety that sets in when this happens during an important competition. At such times your playing partners should assist in the search – make sure that you do the same for them. Do not leave a golfer forlornly looking for a ball by him- or herself; instead, help out. If you do so, when you next lose a ball, there is more chance that your playing partners will help you out, too.

Be careful where you tread

On the green, be aware of where your playing partners' balls have come to rest and avoid treading on the line of their putts. On a soft putting surface your feet can leave marks, albeit temporarily, but these may affect the smooth roll of a ball. Even on a firm green it is courteous to avoid treading on the line of another golfer's putt. Bear this in mind before you march around the green looking at your line and before you stride up to the hole to putt out. If you are unsure whether or not, in adopting your normal putting stance, you will stand on another player's line, it is best to wait before putting out. Many a short putt has been missed by impatient golfers awkwardly straddling the line of another golfer's putt to complete a hole.

MARKING THE CARD

The next tee is the best place to mark your card, rather than on the previous green. This way you will not unnecessarily hold up the group of golfers playing behind you.

THE GOLDEN RULES OF GOLF

GOLF HAS MANY more rules than most other sports, but this reflects the nature of the game. After all, there is much more scope for incident on a 100-acre plot of varied and tree-lined landscape than there is on the relatively sanitized environment of, for example, a billiard table, tennis court, or football field.

Sadly, there is a great deal of ignorance of the rules at amateur level, which is worrying but ultimately not surprising. The rule book itself is a heavily worded and, at times, complex work. Indeed, there is even a supplementary rule book, *Decisions on the Rules of Golf*, which covers bizarre occurrences that require clarification. With such unappealing material available, the rules can take some learning.

This section should change all that, however. It will provide you with a basic understanding of the main rules and will therefore allow you to play the game as it is meant to be played. It should also enhance your enjoyment of the game and save you from the misery of unnecessary penalty shots or even disqualification. Besides, the following pages should also help you realize that the rules do not exist solely to punish you. Instead, with a thorough understanding of the rules, you will find that they can work in your favor, too.

ON THE TEE
Excess baggage
Before you hit your first shot of the day, it is worth checking the number of clubs in your bag. The maximum allowed is 14, and you are penalized if you carry more than that onto the course. In a matchplay competition you will have to deduct one hole for every hole played with the extra clubs, up to a maximum of two holes. This means that if you discover on the 3rd tee that you have extra clubs and you have already lost the first two holes, you will suddenly find yourself four down. In a strokeplay competition you are penalized two strokes for each hole played with the extra clubs, up to maximum of four strokes. It does not matter how many extra clubs you have in your bag – one or 10 – the penalty is the same.

Playing out of turn
In a strokeplay event, if you play out of turn there is no penalty as such, but to do this is poor etiquette (*see p.240*). In a matchplay competition, on the other hand, if you tee off first when it is not your honor, your opponent has the right to cancel that stroke and ask you to play again.

Outer limits
The teeing area is as wide as indicated by the tee markers and two club-lengths deep, creating a rectangular shape within which you must tee your ball. You cannot move the two tee markers, but you can stand either side of them, providing the ball is teed up within the designated area. As discussed in the "Strategy Off the Tee" section (*see pp.218–19*), utilizing the full width of the teeing ground, and therefore

AWARENESS ON THE TEE
You should always pay attention on the tee, as a courtesy to your partners and to insure that you observe the correct order of play.

gaining the best angle of attack, can increase your margin for error or give you a better line into the flag.

If you play from outside the limits of the teeing area, the penalty varies depending on the type of game you are playing. In a strokeplay event you incur a two-stroke penalty and are required to replay the stroke. This is known as playing "three off the tee" (your stroke off the tee counts as your third). In matchplay there is no penalty as such, but your opponent has the right to ask you to play the shot again. The likelihood of this happening probably depends on the quality of your tee shot. If you have played a poor stroke into the trees, for example, it is safe to assume that you will not be given another chance.

Accidental nudge

If, when you address the ball, you accidentally nudge it off the tee with the clubhead, there is no penalty. You simply place the ball back on the tee and start again.

Provisional ball

If you suspect that the ball may be lost from your tee shot, it is advisable to play what is known as a provisional ball (see "Trouble Off the Tee," top right). You must, however, state your intentions to your playing partners or your opponent. Once you have hit your provisional ball, you can begin searching for the first ball. But you are only allowed five minutes in which to find it, starting from the moment you begin looking (not from when you leave the tee). If you cannot find the ball within five minutes, you must declare it lost, add two shots to your score, and continue playing with your provisional ball. This means that if you were to lose your tee shot, your second shot with a provisional ball would count as your fourth. If you find the first ball, though, you may

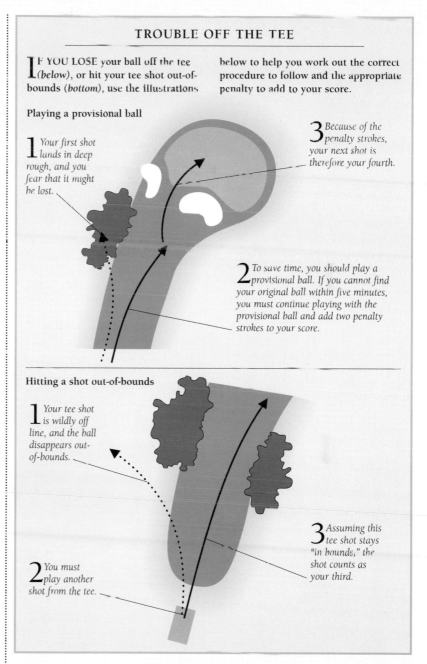

TROUBLE OFF THE TEE

1 IF YOU LOSE your ball off the tee *(below)*, or hit your tee shot out-of-bounds *(bottom)*, use the illustrations below to help you work out the correct procedure to follow and the appropriate penalty to add to your score.

Playing a provisional ball

1 *Your first shot lands in deep rough, and you fear that it might be lost.*

3 *Because of the penalty strokes, your next shot is therefore your fourth.*

2 *To save time, you should play a provisional ball. If you cannot find your original ball within five minutes, you must continue playing with the provisional ball and add two penalty strokes to your score.*

Hitting a shot out-of-bounds

1 *Your tee shot is wildly off line, and the ball disappears out-of-bounds.*

2 *You must play another shot from the tee.*

3 *Assuming this tee shot stays "in bounds," the shot counts as your third.*

play it without penalty and you can then simply pick up the provisional ball. (*Note*: the procedure outlined above for playing a provisional ball is the same if you fear you might have lost your ball as the result of a wayward fairway shot.)

Out-of-bounds

An area of the course on which play is permanently not permitted (as defined by local rules) is described as "out-of-bounds." If you hit a tee shot out-of-bounds (see "Trouble Off the Tee," above), you must replay the stroke from the tee and this counts as your third. This is known as a stroke-and-distance penalty. If you hit that drive out-of-bounds, you will be playing "five off the tee." (*Note:* the penalty is the same if you hit a fairway shot out-of-bounds.)

STRIKING THE BALL

A stroke is defined as the forward momentum of the club made with the intention of fairly striking at and moving the ball. It is useful to recall this description when considering what to do, for example, if you play an air shot. In this situation some believe that because the ball was not hit, the attempt to hit it does not count as a stroke. This is not correct because the intention of striking the ball must be taken into account. A legal strike of the ball also requires a backswing: you cannot scoop or push a ball toward the target. You may be tempted to do so if, for example, your backswing is restricted by a fence or tree – but if you succumb to this urge you will incur a two-stroke penalty.

HAZARDS AND UNPLAYABLE LIES
Bunkers

As mentioned in the "Bunker Play" section, the number one rule in sand

DO NOT TOUCH THE SAND
You must not ground your club in a hazard. In a bunker, the clubhead must not touch the sand either at address or in your backswing.

is to hover the clubhead above the surface, since touching the sand before playing a shot incurs a one-shot penalty (*see the Key Checkpoint on p.145*). There are, however, finer points to consider with bunker play. For example, if the clubhead touches the sand in your backswing, you are penalized just as you would be at address. Equally, you are not allowed to make a practice swing that comes into contact with the sand – but by all means make one that makes contact only with fresh air. (*Note:* the drills in the "Bunker Play" section that involved drawing lines in the

HOW TO TAKE A PENALTY DROP

THE RULES OF GOLF are very strict regarding the exact procedure to follow when taking a penalty drop. First of all, you must signal your intentions to one of your playing partners or your opponent, as it is essential that another player is aware of your intentions. As you make the drop, stand upright with your arm extended in front of you at shoulder height, then let the ball fall out of your hand and drop to the ground.

You are not allowed to influence the ball's flight in any way, for example, by spinning the ball in your fingers or casting it in a particular direction. Just let gravity take its course. If the ball comes to rest nearer the hole, you must redrop. If this happens again, you are permitted to place the ball on any lie you like, so long as you choose a position within two club lengths of your originally identified dropping spot.

MARK THE SPOT *If you have an unplayable lie, and feel that taking a drop from two club lengths away is your best option, mark out this distance with two woods. (You can also drop from behind the ball on an extension of the ball-to-target line, or you can replay the offending shot.)*

DROPPING THE BALL *With your arm fully extended at shoulder height, let the ball fall naturally from your hand – do not attempt to influence the outcome of the drop.*

sand are only suitable for practice. You cannot mark the sand during a proper round.)

The unplayable lie

In the chapter on shotmaking there is a section that describes three escape shots from trees (*see pp.204–5*).

FREE DROPS

THERE ARE MANY situations when you are entitled to a free drop, also known as "free relief," such as when the ground is under repair (*see p.248*), when you come across "casual" water (*see p.247*), or when you encounter certain immovable obstructions (*see p.248*). The most important point to remember is that although a free drop does not incur a penalty, you are allowed only one club length's relief. Also bear in mind that the relief does not take effect from the position of the ball, but from the point where the obstruction or abnormal ground condition ceases to cause a problem.

DROP ZONE *When large areas of ground under repair (or similar) affect play, a drop zone may be introduced. Here Greg Norman is gaining free relief after his previous shot finished in the grandstands.*

WHAT TO DO IN A WATER HAZARD

YOU HAVE three options if your ball lands in a water hazard, which is identified by a yellow painted line or yellow stakes.

1 *You may play the ball in the water – without incurring a penalty. However, as you address the ball, the club must not touch the water. This is a very risky shot.*

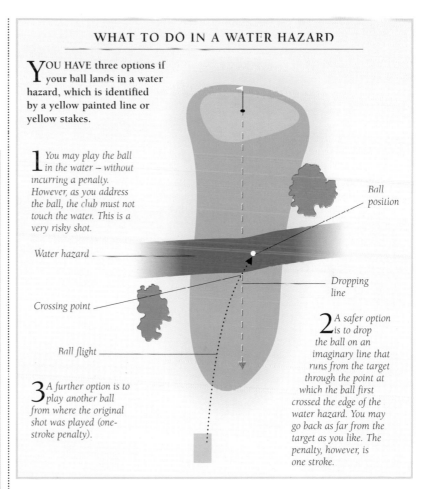

Water hazard

Crossing point

Ball flight

Ball position

Dropping line

2 *A safer option is to drop the ball on an imaginary line that runs from the target through the point at which the ball first crossed the edge of the water hazard. You may go back as far from the target as you like. The penalty, however, is one stroke.*

3 *A further option is to play another ball from where the original shot was played (one-stroke penalty).*

However, if you decide that such shots are too risky (for example in a competition), or that the lie is "unplayable," you could opt for a penalty drop instead (*see "How To Take a Penalty Drop," p.244*). When deciding whether to play or not, only you can decide if a lie is unplayable: it is your choice alone. If you feel that the lie is unplayable, you have three options for a penalty drop.

First, you can drop a ball within two club lengths of where your original ball came to rest (so long as you choose a spot that is not closer to the hole). Measure two club lengths using a couple of woods (the longest clubs in your bag), and mark this spot with a tee before you pick up your ball. Second, you can choose to go back to the spot from where you played the stroke that got you into trouble and take a drop from as near to the original site as you can remember. This is known as a stroke-and-distance penalty. Third, you can imagine a line between the ball and the flag, walk back on an extension of that line, and then drop your ball. There is no limit as to how far back you can go. Each of these three options incurs a penalty of one stroke.

Water hazards

There are two types of water hazard on a golf course: "water hazards" (marked with a yellow stake or a yellow painted line) and "lateral water hazards" (indicated by red stakes or a red painted line). Whenever your ball finishes in water it is important to identify which of the two hazards you are dealing with, as the procedures for each vary slightly.

With a simple water hazard (marked yellow) you have three options (see "What To Do in a Water Hazard," p.245). First, you can play the ball as it lies, without penalty. This is only possible in very shallow water, and even then is not recommended because such a shot usually ends in disaster. Second, you can identify an imaginary line between the flag and where your ball

first crossed the edge of the water hazard, then walk back and drop the ball on an extension of that line (as with an unplayable lie, see p.245). The third option is to return to the spot where you played the shot that ended up in water (this is a stroke-and-distance penalty). These last two options incur a one-stroke penalty.

With a lateral water hazard you can choose from the three alternatives outlined above, or you can drop a ball two club lengths either from where the ball first crossed the edge of the water hazard or from a similar spot on the opposite side of the water (see "What To Do in a Lateral Water Hazard," below). Again, this

incurs a one-stroke penalty. Remember, as with all drops, that you cannot give yourself a lie nearer to the hole.

Playing the wrong ball
It is against the rules to play a stroke with a ball that is not your own. In matchplay the penalty is the immediate loss of the hole, while in strokeplay you receive a two-shot penalty and must take your next shot from where you played the wrong ball. In strokeplay, if you fail to correct your mistake before teeing off at the next hole, you are disqualified from the competition.

ON THE GREEN
What you can do on the green
If you want to clean your ball before putting, mark the ball by placing a coin or ball marker behind the ball before lifting it away. If the ball is damaged, you can replace it with another, providing there is agreement from your fellow competitor or opponent. If your ball marker interferes with the line of a fellow competitor's putt, use your putterhead to measure as far to the side as is necessary and remark (see "Moving the Marker," p.247). Make sure that you do not forget to put the marker back in its original position before you replace the ball.

Regarding obstructions on the line of your putt, you can repair pitch marks and old hole plugs but not spike marks. You can brush aside leaves, twigs, and loose sand, providing you use your hand or the putterhead.

What you cannot do on the green
Being close to the hole does not mean you are entirely safe from penalty. The key points to remember in order to avoid breaking the rules on the green are as follows. First, do not touch the line of the putt,

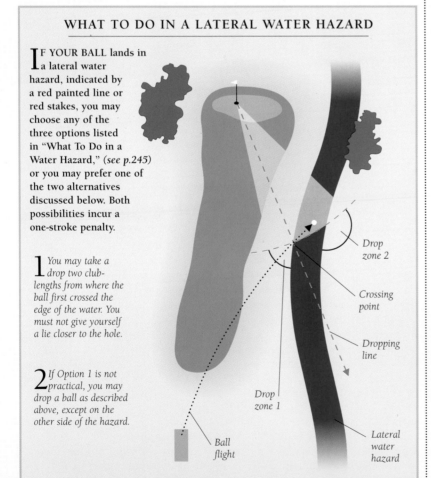

WHAT TO DO IN A LATERAL WATER HAZARD

IF YOUR BALL lands in a lateral water hazard, indicated by a red painted line or red stakes, you may choose any of the three options listed in "What To Do in a Water Hazard," (see p.245) or you may prefer one of the two alternatives discussed below. Both possibilities incur a one-stroke penalty.

1 You may take a drop two club-lengths from where the ball first crossed the edge of the water. You must not give yourself a lie closer to the hole.

2 If Option 1 is not practical, you may drop a ball as described above, except on the other side of the hazard.

Drop zone 2

Crossing point

Dropping line

Drop zone 1

Lateral water hazard

Ball flight

MOVING THE MARKER

YOU SHOULD move your marker if it is on the line of another player's putt or if it interferes with a player's stroke or stance. The procedure outlined below will show you the correct way to do this.

POSITION THE CLUB *If your playing partner asks you to move your ball marker out of the line of his or her putt, begin by carefully placing the toe of your putterhead so that it sits next to the marker.*

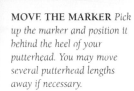

MOVE THE MARKER *Pick up the marker and position it behind the heel of your putterhead. You may move several putterhead lengths away if necessary.*

unless you are brushing aside loose impediments (*see "Impediments and Obstructions," p.248*), repairing a pitch mark or old hole plug, or measuring distance to determine whose putt should be played first. Second, do not test the putting surface by rolling a ball along the green. Third, do not hit your putt while another ball is in motion. And finally, do not brush aside early-morning dew or frost (neither of which are "loose impediments") from the line of your putt (this is a common infringement).

Flagstick misdemeanours

When your ball is on the green, you have only two options regarding the flagstick. If you are a long way from the hole you will probably choose to have it attended (so that you can see where the hole is). In this situation the flag must be pulled out before the ball goes in the hole. Failure to do this incurs a two-stroke penalty. However, if you decide to have the

CASUAL WATER
Before taking a drop, mark the original position of the ball and the area on which you intend to drop, as Per-Ulrik Johansson is doing here.

flagstick taken out, make sure that it is left well out of the way, as there is a two-stroke penalty if your ball hits it. From off the green you have three options. You can have the flag out (two-stroke penalty if your ball hits it), left in (no penalty if the ball strikes it), or you can choose to have it attended (two-stroke penalty).

ABNORMAL GROUND CONDITIONS
Casual water

One of the oldest rules in golf is that you must play the ball as it lies, but there are exceptional circumstances that override this principle. One such situation is if your ball lands in casual water – a temporary accumulation of water (often found after heavy rain). This is a free-drop scenario (*see "Free Drops," p.245*), and whenever it is practical to do so, you must mark the original position of the ball, identify the nearest point of relief (where the water ceases to become an obstruction to either your stance or the lie of the ball), mark that spot with a tee, and drop within one club length of the tee in any direction (so long as you do not end up closer to the hole).

The procedure is slightly different if the casual water is in a bunker. You must identify the nearest dry patch on which to drop the ball, but that spot must be within the confines of the bunker. If the bunker is completely waterlogged, you must either drop the ball into

OBSTRUCTING OBJECTS

THERE ARE MANY different types of object that you might encounter on your journey from the tee to the green. The rules relating to these differ according to the type of object in question. A commonly encountered object is an immovable obstruction, which is a fixed, artificial object. If your ball comes to rest near such an obstruction and your stance or swing is impeded, you are allowed free relief.

IMMOVABLE OBSTRUCTION *As a fixed sprinkler head may impede your stance or swing, you are allowed to take a free drop.*

the shallowest area of water or drop it outside the bunker and incur a one-stroke penalty. This is one of the harshest rules in golf.

Ground under repair
Any portion of the course that would be damaged if played on, for example a patch of newly planted grass, can be declared "ground under repair." Such areas are encircled by a white line, and often have the letters "GUR" painted alongside. If your ball lands inside the white line, measure one club length from the point where the ground under repair no longer interferes with either your stance or the ball, and take your drop from there.

Plugged ball
When a ball plugs in its own pitch mark on a closely mown area of grass, you are allowed a free drop. You simply mark the position of the ball, lift it, clean it if necessary, and drop it as close as possible to where it became plugged. If a ball plugs in its own pitch mark in the rough, the Rules of Golf do not permit a free drop. However, during winter months, when plugged balls are most common, golf clubs often introduce what are known as "Winter Rules," which allow free relief in the

rough. It is usually stipulated that you may not clean your ball, as you can if your ball becomes plugged on a closely mown part of the course.

IMPEDIMENTS AND OBSTRUCTIONS
Loose impediments
Movable natural objects – leaves, twigs, branches, stones, and so on – are described as loose impediments. Providing the object is not growing and is not solidly embedded in the ground, you are allowed to move it without penalty. However, you will be penalized one shot if the ball moves as you clear the object away (unless you are on the green).

You cannot move loose impediments in a hazard. The one exception to this rule is that you can move stones from around the ball in a bunker (for safety reasons).

Finally, sand and loose soil are defined as loose impediments on the green, but not off the green. Make sure that you remember this if you are putting from the apron of the green, which is technically not part of the green.

Immovable obstructions
Obstructions are defined as artificial objects; typical immovable obstructions include fixed sprinkler heads around greens (*see "Obstructing Objects," left*) and the concrete tee boxes to the side of a teeing area that provide information about the hole. If such an obstruction interferes with either your stance or your intended swing, you are entitled to free relief. Since the obstruction is immovable, you can move your ball (no nearer the hole) within one club length from the spot where the obstruction no longer interferes with your stance or swing. You are not allowed relief, however, if the obstruction is merely in the flightpath of your next shot.

Movable obstructions
Empty cans and bunker rakes are common examples of movable obstructions. If your ball comes to rest touching a movable obstruction or in such close proximity to the obstruction that it interferes with your stance or swing, you are allowed to move the obstruction. Before you do so, it is wise to mark the position of your ball with a tee, so that if the ball moves during the process of lifting away the obstruction you can simply place the ball back on its original spot, without penalty.

DEFLECTED BALLS
Ball deflected while in motion
If your ball is deflected while in motion, the correct procedure varies according to the cause of the deflection.

LOOSE IMPEDIMENTS
A natural object, such as this small branch, is classed as a loose impediment and may be shifted, provided the ball does not move.

BUNKER DISTRACTION
A bunker rake is classed as a movable obstruction and can be moved so that it does not interfere with your stance or swing.

If your ball hits something natural, such as a tree, you must play the ball from where it comes to rest. The same is true if your ball hits an "outside agency," examples of which include greenkeeper's equipment – such as a mower – or a spectator.

If an animal intercepts your ball while it is in motion, you must replace the ball on the spot from where it was first taken. Although this may be short of where your shot might have finished, if the ball was heading toward a hazard or the rough, this rule can work in your favor. If an animal steals your ball on the green while you are putting, you can replay the stroke without penalty.

If your moving ball hits a ball at rest, you must play your ball from wherever it finishes. On the green, if your putt strikes a ball at rest, you are penalized two strokes, and the struck ball should be replaced in its original position. Always ask a ball to be marked, even if you think there is only a remote chance of hitting it.

Stationary ball deflected or moved
If your ball, while at rest, is moved by an outside agency, such as an animal, there is no need to panic. Simply replace the ball as close as possible to the spot from where it was moved (there is no penalty). Even if the ball disappears forever (if,

for example, a crow flies off with it – which is not as unusual as you might think), you can take another ball from your bag, place it where the original was, and proceed without penalty.

The rules are not so benevolent if a ball is moved by you (for example, if you kick the ball while searching for it in deep rough), your caddie, your partner, or any piece of equipment belonging to you or your partner. In this situation there is a one-stroke penalty, and you must replace the ball in its original position. However, there are exceptions to this rule. You are not penalized if, so long as you return the ball to its original position, your ball is moved during the process of:
• measuring putts on a green to

determine the playing order
• repairing a pitch mark on the green
• moving an obstruction (see "Movable Obstructions," p.218), such as a bunker rake, out of the way
• searching for a ball in a hazard, such as a bunker
• brushing aside loose impediments, such as leaves or sand, on the green
• moving a ball that is interfering with play
• lifting, placing, or replacing a ball during the course of taking free relief.

COLLISION ON THE GREEN
In the 1997 US Open, Jack Nicklaus's and Hale Irwin's balls collided. Officials had to decide where to replace the struck ball.

GLOSSARY

ADDRESS
An alternative word used to describe a golfer's **setup** position.

ADVANCEMENT SHOT
A stroke, such as the second shot on a long **par 5**, played where the intention, either through choice or necessity, is not to reach the **green**.

AIR SHOT
A stroke whereby the clubhead fails to make contact with the ball.

ALBATROSS
A score of three under **par** on one **hole**.

APPROACH SHOT
A stroke played with the intention of hitting the **green**.

APRON OF THE GREEN
The closely mown area of grass between the **rough** and the putting surface.

BALATA
An artificial rubber compound used to cover balls designed for maximum control.

BARE LIE
A situation where the ball is sitting on a patch of ground with very little or no grass on it at all.

BIRDIE
A score of one under **par** on a **hole**.

BLADE
A forged iron clubhead thought to offer superior feel off the clubface but is less forgiving to off-center strikes. Also the bottom edge of an iron.

BOGEY
A score of one over **par** on one **hole**. Also a **matchplay** competition played against the par of the course.

BORROW
Another word for **break**.

BOUNCE
The wide flange at the base of a sand wedge.

BREAK
The deviation left or right made by a ball rolling along a **green** as a result of the slopes on the putting surface.

CARRY
The distance a ball flies through the air.

CAVITY BACK
A design where the middle of the back of an iron's head is hollowed out, allowing weight to be positioned around the perimeter

of the clubhead. This increases the mass of clubhead behind off-center strikes.

CLOSED STANCE
An **address** position where the golfer's alignment is to the right of the target.

CLUBBING DOWN
A situation where a golfer takes a more-**lofted** club, for example an 8-iron instead of a 7-iron.

CLUBBING UP
A situation where a golfer takes a less-**lofted** club, for example a 5-iron instead of a 6-iron.

COLLAR OF ROUGH
The area of grass where the **apron of the green** joins the **rough**.

COURSE PLANNER
A booklet with a diagram of each hole that shows the distinguishing features of the hole, as well as the distances from various points between the **tee** and the **green**.

CUP
Another word used to describe the **hole**.

Distance chart
Another term for a **course planner**.

DIVOT
The turf dislodged at impact while playing a shot.

DIVOT MARK
The hole in the ground left as a result of a **divot** being taken.

DOGLEG
A hole, either a **par 4** or **par 5** (but never a **par 3**), where the fairway bends from left-to-right or from right-to-left at some point between the **tee** and the **green**.

DORMIE
The state of play in a **matchplay** competition where a player is up by as many **holes** as there are left to play in the round. For example, four-up with four holes to play is described as "dormie four."

DOUBLE BOGEY
A score of two over **par** on one **hole**.

DOUBLE EAGLE
Another word used to describe an **albatross**.

DRAW
A shot where the ball moves from right-to-left through the air, as a result of sidespin imparted at impact.

DRIVER
The longest club in the bag, designed for hitting tee shots.

EAGLE
A score of two under **par** on one **hole**.

FADE
A shot where the ball moves from left-to-right through the air, as a result of sidespin imparted at impact.

FAIRWAY
The closely mown area of grass bordered on either side by longer grass (**rough**).

FELLOW COMPETITOR
A person with whom you play in a **strokeplay** competition.

FOURBALL BETTERBALL
A competition played in pairs, where the best score of the two partners on each **hole** counts.

FOURSOMES
A game of pairs where two golfers share the same ball, one teeing off on odd-numbered **holes** and the other on even-numbered holes. After the tee shot the pair play alternate shots.

FRINGE
Another word for the **apron of the green**.

GAP WEDGE
A club designed to bridge a gap in terms of **loft**, usually between a sand wedge and a pitching wedge.

GREEN
The putting surface. (The **hole** is located on the green.)

GREENSOMES
A type of play where partners both tee off on each hole. They then select the more favorable of the two balls and play alternate shots with the same ball until the **hole** is completed.

GRIP
The rubber handle at the top of a club. Also, both hands positioned on the club's grip are referred to as the grip.

GROUNDING THE CLUB
Resting the clubhead on the ground behind the ball at **address**.

HALVED
In a matchplay competition, if opponents register the same score on a **hole**, the hole is said to be "halved."

HANDICAP
A figure that reflects a golfer's ability relative to the **par** of the course.

HEAVY
A shot where the clubhead strikes the ground before the ball.

HEEL
The area of the clubface nearest to the **shaft** of the club.

HEEL-TOE WEIGHTING
Another term for **peripheral weighting**.

HOLE
The hole itself (which is located on the **green**). Also a general term used to describe the area between the **teeing ground** and the green, for example: "the first hole."

HOLING OUT
The actual process of getting the ball into the hole.

HOOK
A shot where the ball moves from right-to-left through the air as a result of sidespin imparted at impact. An exaggerated version of a **draw**.

HOSEL
The part of the clubhead into which the **shaft** is secured.

LAYING UP
Playing a shot short of the **green**, either through choice or necessity.

LIE
Where the ball comes to rest on the course. Also the angle at which the bottom edge of the clubhead sits relative to the **shaft**.

LINKS COURSE
A golf course by the sea.

LOFT
The angle at which the clubface sits relative to perpendicular. This determines the ball's **trajectory**.

LOOSE IMPEDIMENT
A term used in the Rules of Golf to describe a movable natural object, such as a leaf or twig, interfering with the line of play.

MATCHPLAY
A game played between single opponents or pairs where holes are won, lost, or **halved**.

OBSTRUCTION
A term used in the Rules of Golf to describe anything artificial that might interfere with play, such as a fixed sprinkler head (an immovable obstruction) or an empty can (a movable obstruction).

OPEN STANCE
An **address** position where the golfer's alignment is to the left of the target.

OPPONENT
A person whom you play against in a **matchplay** situation.

OUT-OF-BOUNDS
A designated area of a golf course where play is permanently not permitted. The penalty for hitting a ball out-of-bounds is **stroke and distance**.

PAR
The standard score for a **hole**, based on the number of shots an accomplished player would normally take to complete the hole. Also a score equal to the par on a hole

PAR OF THE COURSE
The total of the **pars** of all 18 holes.

PAR 3
A **hole** that should be completed in three strokes. To achieve **par**, usually the **green** should be hit in one stroke, followed by two putts.

PAR 4
A medium-length **hole**, which should be completed in four strokes. To achieve **par**, usually the **green** should be hit in two strokes.

PAR 5
A long **hole**, which should be completed in five strokes. To achieve **par**, usually the **green** should be hit in three strokes.

PERIPHERAL WEIGHTING
The principle of distributing the mass of a clubhead around its edges to allow for a degree of forgiveness for off-center strikes.

PGA
The Professional Golfers' Association, which looks after the interests of professional golfers in the UK. Each country has its own PGA, for example the Australian PGA.

PIVOT
The coiling and uncoiling of the upper body in the swing, combined with the correct **weight transfer**.

PLAYING PARTNER
A person with whom you team up in a game played in pairs, such as **foursomes**.

POSTURE
The overall position of the body and legs in the **setup**.

PREFERRED LIES
A local rule often introduced during the winter months when ground conditions are usually poor. The rule permits golfers to move their ball

onto a more favorable lie, so long as this is within 6 in (15 cm) of the spot where the ball originally came to rest. The rule usually only applies on closely mown areas of grass, such as the **fairway** or the **apron of the green**.

PULL
A shot where the ball starts left of target and continues to fly in that direction.

PUSH
A shot where the ball starts right of target and continues to fly in that direction.

READING A PUTT
The process of studying the line of a putt to identify possible **breaks** that might occur as the ball moves towards the **hole**.

RELEASING THE CLUB
A phrase that describes how the right hand rolls over the left through impact, which indicates a powerful and free swing of the clubhead.

REVERSE PIVOT
A swing where the weight moves in the wrong direction: onto the front foot in the backswing and onto the back foot in the downswing. Such a swing results in a loss of power and poor strikes.

ROUGH
The thicker grass either side of the **fairway** and around most **greens**. The rough is designed to penalize wayward shots: it is more difficult to play from than the closely mown grass of the fairway.

ROYAL & ANCIENT
The governing body for amateur golf all over the world, except in the US. The Royal & Ancient, commonly referred to as the R&A, administers the official Rules of Golf.

RUN
The portion of a ball's journey from the moment the ball first hits the ground to the point where it eventually comes to rest. More **lofted** clubs produce less run; less-lofted clubs, such as the driver and long irons, tend to generate more run.

SCRATCH
A **handicap** of zero.

SETUP
The position you adopt before striking the ball, including your grip, aim, stance, and posture. Also known as the **address** position.

SHAFT
The part of a club between the **grip** and the clubhead.

SHANK
A shot where the ball is struck from the **hosel** of the club, causing the ball to fly sharply to the right of the target.

SKY
A tee shot played with either a driver or lofted wood where the top edge of the clubhead strikes the bottom of the ball, which flies steeply upwards.

SLICE
A shot where the ball moves from left-to-right through the air as a result of sidespin imparted at impact. An exaggerated version of a **fade**.

SPLASH SHOT
A bunker shot where the clubhead strikes the sand behind the ball, and a wave of sand propels the ball out of the bunker.

STABLEFORD
A type of play where points are awarded according to the score relative to **par** on each **hole**. The golfer with the most points after 18 holes is the winner.

STANCE
The width your feet are apart at **address**, and the position of the ball relative to your feet.

STANDARD SCRATCH SCORE (SSS)
A figure calculated on the basis of the length of the course. The SSS, which is used in the calculation of **handicaps** during competitive **strokeplay**, is not always equal to the **par** of the course.

STROKE AND DISTANCE
A penalty where the golfer must return to the spot from which the last stroke was played (conceding the distance gained) and add one stroke to his or her score for that **hole**.

STROKEPLAY
A type of play in which each competitor records his or her score for each hole. The golfer with the lowest total is the winner.

SWEET SPOT
The centermost portion of the clubface, where the majority of the clubhead's mass is usually positioned.

TEE
A common abbreviation for either a **tee** or the **teeing ground**.

TEE BOX
Another term used to describe the **teeing ground**.

TEEING AREA
The part of the **teeing ground** from which golfers must hit their tee

shots. The teeing area is two club lengths deep and its width is defined by two tee markers.

TEEING GROUND
The whole area of closely mown grass on which the designated **teeing area** is situated.

THIN
A shot where the bottom edge of the clubhead strikes on or above the equator of the ball, causing it to fly on an uncharacteristically low **trajectory** (or even along the ground).

TOE
The area of the clubface that is furthest from the shaft of the club.

TOUR EVENT
A professional tournament usually played over four rounds, where the golfer with the lowest 72-hole score is the winner.

TRAJECTORY
The arc on which the ball flies through the air. The higher-numbered irons, which have more **loft**, propel the ball on a higher trajectory. The lower-numbered irons, which have less loft, send the ball on a lower trajectory.

TRIPLE BOGEY
A score of three over **par** on one **hole**.

USGA
The US equivalent of the **Royal & Ancient**.

USPGA
The United States Professional Golfers' Association. An organisation that looks after the interests of professional golfers in the US.

UTILITY WOOD
A lofted metal-wood, such as a 7-wood, that features a small clubhead. Utility woods are designed for **advancement shots** from the **fairway** and light **rough**.

WEIGHT TRANSFER
The process whereby the bodyweight moves from one foot to the other during the process of swinging a club.

WINTER RULES
Local rules introduced by a golf club's committee during winter to allow **preferred lies** on closely mown areas of grass.

INDEX

Page numbers in *italic* refer to the photographs of named players and courses

A

abnormal ground conditions, rules 247–8
accidental nudges 243
address
  back-handed chop 204
  ball above your feet 201
  ball below your feet 200
  bunker play 134, 156
  chipping 108
  freezing at 57
  improving with videos 60
  iron shots 78
  iron shots from thick rough 203
  pitching 104
  preshot routine 216–17
  putting 161
  restricted backswing 205
  shaping shots 211
  spine angle 45
  swing zone 26
  tee shots 31, 34, 39, 50, 52
  waggle 36
  wind play 206
adrenaline 217
advancement shots, iron play 54
aggression
  chipping 125
  pitching 91
aim 20–1
  improving with divot marks 38
air shots 205, 244
albatross 236
angle of attack, pitching 97, 101
animals, deflected balls 249
anxiety
  freezing at address 57
  tee shots 32
Aoki, Isao 151
arms
  chipping 117

iron play 73
putting 161
straight-armed swing 204
straight left arm 72
stretching exercises 214
swing 45
in takeaway 75
tee shots 40–1
"thumbs up" drill 74

B

back *see* spine
back-arches 214
back-handed chop 204
backspin
  bare lies 202
  chipping 117, 121
  pitching 97, 98, 101, 103
  shaping shots 211
backswing
  box at top 48
  bunker shots 141, 156
  chipping 116
  flexing knees 78
  grounding heels 42–3
  head movement 67
  improving with videos 61
  iron shots 78–9
  loss of power 192
  pausing at top of 38
  pitching 86–7, 95, 96, 105
  putting 161, 164
  restricted backswing 205
  shoulder position 49
  speed 66
  staying connected 71
  straight left arm 72
  swing zone 26
  tee shots 41, 53
  transition to downswing 68
  turning your back on the target 44
balance *see* weight distribution
balata balls 235
  chipping 117
  pitching 93
Ballesteros, Seve 151, 209
balls

above your feet 148, 201
accidental nudges 243
bare lies 202
below your feet 149, 200
bounce 122
bunker shots 137, 139
chipping 110–11, 115, 117
choosing 235
deflected balls 248–9
direction 59
downslope lies 198
escape shots 204–5
free drops 245
"heavy-contact" chip 188
high shots 208
history 9
hitting with heel of club 44
hook 187
iron play 57
launch angle 77
lost balls 240–1, 243
low shots 209
penalty drops 244, 245
pitching 83, 93
playing out of divot marks 203
plugged balls 248
provisional balls 240–1, 243
pull shot 195
push shot 194
putting 161, 162, 165, 173
rules 244, 246, 248–9
safety 241
shanked iron shot 189
shaping shots 210–11
sideslope lies 199
skied drive 190
slicing 36, 39, 186
stance 22–3
tee shots 33, 39
teeing up 31, 50
topped shots 191
upslope lies 198, 199
weak shots from rough 193
wind play 206–7
winter golf 224
bare lies 202
baseball grip 19
"Bellied Wedge" shot 125
beryllium-copper heads,

wedges 98, 234
birdie 236
Bjorn, Thomas 180
blades 232–3
body pivots, stretching exercise 214
body turn
  chipping 109–10
  loss of power 192
  pitching 96, 104
  preshot routine 216
  swing 40–1
bogey 219, 236, 237
bounce, sand wedges 135, 144, 154, 234
bunker play 132–57
  balls 137, 139
  casual water 247–8
  "clubbing up" 153
  clubs 135, 144, 153–5
  covering your tracks 141, 238–9
  flop shots 121
  grip 142, 151, 152, 153
  hard-packed sand 144
  hovering the club 145
  intermediate shots 143
  judging distance 145
  long-range shots 142
  monitoring your performance 227
  pitching over 90
  plugged lies 150
  "punch-and-spin" shot 154
  putting from sand 153
  rules 244–5
  short-range shots 151–2
  slopes 145–9
  strategy 220
  swing 136, 138–41, 156–7
  winter golf 225

C

Canada Cup *10*
cards, marking 241
casual water, rules 247–8
"cavity backs" 233
center of gravity, drivers 230–1
center-shafted putters 234–5
chipping 106–31

address 108
balls 110–11, 115, 117
chipping contest 123
downslope lies 118
flop shots 121
from rough 121
grip 124, 126
"heavy-contact" chip 188, 198
holing a chip shot 125, 128
hovering the club 129
landing errors 120
loft 123
with lofted woods 129
minihook shot 128
monitoring your performance 227
putting technique 126
reading the green 127
swing 109, 114, 116–17
upslope lies 118
warming-up exercises 215
choking down
  ball above your feet 201
  bunker shots 142, 153
  drivers 35
  wedges 87
  wind play 207
chop, back-handed 204
Christine, Jim 64
Clark, Howard *212–13*
clock face drill
  chipping 116
  pitching 101
clubface
  aim 20–1
  ball below your feet 200
  bunker shots 152
  chipping 124
  hook 187
  pull shot 195
  push shot 194
  putters 162, 234
  slice 186
  sloping lies 199
  staying square 70
  tee height 31
  tee shots 36–7, 50
clubhead
  "bounce" 135, 144
  bunker shots 141
  chipping 113, 114
  drivers 230
  "heavy-contact" chip 188

irons 232, 233
lofted woods 232
pitching 83, 100
push shot 194
putting 161
shaping shots 210–11
skied drive 190
slices 41
swing 46
topped shots 191
weak shots from rough 193
wedges 234
clubs
bare lies 202
bounce 154
bunker shots 135, 144, 153–5
chipping 115, 119
choosing 230–5
downslope lies 198
grip 18–19
grip size 230
high shots 208
history 9, 10
hitting with heel of 44
junior players 59
lie angle 232
low shots 209
materials 231
playing out of divot marks 203
posture and 25
putting 179
restricting numbers 209
rules 242
shafts 231
shanked iron shot 189
slice 186
stance 23
upslope lies 199
waggle 36
wind play 206
winter golf 224
see also drivers; irons; putters; wedges; woods
coaches 10–11
concentration 164, 223, 240
control balls 235
Couples, Fred 78, 78
course planners 221
crosswinds 207
Cypress Point 8

D

deflected balls, rules 248–9
distance

irons 233
wedges 234
woods 231
distance balls 235
distance charts 56
divots
etiquette 238
"heavy-contact" chip 188
improving aim with 38
iron shots 61
pitching 88–9, 101
playing out of 203
dogleg fairways, strategy 219
downslope lies 198–9
bunker shots 145, 147
chipping 118
putting 176
downswing
bunker shots 156–7
head movement 67
iron shots 78
"late hit" 72
loss of power 192
pitching 85, 96, 99, 101
slices 41
speed 66
swing zone 27
tee shots 41, 52, 53
transition from backswing 68
draw 207, 210
strategy 218
drivers
choosing 230–1
posture and 25
shafts 231
skied drive 190
slice 186
stance 23
tee shots 28–53
wind play 206
driving, monitoring your performance 226
Duval, David
putting 182-3

E

eagle 236
Eales, Paul 225
elbows, squeezing 71
Els, Ernie 7
grip 19
rhythm 78
swing 48
tee shots 52–3
equipment 230–5
escape shots 204–5
etiquette 141, 238–41

eyes
focusing left eye 69
putting 162, 166, 169
"tunnel vision" 175

F

fade 207, 211
strategy 218
fairway bunkers 142, 153
see also bunker play
fairway woods 231–2
fairways
divots 238
doglegs 219
strategy 220
Faldo, Nick 10, 156, 184
grip 19
pitching 91, 104–5
putting 164, 164, 171
tee shots 47
faults 185–95
Faxon, Brad 237
"fear shots" 90
"feathery balls" 9
feet
grounding heels 42–3
iron play 73
lifting heels 43
posture 24–5
stance 22–3
weight distribution 58
"five off the tee" 244
flags
chip shots 128
etiquette 239
"go-for-the-flag" range 65
rules 247
flex, shafts 231
flop shots 121
followthrough
bunker shots 141, 157
chipping 116
improving with videos 61
low shots 209
pitching 99, 105
putting 161
swing zone 27
football drill 69
footprints
in bunkers 238–9
on green 241
"fore!" 241
forearms, swing 45
fourball betterball 237
foursomes 237
free drops 245
freezing at address 57
Furyk, Jim 180

G

game plan 222
gap wedges 91
"getting ahead of the ball" 69
gloves, chipping 111
graphite shafts 231
grass
chipping 113
monitoring iron shots 65
Texas Wedge shot 112
see also divots; rough
greens
chipping 122, 127
flags 239
monitoring your performance 226
reading 163
repairing pitch marks 239
rules 246–7
slope 103, 122
greenside bunkers
judging distance 145
see also bunker play
greensomes 237
grip 9, 18–19
and aim 21
ball above your feet 201
baseball grip 19
bunker shots 142, 151, 152, 153
chipping 124, 126
interlocking grip 19
overlapping grip 9, 19
pitching 83–4, 87
pressure 19, 83
putting 160, 180
strengthening 36
tee shots 36–7
weakening 37
grip size
clubs 230
putters 235
ground under repair
rules 248
gutta-percha balls 9

H

Hagen, Walter 139
handicaps 236
hands
chipping 111
palm position 75
"thumbs up" drill 74
see also grip
hard balls 235
chipping 117

pitching 93
hard surfaces, chipping drills 119
Harmon, Butch 10, 11, 11
hazards, rules 244–6
head
during swing 67
focusing left eye 69
putting 165–6, 168–9
"swing triggers" 85
"heavy-contact" chip 188, 198
heels
grounding 42–3
heel-toe weighting 58
lifting 43
high shots 208–9
hips
grounding heels 42
iron shots 70
lifting heels 43
posture 24
stretching exercises 214
history 8–10
"hitching a ride on both sides of ball" 74
hitters 48, 49
hitting zone
pitching 99, 101
swing paths 27
Hogan, Ben 10, 10, 18
hole
chipping 125, 128
putting 167–8, 175
size 167
honor on the tee 240
hook 187
minihook shot 128
tee shots 37
hosel, shanked iron shot 189
"hovering the club"
bunker shots 145
chipping 129
pitching 100
putting 177

I

immovable obstructions, rules 248
impediments, rules 248
inserts, putterface 235
interlocking grip 19
irons 54–79
ball position 57
bunker shots 153, 155
chipping 115, 119, 122
choosing 232–3
divots 61

downslope lies 198
iron shots from thick
    rough 203
launch angle 77
loft and distance 75,
    233
long irons 25, 224
peripherally weighted
    irons 233
posture and 25
range 56, 77
shafts 231
shaping shots 211
slice 186
stance 23
tee shots 50
upslope lies 199
weak shots from rough
    193
weight distribution 58
wind play 206
Irwin, Hale 249

J

Jacobs, John 10
Johansson, Per-Ulrik
    78–9, 247
Jones, Bobby 9, 9, 10
    bunker shots 140
    swing 66
junior players, clubs 59

K

knees
    flexing 78
    stretching exercises
        214
    swing 41
"knockdown-punch
    shot" 209

L

"lag," putting 163, 174
Langer, Bernhard 100,
    236
"late hit" 72
lateral water hazards 246
launch angle, ball 77
Leadbetter, David 10, 47
left-handed players 12
    grip 18
legs
    iron shots 78
    pitching 104
    posture 24
    sloping lies 199
Lehman, Tom 49, 49
lie angle, clubs 232

lob wedges 91, 234
loft
    bunker shots 153
    chipping 118, 123
    downslope lies 198
    drivers 230
    high shots 208
    hooks 187
    irons 75, 233
    lofted woods 232
    low shots 209
    shaping shots 211
    slices 186
    tee shots 34
    upslope lies 198, 199
    wedges 91, 234
    woods 231
lofted woods 63
    chipping with 129
    choosing 231–2
    winter golf 224
long holes, strategy 220
long irons 25, 224
long putters 179, 235
loose impediments, rules
    248
loss of power 192
lost balls 240–1, 243
Love, Davis 48, 48, 63
low shots 209

M

mallet-headed putters
    234, 235
maps, course 221
markers, rules 247
matchplay foursomes
    237
matchplay singles 236–7
mental approach 222–3
metal drivers 230
minihook shot 128
mirrors, putting drill
    169
monitoring your
    performance 226–7
Montgomerie, Colin
    179, 237
Morris, Old Tom 9, 9
movable obstructions,
    rules 248
"multiple-target" drill
    103
muscles, warming up
    214–15

N

Nelson, Byron 9–10
Nicklaus, Jack 10, 10, 249

address 216
lifting heels 43
recovery shots 196–7
"spot marking" 20
"swing triggers" 85
Norman, Greg 20, 129
nudges, accidental 243

O

obstructions
    escape shots 204–5
    rules 248
Olazabal, Jose Maria 237
    pitching 91
    rhythm 78
O'Meara, Mark 228–9
out-of-bounds 219,
    243–4
overlapping grip 9, 19

P

Palmer, Arnold 174
par-3 holes, teeing up 50
par-5 holes, strategy 220
Park, Mungo 9
Pelz, Dave 128
penalty drops 244, 245
Penick, Harvey 215
perfect parallel
    alignment 21, 82
peripherally-weighted
    clubs
    irons 233
    putters 234
personal distance
    iron shots 56, 77
    pitching 82
pitch marks
    plugged balls 248
    repairing 239
pitching 80–105
    accuracy 90
    angle of attack 97, 101
    balls 93
    divot marks 88–9, 101
    from rough 100
    grip 83–4, 87
    hovering the club 100
    over bunkers 90
    personal distance 82
    speed 84
    stance 82
    swing 85–7, 92–105
pitching wedges
    bunker shots 144, 155
    chipping 115, 119,
        122
    loft and distance 234
Player, Gary 85, 174

plugged balls
    bunker shots 150
    rules 248
posture 24–5
    at address 45
    iron shots 78
    pitching 96
    putting 161
    tee shots 52
    weight distribution 58
power, loss of 192
practice strokes 63
    putting 172
    warming-up exercises
        215
preshot routine 216–17,
    219
Price, Nick 10, 78
    chipping 130–1
problem shots 202–3
provisional balls 240–1,
    243
pull hook 195
pull shot 195
"punch-and-spin"
    bunker shot 154
push shot 194
putters
    choosing 234–5
    grip size 235
    long putters 179, 235
    "toe poke" 127
putting 158–83
    balls 161, 162, 165,
        173
    chip shots 126
    close-range putts 177
    clubs 179
    from sand 153
    grip 160, 180
    holing putts 167–8,
        175
    hovering the club 177
    monitoring your
        performance 227
    pace and line 181
    posture 161
    practice strokes 172
    reading the green 163
    slopes 170, 176
    speed 173
    sweet spot 165
    swing 161, 164, 176
    Texas Wedge shot 112
    three-putting 172, 173
    "tunnel vision" effect
        175
    wind play 207
    winter golf 224

R

rakes 141, 238–9, 249

records, chipping drills
    120
release
    football drill 69
    right-armed swings
        100
restricted backswing 205
reverse overlap grip 160
reverse pivot, loss of
    power 192
rhythm
    iron play 78
    swing 41
    tee shots 32
Robertson, Allen 9
Rocca, Costantino 237
rope, practice swings
    with 64
rough
    "Bellied Wedge" shot
        125
    chipping 121
    hovering the club 100,
        129
    iron shots from thick
        rough 203
    lost balls 241
    pitching from 100
    strategy 221
    "toe poke" 127
    weak shots from 193
routine, preshot 216–17,
    219
rules 242–9
Ryder Cup 6, 104, 237

S

safety 241
sand see bunker play
sand saves 227
sand wedges 91
    bare lies 202
    bounce 135, 144, 154,
        234
    bunker play 134, 135,
        152
    chipping 115, 119
    choosing 234
    on hard-packed sand
        144
Sarazen, Gene 135, 154
scoring
    bogey 237
    fourball betterball 237
    handicaps 236
    marking cards 241
    matchplay singles
        236–7
    mental approach 223
    stableford format 236
    strokeplay 236

scoring shots, iron play 54
Scotland 8–9
self-assessment 226–7
setup see address
shadow, learning about your swing with 66
shafts, clubs 231
"shaking hands with the target" 46
shanked iron shot 189
shaping shots 210–11
shotmaking 197–211
  escape shots 204–5
  high and low shots 208–9
  problem shots 202–3
  shaping shots 210–11
  sloping lies 198–201
  wind play 206–7
shoulders
  backswing 49
  swing 40
side bends 214
sideslope lies 148, 198, 199
sidespin
  shaping shots 211
  tee shots 32, 34
skied drive 190
slice 186
  causes 41
  tee shots 36, 39
sloping lies 198–201
  ball above your feet 148, 201
  ball below your feet 149, 200
  bunker shots 145–9
  chipping 118
  greens 103, 122
  putting 163, 170, 176
Snead, Sam 83
soft balls 235
Spearman, Mitchell 184
speed
  putting 173
  swing 66
spin, pitching 93
spine angle
  at address 45
  iron shots 79
"spot marking" 20–1, 217
stableford format 236
stance 9, 22–3
  aim 21
  ball above your feet 201
  ball below your feet 200
  bunker play 134, 137
  chipping 108

iron play 57, 73
iron shots from thick rough 203
pitching 82, 94, 101
preshot routine 217
putting 161
sloping lies 199
tee shots 30–1
wind play 206, 207
steel
  shafts 231
  wedges 234
straight-armed swing 204
Strange, Curtis 104
strategy 218–23
strengthening grip 36
stretching exercises 214
stroke-and-distance penalty 244
strokeplay 236
strokes, rules 244
sucker pin placements 220
sweet spot
  pitching 83
  putting 165
swing 9–10
  aim 20–1
  ball above your feet 201
  ball below your feet 200
  bunker shots 136, 138–41, 156–7
  chipping 109, 114, 116–17
  freeze-frame practice 62
  freezing at address 57
  grip 18–19
  grounding heels 42–3
  hand position 75
  head movement 67
  high shots 208
  improving with divot marks 38
  improving with videos 60–1
  iron shots 78–9
  iron shots from thick rough 203
  "late hit" 72
  loss of power 192
  low shots 209
  pitching 85–7, 92–105
  posture 24–5
  practice swings 63
  pre-shot routine 216
  putting 161, 164, 176
  releasing clubhead 46
  restricted backswing 205

rhythm 78
rope practice 64
speed 66
stance 22–3
straight-armed 204
swing paths 27, 44
swing zones 26–7
takeaway 47
tee shots 32–3, 38, 40–9
"thumbs up" drill 74
transition 68
triggers 85
using shadow 66
weight distribution 50
see also backswing; downswing
swingers 18

T

takeaway
  arm position 75
  freezing at address 57
  hovering the club 129
  staying square 70
  swing zone 26
  tee shots 47
targets
  aim 20–1
  "multiple-target" drill 103
tee markers 242
tee shots 28–53
  address 31, 34, 39, 50, 52
  aim 38
  balance 37
  choking down 35
  choosing clubs 51
  honor on the tee 240
  hook 37
  loss of power 192
  par-3 holes 50
  push shot 194
  releasing clubhead 46
  slice 36, 39
  stance 30–1
  strategy 218–19, 222
  swing 32–3, 38, 40–9
  takeaway 47
  tee height 31
  teeing up 50
  waggle 36
  wind play 206
teeing area
  divots 238
  rules 242–3
tendons, warming up 214–15
Texas Wedge shot 112
"three off the tee" 243

"thumbs up" drill 74
titanium clubs 231
"toe poke" 127
toes, touching 214
topped shots 191
Torrance, Sam 63
tournaments, formats 236–7
trajectory, launch angle 77
transition, swing zone 27, 68
trees, escape shots 204–5
Trevino, Lee 84, 209
triggers, swing 85
"tunnel vision" effect, putting 175
two-piece balls, pitching 93

U

umbrellas
  chipping drills 113
  pitching drills 94
unplayable lies, rules 245
upslope lies 198–9
  bunker shots 146
  chipping 118, 122
utility woods 232

V

Vardon, Harry 9, 11, 41
Vardon grip 9
videos, improving swing with 60–1

W

waggle, tee shots 36
warming up 214–15
water hazards
  casual water 247–8
  rules 245–6
  strategy 220
Watson, Tom 43, 116
weak shots from rough 193
Webb, Karrie 11
wedges
  bare lies 202
  beryllium-copper heads 98
  bounce 154, 234
  bunker play 134, 135, 152
  chipping 115, 119, 122

choosing 234
loft and distance 91, 234
pitching 80–105
tee shots 33
see also sand wedges
weight distribution
  iron play 58
  loss of power 192
  moving head 67
  posture 25
  swing 26
  tee shots 34
Westwood, Lee 156–7
wind 206–7
winter golf 224–5
"Winter Rules" 248
woods
  chipping with 129
  choosing 231–2
  loft and distance 231
  posture and 25
  skied drive 190
  slice 186
  tee shots 34
  wind play 206
  see also lofted woods
Woods, Tiger 10, 11, 192
  chipping 129
World Matchplay Championship 237
Wright, Mickey 99
wrists
  playing out of divot marks 203
  putting 163, 174

Z

Zoeller, Fuzzy 44

AUTHOR'S ACKNOWLEDGMENTS

In time-honored fashion there are many people to whom I would like to express my thanks for their tremendously valuable contributions to this book. First and foremost to Arthur Brown, who set the wheels in motion for this project and helped me to develop it from concept to completion. Thanks to David Lamb of Dorling Kindersley for believing in our idea and giving Arthur and myself the opportunity to run with it.

Once the book was up and running I was fortunate to have on board a team of talented golfers, all of whom did a fantastic job of demonstrating their skills in every department of the game, unperturbed by the high-speed whirrs and clicks of the nearby cameras. In particular to Michael Welch, boy wonder of the early 1990s and now a tour professional who, for the best part of three days, toiled under the Dubai sun and whose classic swing should be an inspiration to all who read this book. I would also like to thank Sandy Meyer, a teaching professional at Dubai Creek GC, who in her debut performance in front of a camera made it all look easy.

My dream team in the studio also successfully made a tough job look easy under the glare of our photographer's bright lights. Italian Open champion Samantha Head found time in her busy schedule to spend a day in the studio, and I thank her for her skills and enthusiasm. Also to teaching professional Nigel Pinhorne, who frequently set off at the crack of dawn from his home in Portsmouth to the studio in London, and did not put a foot wrong. My thanks go also to Yaz Ali, a hugely talented young golfer from Ealing, England and surely a star of the future. And to Michael Katzler, whose first task on arrival was to hit chip shots off a paving slab with tens of thousands of pounds of camera and lighting equipment only feet away … and no damage was done. Nice going, Michael.

On the other side of the camera were two wonderful photographers, and the hundreds of specially commissioned images you see in this book are a tribute to their talents. In Dubai we had the services of the world's leading golf instruction photographer David Cannon, a good friend and a skilled golfer who knows exactly what to look for in a golfing image and how to capture it perfectly through a lens. The book also features some innovative studio photography by the talented Steve Gorton, whose skill at producing pure, uncluttered images brings a fresh focus to golf instruction. My thanks go to both David and Steve.

Thanks to the master of attention to detail, Sean O'Connor, whose meticulous and skillful editing, along with a clear understanding of what we were trying to achieve with this book, added polish to the finished product. Thanks also to Alistair Plumb for his considerable efforts in the book's design.

We could not have found a better location than Dubai for the bulk of the photography, and this trip would not have been possible without the assistance of Michelle Chedotal, Dubai Golf sales & marketing director, who helped to coordinate the many different elements that make up a successful trip. My thanks to her and also to Jacqueline Campbell for allowing us to stay at the glorious Jebel Ali Hotel and Golf Resort, our only regret being that we could not find enough time to spend on their wonderful beach! We were indeed lucky to be able to spend as much time as we needed, though, on the resort's fine nine-hole golf course, and my sincere appreciation goes to director of golf James Williams, who could not have been more accommodating and helpful. I would also like to thank Adrian Flaherty, the director of golf at The Emirates Golf Club in Dubai, who hosted us at such short notice and made available for photography the stunning Desert Course. And we would not have arrived in such comfort were it not for the excellent and efficient Emirates Airlines.

Finally, thanks to my dad for introducing me to golf all those years ago and to my wife, Chantal, for tolerating a husband whose hermitlike existence for the best part of seven months – the time spent writing this book in the office in our spare room at home – must have made her feel like she was living the life of a single woman.

Picture credits

Allsport: Andrew Redington 104/105; **Dave Cannon** 7, 11br, 52/53, 78/79, 130/131, 182/183, 228/229; **Stephen Munday** 164bl; **David Rogers** 196/197; **Dave Cannon**: 4, 5tl, 18-25, 28/29, 30tl, 38bl, 50l, 51b, 54/55, 56l, 59, 65, 66r, 69t, 71r, 73b, 77, 80/81, 82t, 83, 88-90, 91l, 92-94, 98r, 100t, 101r, 103, 105br, 106/107, 109/110, 111l, 112/113, 114t, 115, 117, 118, 120-125, 127/128, 129r, 132-147, 150-159, 162b, 164r, 167-175, 176l, 177, 179, 181, 185tr, 186-195, 197cra, 197br, 198/199, 200-211, 213cra, 213br, 214-224, 226/227, 230bl, 232bc, 235br; **Peter Dazeley:** 236; **DK Picture Library: Dave Cannon** 244bl, 248, 249tl; **Steve Gorton** 229br, 234bl, 234br, 238-243, 244c, 244br, 247tl; **Golf World:** 229tl, 230br, 231tl, 232tr, 232bl, 233tl, 235tl; **Steve Gorton:** 1, 3, 5b, 26/27, 30b, 31, 32-37, 38br, 39-47, 48r, 49tl, 49bl, 50bc, 53r, 57/58, 61, 62-64, 66l, 67/68, 69b, 70, 71l, 72, 73t, 74/75, 76r, 79cr, 79br, 82b, 84-87, 91r, 95, 96/97, 98l, 99, 100b, 101l, 102, 105cra, 105crb, 108, 110t, 111r, 114b, 116, 119, 124t, 126, 129l, 131cra, 160/161, 162t, 163, 165/166, 174t, 176r, 178, 180, 183cra, 183br, 226tr, 231cr; **Hulton Getty:** 9tc, 10tr; **Golf Picture Library: Matthew Harris** 16/17; **Phil Sheldon:** 6, 8, 10bl, 48l, 49br, 76bl, 184, 212/213, 225b, 225t, 237tr, 237bl, 247br, 249br; **Dale Concannon Collection** 9br; **Jan Traylen** 245bl; **Sporting Pictures (UK) Ltd:** 11tc.